Francis Gabrini

Saturday, the day consecrated to Mary : or, Meditations on the greatness, the virtues, and the glories of the Most Holy Virgin for every Saturday in the year

Francis Gabrini

Saturday, the day consecrated to Mary : or, Meditations on the greatness, the virtues, and the glories of the Most Holy Virgin for every Saturday in the year

ISBN/EAN: 9783743657991

Printed in Europe, USA, Canada, Australia, Japan

Cover: Foto ©Lupo / pixelio.de

More available books at **www.hansebooks.com**

"HAIL! MARY, FULL OF GRACE!"—*Luke*, i. 28.

SATURDAY,

THE

DAY CONSECRATED TO MARY

OR,

MEDITATIONS

ON

THE GREATNESS, THE VIRTUES, AND THE GLORIES

OF THE

MOST HOLY VIRGIN.

FOR EVERY SATURDAY IN THE YEAR.

COMPOSED BY

REV. FRANCIS GABRINI, S.J.

TRANSLATED FROM THE GERMAN BY

REV. EUGENE O'KEEFFE.

WITH AN ENGRAVING.

"What mortal could, unless he were sustained by a divine declaration, embolden himself to say, with his unclean lips, anything, whether little or great, of her who brought forth the God Man? Yes! she it is whom God the Father, from all eternity, fore-ordained to be a virgin ever, and most worthy; whom the Son chose to be his mother; and whom the Holy Ghost prepared, that she might be the abode of every grace. With what words shall I now, an insignificant man, give expression to the supremely exalted dispositions of that virginal heart—dispositions which she, with her most holy mouth, revealed? Yes! to give adequate expression to such dispositions would be a task, for the accomplishment of which neither the tongues of all men nor the tongues of all angels were sufficient."
—St. Bernard of Sienna (9th Sermon on the Visitation).

—

1872.

To the Dear Memory

OF

HIS FATHER,

ULICK O'KEEFFE,

WHOSE HARD-WORKING HANDS, IN THE POOR, DESPISED, AND

FIENDISHLY MISGOVERNED ISLAND OF HIS BIRTH,

GAVE HIS CHILDREN A CATHOLIC

EDUCATION,

—NOT A MIXED OR GODLESS ONE,—

AND WHOSE SOUL, IN REWARD OF HIS HAVING DONE SO, NOW,

AS MAY BE HOPED, DWELLS IN LIGHT INACCESSIBLE,

THIS TRANSLATION IS,

IN THE SPIRIT OF FAITH, AND IN THE SPIRIT OF FILIAL

GRATITUDE,

DULY INSCRIBED BY THE TRANSLATOR.

DEDICATION.

Most Exalted Mother of God, Queen of Heaven and of Earth, and our Most Loving Mother!

Behold at thy feet, most exalted Queen, a poor gift from the most miserable of thy servants. It is thine, O Lady! and though it is not worthy of thee, yet can it belong to no one else than to thee; for it is thine. Thou knowest that in the troubles of this life I have found no dearer refuge than thy protecting mantle, and no greater consolation than that which I have found in recurring to thy graciousness, and in entreating thee to excite in my heart the most lively confidence in God. The multitude of the mercies which thou hast shown me, produced in me the most ardent desire to offer thee a small tithe of my thanks—thanks which on so many grounds I owe thee, and which I can never sufficiently express. With the view to satisfy this desire, I resolved to compose a book that might be promotive of thy honor, and conducive to the end that all souls may be encouraged to build their hopes chiefly on thee, next after building them on God himself. Behold this little gift, O Lady! such as it is, here at thy feet. Deign to accept it with that condescension with which thou acceptest the things that are agreeable to thee; for more, far more, would I delight to bestow on thee were it but in my power to do so. Look upon it as thy own, and as such, bless it by showering upon all who shall use it abundance of graces and favors! Impart to these poor prayers such efficacy that they may inflame the coldest and most unfeeling souls with love for thee! The grace, O Mary! to know thee and to love thee—this grace is the recompense which I earnestly entreat of thee for others and for myself. Grant it me, O Mistress! for if I love thee on this earth, I am assured I shall love thee for all eternity in heaven; and should I be successful in inducing others to love thee, I shall be certain of co-operating to their eternal salvation. Amen.

PREFACE.

We have already very many books treating of the most holy Virgin,—books, too, which are most estimable in every regard. Some persons, in view of this fact, will perhaps say: Is not a new book on our Blessed Lady at best useless? A great blessing to the world were it, if freethinkers acted on this principle; for then they would cease to multiply every day the number of those impious and corrupting books which are so baneful at once to religion and to society. But to the great misfortune of mankind, freethinkers take not this view of the matter; and consequently we see published nearly every day a countless multitude of books, which ruin the mind and corrupt the heart of those who touch them.

Many families are aware of this, who, with tears of blood, deplore the foolish waywardness with which children betake themselves to reading of such books. And even should the streets and the houses teem with those publications, neither their authors, nor their distributors, nor their readers, ever say, "We have enough of them." Yea! even every trouble is taken to maintain in constant fruitfulness the impure vein which produces them, and no expense is spared to facilitate their circulation. And when a new book appears, having for aim to promote that which is good, should well-meaning persons look upon the publication as superfluous for the mere reason that there are already extant a multitude of such books? Oh, how true is it that "The children of this world are wiser in their generation than the children of light." Luke, xvi. 8 v.

Because of the difference in the tastes and constitutions of individuals, variety of food is of very great utility, for that which is agreeable to some is not palatable to all; and so in like manner, variety of books is very profitable by reason of the different tastes and of the different necessities of souls. This person prefers to use one book, that another: one finds more consolation in this, another in that. Hence the saying of St. Augustine: "To the end that one and the same thing may be communicated to very many persons, to some in this way, to others in that, many books written by many authors, in different styles, but not in different faith, are useful, even though such books treat of the same subjects." (Book 1st, ch. 3rd, on the Trinity.)

On the other hand, there is not of plain and cheap books on the Virgin, any such superabundance that many other books might not usefully occupy hitherto unoccupied ground. At all events, devout reader, the love which thou conceivest to the most holy Mother of God, will make this book acceptable to thee, at a time at least, when we all, in extreme need of her most powerful intercession, should, with tearful eyes, turn to her who is the anchor of our common salvation.

Little or nothing of what is new will be found in this little work; for I did not contemplate the composition of a book which should contain nothing that had been said and repeatedly said by others before, but rather the composition of a book, calculated to promote love and devotion to Mary. Thou wilt, then, in these pages meet many things which thou hast, ere now, perhaps frequently read in most approved authors. To every one that which belongs to him, and to God all honor!

There are here fifty-two meditations, as many as there are Saturdays in the weeks of the year; not that those meditations are not appropriate for all the days of the week,—since the Virgin Mary should be every day honored;—but because Saturday is consecrated to her by the Church, and pious souls are accustomed to distinguish this day by performing special works of devotion in honor of their Mistress. Since, furthermore, the honoring of the Virgin,—to advance which is the aim of this little work,—comprises in it, as so many parts, high esteem of her, imitation of her, and confident recourse to her goodness; so in the order of those meditations, I have followed to some extent this division which appears advantageous, as well according to the natural course of the life of the most holy Virgin Mary, as in regard to those moral considerations which, deduced from the truths meditated, are applied to the necessities of the soul.

For this reason I set forth in the first place her principal dignities; then her virtues; and lastly, the benefactions which her hands pour forth upon us in abundance.

Each meditation is divided into three points—a plan which will be found convenient for priests who have to preach or otherwise to speak on the Virgin. It will not be difficult for them to find, in such a variety of matter, what they are in quest of; and since the division is already made, and the matter already in order, they can have no further trouble than to develope, a little more, the matter furnished them in these pages.

The three first meditations are, as it were, the keys to the others, because they touch in a general way the subjects which are afterwards to be developed in their proper places. In them all, especially in those which treat of Mary's benefactions, an endeavor has been made to infuse courage into those who are in sin and in affliction, and to encourage all to place confidence in this most sweet mother. And, in truth, who in this valley of tears, is our dearest refuge and the sweetest attraction for the purpose of leading souls to

God? We are indeed astonished at Mary's dignities; but, to the miserable, the thought of her mercies is sweeter and more welcome. "Her virginity," says St. Bernard, "her humility, we marvel at; nevertheless, her mercy speaks more affectionately to the wretched." (Fourth Sermon on the Assumption).

This reflection occasioned yet another, to wit, that those meditations should be plain and intelligible to every class of persons. Let then the reader not be astonished at not finding any great exhibition of Latin sentences, and of such principles and proofs as are too subtle and scientific, and are hence not adapted to the comprehension of all. May it please the Lord that the holy desire to advance in the knowledge and love of the Virgin Mother may burn in all the faithful, since indeed they all are her children! Oh, how condescendingly would she from on high comply with that wish! How much good would accrue unto souls therefrom!

But in order that the reader may obtain from this book the wished-for fruit, the Virgin must be accompanied with different dispositions, according to the virtues and the mysteries meditated upon. "If the psalm pray," said St. Augustine, "pray also; if the psalm lament, lament also; if it congratulate, then rejoice," &c.

Let us, accordingly, rejoice at her joys; let us mourn

over her sorrows; and let us congratulate ourselves on her glories. In one word, those meditations will be beneficial to us, if, in all earnestness, we excite ourselves to love Mary, and if we determine to imitate her example by means of practical resolutions. Let us then admire her unspeakable dignities; let us felicitate ourselves with her on the great privileges which God conferred upon her; let us affectionately dwell upon her actions and words, in order to form in us her virtues, in order to render our life comformable to hers in the best manner possible. Let us promise ourselves that we shall receive every grace from her; and let us, with unbounded confidence, place ourselves and all that we have, in her hands. In one word, let us render to her all the interior and all the exterior homage which holy Church requires, and which is so agreeable in the eyes of God.

If we meditate on Mary's life in this manner, we shall grow in virtue; and growth in virtue is the precious fruit of honoring her. If we meditate on her life in this way, we shall in life and death enjoy her special protection, and be one day infallibly called to the enjoyment of the eternal happiness which we await, and which the most holy Virgin, in her mercies, aims at obtaining for us. Amen.

CONTENTS.

Subjects of the Meditations, arranged according to the order of the Festivals which are celebrated throughout the year in honor of the Most Holy Virgin.

Movable Feasts referred to in this Work.

SATURDAY.

FIRST MEDITATION.

THE PRIVILEGES OF MARY.

FIRST POINT.

THE ORIGIN OF MARY'S PRIVILEGES.

THE fountain whence flowed the privileges which adorn the Virgin, is no other than the especial love which God bears to her, a love which neither human nor angelic tongue can ever adequately portray. God loves her alone more than he loves all the hosts of blessed spirits in heaven, and all the hosts of just souls militant on earth. Numberless, says the Lord, are the souls whom I love: "There are young maidens without number:" Cant. vi. 7 v. One, however, has succeeded more than all others in winning my heart: "One is my dove, my perfect one is but one:" Cant. vi. 8 v. Such is the teaching of the holy fathers,—St. Augustine, St. Bernard, St. Anselm—and among divines, Suarez, one of the chief, maintains that "God loves the Virgin Mother more than he loves all the other saints."

And still how exceeding great must not be his love of them! The apostles, for example, who with so many labors and toils converted the world! the martyrs who so heroically laid down their lives for him! the virgins who, out of love for him, preserved the lily of their purity spotless at the expense of long and sharp conflicts! the hermits, the confessors; in short, all others who gave him so many proofs of their fidelity and love! Now say to thyself: the love which God conceives towards all the saints taken together is, in comparison with that which he bears to the Virgin alone, as a spark to a conflagration; so that, if, what however is impossible, he were obliged to choose between giving up Mary and giving up all the other saints, He would prefer being deprived of them all, rather than that He should suffer the loss of her alone.

"Who," cries out in astonishment St. Anselm, "can measure this love?" Our Lord in the effusion of his love said one day to St. Theresa: "Had I not yet created the world, I would now create it for thy sake alone." What then would He have said or done had He been obliged to attest to Mary the love which He bore her? to Mary, who is dearer to Him than all the saints, and in the presence of whom they all pale as stars before the sun? We have no plummet which can enable us to investigate the depths of this sea of love; as we contemplate it, our understanding becomes confounded: so answer the holy fathers who, after having said all they knew of God's love to her; still further declare that they had said nothing, and that they could not find words to give due utterance to their conceptions.

What thinkest thou during this meditation? What is the character of the feelings which arise in thy heart? Be glad and rejoice at her beautiful lot; exult with her; render her thy most cordial felicitations; say unto her what thou wouldst say to a person who was exceeding dear to thee, and whom the greatest good luck imaginable had befallen. Oh, how soon wouldst thou in such contingency have dispositions and words at hand!

SECOND POINT.

THE FULNESS OF MARY'S PRIVILEGES.

Who glows with warm love, acts not with niggardly reserve when there is question of communicating his goods to the object of his affection. This observation applies to God in his dealing with the most holy Virgin. So many privileges and so many treasures did he bestow on her that their only measure is the love he bore unto her.

What, in fact, has he not conferred on this incomparable creature? Ever from eternity, her among all he singled out to be the mother of his only begotten Son; he elected her from all flesh; he fore-ordained her to the enjoyment of the highest degree of glory; to the rule which governed all the other descendants of Adam he made her a solitary exception, by singularly preserving her from the stain of original sin, which is inherited by each and every one of them; ever from eternity he wished she should in the first instant of her conception be all immaculate, all pure, and all holy. He filled her with grace, and confirmed her in its fulness. He wished such superabundance of this grace to inhabit her, that already, at the beginning of her existence, she was richer in graces than is any other saint at the close of his career. He wished that in her should be united two extremely incompatible privileges, namely, virginity and motherhood; but united so that she should have the fruit of motherhood, yet not contract the defilement attaching to motherhood; and also that she should enjoy the honor accorded to virginity without inheriting the fruitlessness which is virginity's concomitant. He desired to behold her honored and revered in heaven as supreme mistress and lady; he desired to know that she was honored and invoked on earth, as the refuge of the miserable, and as the consolation and the salvation of all.

The infused gifts of body and mind he imparted to her in measure so overflowing, that all those which divine generosity conferred on all other beloved souls would not, were those gifts put together, nearly equal those with which Mary was endowed. "Many daughters have gathered together riches; thou hast surpassed them all:" Prov. xxxi. 29 v. On some persons God bestowed—who knows it not?—such splendid gifts, that the recipients, even during their earthly life, excited universal astonishment. Call to mind, for example, a Bernard of Clairvaux, a Philip Neri, a Francis of Sales, a Francis Xavier, a Theresa of Jesus, a Stanislaus Kostka, though so very youthful:—hearts were won by the heavenly countenance of saints such as they, so eminently shone forth in those holy personages the gifts of the Lord. Now imagine all those gifts united together which in so many centuries he conferred on so many millions of saints of both sexes, and then, without fear of error, say to thyself: "Mary alone received an incomparably greater multitude of gifts." "She outstripped," says St. Bonaventure, quoted by Cornelius A. Lapide, "in natural gifts all daughters; she outstripped them all in grace likewise; she outstripped in glory all daughters, that is to say, all human souls and all angelic spirits."

Oh, what a treasure! immeasurable, sovereignly precious, unspeakable! Oh what fulness of privileges and of greatness! What oughtest thou to do on contemplating this fulness? To praise God, to glorify him, and to thank him for the generosity with which He enriched Mary. This manner of honoring her is most acceptable to her, as she often informed souls devotedly attached to her service. Say therefore: "I thank thee, eternal Father, for the privileges which thou hast accorded to thy first-born daughter; divine Son, I thank thee for the greatness imparted to thy most holy Mother; divine Spirit, I thank thee for the treasures communicated to thy beloved spouse. Praise, glory, and thanks be to thee, O most exalted Trinity, for the generosity which thou hast exercised towards Mary."

THIRD POINT.

THE EXCELLENCE OF MARY'S PRIVILEGES.

So splendid and so glorious are the privileges which God conferred on the Virgin, that by them she was elevated to a sphere peculiarly her own in this world, and was constituted a subject of admiration to even the angels of heaven.

Quite too feeble are our comparisons to convey a just idea of the sublimity of the treasures with which Mary was enriched. Those treasures were indeed quite other than heaps of gold and multitudes of most precious pearls, obtained from the seas and from the mountains. God elevated her in such a manner that among all mere creatures she should become the most exalted, the most holy, and the most worthy of his love: "worthy of the worthy," to use the characteristic expression of St. Augustine. When he created the heavens he fashioned them with his fingers: "For I will behold thy heavens, the works of thy fingers:" Prov. viii. 4 v. And when he afterwards formed Mary it is said that, by reason of her exaltation, he brought into requisition the might of his arm—"He hath shown might in his arm:" Luke i. 51 v.—so excellent are the treasures which he poured forth in the work of her composition. St. Gregory likens her to a high mountain which, on account of the elevation of its peaks, rises above all other mountains: "Mary was a mountain, in that, by her high election, she towers above all the dignities of chosen creatures."

The holy evangelist, John, represents her to us as illumined with a crown of stars, the moon as her footstool, clothed with the sun, in order to discriminate between her and the other saints, who also have their being in an atmosphere of light. So exalted, therefore, and so admirable does she appear, that she goes forth not only as one adorned for the bridegroom, but as *the one* adorned by the bridegroom; as another interpreter puts it: "Prepared as a bride adorned by her husband." The same thought is to be met with in the holy fathers, and is by them expressed in most ingenious terms—terms which can apply to Mary alone. They call her: the most splendid of miracles; the miracle of the miracles of God; the solicitude of the eternal council; the most beautiful work which issued from the Creator's hands; the one, all created for the one; the beautiful rainbow of salvation; the production of the pure divine sun; the splendor of the omnipotence of God; the temple of his grace; the theatre of his glory; the delight of the divine heart; the ever lovable and ever beloved Virgin: and finally they declare that she is the one, the only one, worthy of the Creator. These, and a thousand other expressions of a like nature which are frequently to be found in the works of the fathers, give us to understand how exalted are her privileges and how highly were they esteemed by those learned and sainted authors.

Now what follows from all this? When thou meetest a person distinguished by privileges, thou renderest honor to that person in the best manner thou knowest how. This do proportionally towards the most holy Virgin—honor her all thou canst with all homage; and be not afraid that thou shalt overstep the just limits. Who, after God, is more deserving of all worship? Examine the character of thy interior and exterior worship in the past; examine whether thou hast at all times, and in mind and heart, esteemed and honored her; whether, in her churches, at the foot of her altars, and before her images, thou hast evinced that modesty and respect to which she is on so many grounds entitled.

Oh, exalted lady! worthy the veneration of angels and of men, I confess my negligence and callousness; the angels are never tired of contemplating with astonishment thy manifold greatness, and always count it an honor to them to offer thee their homage; and yet I was so devoid of feeling, and so lukewarm! Ah! pardon me my blindness—henceforward, matters shall be otherwise; next after God, thou shalt be the most exalted object of my reverence; and that thou shalt be such I promise to evidence both in private and in public, both by my words and by my actions. Amen.

SECOND MEDITATION.

THE VIRTUES OF MARY.

FIRST POINT.

MARY POSSESSED ALL VIRTUES.

As the Lord desired to see the most holy Virgin more honored than all other creatures, so He willed also that she should on her side merit this honor by the full possession of all virtues. "An astonishing creation," says the amazed John of Damascus, "whom the beauty of the virtues inhabits!" But why wilt thou inquire if there are virtues in Mary? Yea, in her, says St. Ambrose, is mirrored forth the genuine emblem of virtue; she is "the type of virtue; in her as in a most exquisite model are the lessons of righteousness set forth." It would appear that God himself wished to point this out to us, since in the inspired writings he calls her "an enclosed garden:"—"My sister, my spouse, is a garden enclosed, a garden enclosed, a fountain sealed up:" Cant. iv. 12 v.

And that was no common garden which lies open to the eyes of the curious, but rather a garden reserved for the divine majesty alone, as is the case with the royal gardens which, on account of the preciousness of the flowers to be found therein, and of the distinguished character of the persons for whom they are preserved, are with every possible solicitude watched and kept close. Dost thou imagine that if she had not all virtues, that if even one of them were lacking to her, she would be the most delightful garden of the majesty of God, and a garden laid out merely for his enjoyment? Certainly not; for otherwise she would have been in no way so perfect that she had left nothing more to be desired; she would have had in her nothing so worthy as to induce him to exclaim, "My sister, my spouse, is a garden enclosed."

Run over now in thought all the virtues—the infused, as well as the moral—faith, hope, and charity, which are called divine virtues because they are proper to man, inasmuch as he becomes, by grace, partaker of the divine nature—prudence, justice, temperance, fortitude, which are called human or moral virtues, because they may be met with in man in his natural state, even when he is not elevated to a supernatural condition; so all the other virtues which emanate from these—virtues such as humility, patience, resignation, morality, virginity, love of one's neighbor, and the other virtues to the very last—and having looked over them all, say with St. Jerome: "No virtue, no beauty, no splendor, no glory is there which shone not forth in her." Yes, all the virtues, without a single exception, flourished in Mary, and without the least defilement of fault, or defect of any kind whatever; and in blooming in her they bloomed in so pure and delicious an atmosphere, under such fresh and invigorating influence, that she became by them what St. Gregory of Cæsarea styles her, "the paradise of God."

Meditate attentively on such beautiful virtues; be

astonished at them; esteem them: however, content not thyself with doing all this—for if thou wilt pass for her true servant, thou must form all those virtues in thyself. Mary assuredly possessed them all. How many of them dost thou possess? How many of them are wanting to thee? Were all of them lacking in thee, yet shouldst thou not lose courage; if thou hast a good and upright will to honor her in so excellent a manner as by imitating her, then will she trace out for thee the path to her imitation, and then too will she bless thy efforts. In moments when thou desirest more than at other times to secure her protection,—for instance, in the exercise of the nine days' devotion with which thou preparest to celebrate her festivals, offer her this homage; I mean the homage of being very assiduous in imitating one of her most conspicuous virtues, say one of those three, her humility, her patience, her love of her neighbors,—and believe it firmly, this practice will prove to her very acceptable.

SECOND POINT.

MARY POSSESSED ALL VIRTUES IN THE MOST PERFECT DEGREE.

The Lord himself established, in the soul of the Virgin, all virtues; and he established them by the most signal and pre-eminent confirmation in grace, of which there was ever an example. This confirmation consists in the fact that no attraction, of any kind whatever, to sin of any description whatever, had any place in her. Thence comes it that her virtues were of so heroic and of so extraordinary a nature; thence comes it that she possessed them in a far higher degree of perfection than that in which they are possessed by any other just souls. Who then can measure the excellence and the eminence of those her virtues? Albert the Great says that Mary possessed the virtues in the same perfection as the blessed citizens of heaven; and she possessed them whilst she was in that state which is proper to earthly pilgrims, and this state is that of merit. She possessed the virtues in the perfection of their acts, as do those who enjoy the vision of God; and she possessed them with the capability to acquire merits, as acquire those who are pilgrims on earth. And Sophronius takes occasion to remark that as in comparison with God no creature is good, even so is it true to say that, in comparison with the Mother of God, no creature is perfect, even though it were adorned with all virtues: "As no one is good compared with God, so is no creature perfect compared with the Mother of the Lord; and were there one such creature, that creature should be embellished with very extraordinary virtues."

The glowing virtues of the saints are worthy of admiration; but how far removed are those virtues from the perfection which they reached in Mary! There is not one saint who approached the Virgin in unlimited and perfect possession of all the virtues; there is not a single saint who in the perfection of even a single virtue could bear any comparison with her. Not one of the saints is so perfect in humility as is the Virgin; in obedience, in virginity, in patience, in love, in strength of mind, in heroism—in all these virtues, not one of the saints is so distinguished as Mary. Even in the special virtue in which each stood pre-eminent, she shines among them as the sun among the stars. Oh, what a wonderful phenomenon must she have been, and how precious must have been the spiritual jewelry with which she was adorned!

Notwithstanding all this, it may be said rather that the virtues were adorned by Mary, than that she was adorned by the virtues; and this is an observation similar to that which St. Bernard makes of the stars which form a halo of light around her head in heaven: "Much truer is it to say that she adorns them, than that she is adorned by them."

Hast thou one virtue—one virtue at least—in a perfect degree? Dost thou desire, dost thou at least endeavor to advance, or art thou one of those who, in order to avoid offering themselves any violence, lag behind in that lukewarmness and miserable indifference in which they find themselves? Remember that, in the path of virtue, not to advance is the same as to go back:—"Not to progress is to retrograde."

Bear also in mind that if thou wilt honor Mary in an especial manner, thou must take pains to imitate her as perfectly as possible, by endeavoring for instance to exercise more charity towards thy neighbor, and more vigilance over all thy actions. Oh! with how many precious jewels wilt thou be one day adorned, when thou shalt appear in presence of the Virgin Mary!

THIRD POINT.

MARY PRACTISED ALL THE VIRTUES IN SUCH MANNER AS TO ACQUIRE FOR HERSELF INCOMPARABLE MERITS.

In Mary the virtues were not inactive, but rather were constantly exercised; and as Richard of Saint Victor well said, "they poured themselves forth in continuous exercise." Their worth consisted not merely in that they adorned her, but rather in that they were ceaselessly and uninterruptedly reduced to practice. As God subjected the Virgin on earth to all the eventualities which are incident to human life, so had she an opportunity to cultivate all the virtues; and as he deigned to place her in situations even the most extraordinary and most trying, so found she occasions of practising the virtues in their very most difficult form.

Briefly ponder the principal actions and mysteries of her life—consider her in the most trying circumstances in which she was placed; when her most pure spouse struggled with the thought to put her away, when she was cruelly refused admission into the inn by the Bethlehemites, when the divine child was born in so unworthy and rude a cavern, when she, at only a few moments' notice, fled into Egypt —consider her present at the passion and death of her Son; and also consider her in the midst of the other difficult and continuous troubles which were distinguishing characteristics of her life. Behold how she bore herself through them all. Oh, what persistent exercise of heroic virtues! what great faith! what great resignation! what great fortitude! what blind obedience! what complete surrender into the hands of God!

Nor was it only on very solemn and extraordinary occasions that she practised these virtues; no, she practised them on the simplest and the most common place occasions. "In every sterling virtue she was perfect," says Richard of St. Victor; "she was perfect in her speech, perfect in her going out and coming in, perfect in the humble services which she rendered her family." Yes; as in all things she strove after nothing but the accomplishment of the divine will, so she proposed to herself to embrace nothing but what the wisdom of God pointed out to her! Inflexibly adhering to this heavenly rule, she ordered not only her words and works, but also her wishes, her thoughts, her inclinations, and all else exterior and interior, in the most perfect manner possible.

Who then can form an idea of the merits she acquired during so many years of her life, in every moment of which she corresponded so faithfully with grace, co-operated with it so assiduously, and glowed with such great zeal infused into her by the spirit? "Mary," says the holy Bernardine, already quoted, "infinitely transcends in merit whatever can be said or imagined of all creatures, whoever they be that are inferior to the God-Man."—Gifted already at the first moment of her existence with the most profound knowledge of God; animated with prevenient, operating, all-penetrating grace; already she resigned herself wholly and entirely into his hands, and enriched herself more and more with virtues, so that, as says Suarez, she could, at the close of her life, acquire by a single action as many new de grees of grace as she had acquired in all her life before.

This, exclaims St. John of Damascus, is an abyss which we cannot fathom. Human life is not exempt from painful experiences—from painful experiences which cannot be meritoriously undergone by a person devoid of healthy and robust virtue. Perhaps some such experiences have already traversed thy career, and perhaps some such will traverse it hereafter. How hast thou conducted thyself on those occasions? With what resignation to the hands of Providence? Oh, what a difference is there between the desire to imitate Mary, and the actual imitation of her by the exercise of virtue in even the most trying moments! Acknowledge that up to the present thou hast been weak; and entreat the Virgin to give thee her assistance for the future.

Oh, exalted lady, alike admirable in the privileges thou hast received from God, and in the virtues thou hast practised, cast a glance at this poor wretch who stands before thee, and who has the desire to honor thee after the manner which is most pleasing in thy sight! Oh, yes, in order to cause thee to rejoice, I will imitate thy virtues as well as I can; but do thou assist my weakness on all occasions. Strengthen then my will in the most difficult circumstances; and relying on thy protection, I promise thee that I shall bid farewell to my supineness, and that I shall become an active and industrious servant of thine. Amen.

THIRD MEDITATION.

THE BENEFITS WHICH MARY CONFERS.

FIRST POINT.

MARY CONFERS HER BENEFITS WITH UNSPEAKABLE LOVE.

No sooner is mention made of the most sweet name of Mary than there flits before the mind's eye the form of a most amiable creature—of a creature as elevated in position as she is merciful in disposition. When one looks upon her image with the eye of faith, then instantly the heart takes courage, and heavenly balm is infused into the whole soul. The faithful behold in her nothing else than an extremely loving mother, who for us is all sympathy, all mildness, all love: this is the conception which they most easily form to themselves of her, and so deeply rooted in them is this conception, that they can form to themselves no other.

The Church confirms them therein, by exhorting them to take refuge in her heart with all confidence. She even represents our blessed Lady as the mother of mercy, as the dearest hope after Jesus, as the fountain of tenderness, and invokes her under these encouraging titles: "O good, O mild, O sweet Virgin Mary!" The holy fathers let slip no opportunity that presents itself, of extolling her goodness; and though they have already said everything of her that can be said, they yet assure us that they could not find words fit to convey a just idea of the goodness and generosity of her heart. "Oh, thou who art worthy of all praise," exclaim St. Augustine and St. Bernard, "thou art that lauded land which flows with milk and honey, and in which every one finds a remedy for his evils and relief from his necessities."

What, wilt thou after all this inquire into the dispositions with which she distributes her graces? She distributes them cheerfully, and with more than a mother's love, without, however, arrogating to herself any credit for what she does, without reproaching us with our needy condition, and without being disgusted at our manifold wretchednesses. Yea, like her dear Son, she even goes in quest of the poor, in order that she may be the better help to them. She invites them to assemble around her throne; she gladly accepts their services; she is not put out of humor with their frowardness; she at times anticipates their request by her benefactions; and she rejoices when she is invoked and petitioned, because such petition and invocation give her meet opportunity to distribute her merciful favors with more profusion. Oh! with how much right does her servant Bonaventure say to her: "Thou, O Mary! art amiable towards all; thou givest sweet consolation to all; towards each one thou art affectionate; towards each one friendly; to every one thou grantest enjoyment!"

Let so great a love incite thee to flee to the Virgin in all thy necessities, but to flee to her with plenary and immovable confidence. Do this, and thou hast the key which will open to thee the treasures of all her mercies. Is it possible to cause greater pain to a loving and generous heart, than by calling in doubt its love?

Beware, therefore, lest thou become guilty towards the Virgin of committing so great a crime as that of calling in doubt the love of her heart.

But, truly, what hast thou to fear? In her surely there is nothing morose, nothing repulsive: "She is all charming, and offers to every one milk and honey." She is all mildness and grants her protection to all; therefore, repose thy trust in her always, be thy troubles ever so weighty, be the graces which thou obtainest, ever so great. Cast thyself entirely and without reserve into her holy hands: say to her that thou expectest everything which is good from her; and thou shalt, in the end, infallibly experience the exceeding greatness of the love which glows in the heart of Mary.

SECOND POINT.

MARY CONFERS HER FAVORS WITH ALL-EMBRACING LOVE.

Since all graces pass through Mary's hands, there is no grace dispensed save through the medium of her instrumentality; and hence it follows that there is no rational creature who has not to some extent had a share in her benefactions. As her divine Son excluded no one from the benefit of redemption, so in like manner her love excludes no one. "To all she opens the bosom of her mercy, in order that all might receive of its fulness."

Who in fact is it that has not tasted of its exuberance? In her the afflicted find consolation; the sick, health; the poor, support; the oppressed of every condition, assistance and strength: "the captive finds emancipation; the sick, recovery; the mourner, consolation." She gives her graces to the just that they may persevere and advance in virtue: she gives them to sinners, in order that they may be converted. "The sinner obtains pardon; the just, grace," says St. Thomas, archbishop of Valencia. Yes, she confers favors on those even who are not in the way of salvation; and this she does with a view to their enlightenment and eventual glorification. "She despises no one; she refuses her mercies to no one; she consoles all;" as Blosius happily observes. Amadeus compares her to a very beautiful tree which grows out of the middle of the earth towards heaven, and extends to the extreme confines of the world its branches, so that all might take secure refuge beneath them. "The very noble plant which sprouted upon the root of Jesse, ramifies by reason of the amazing magnitude of its branches, to all the countries of the earth, in order by its delightful shade to preserve from cold, storm, and rain, the children of Adam that are dispersed; and also in order with its most wholesome fruit to nourish them who are hungry."

What a noble figure is this employed by Blosius for the purpose of setting forth the all-embracing love of Mary! Who ought not to flee under the shadow of this tree? Who ought not to rejoice at having so secure a city of refuge? And who ought not to make an effort to enjoy its precious fruits? Let him be, in consequence of the darkness of his understanding and of the perversity of his heart, an unworthy commiserable sinner—if he flees to her, he will find every good: "He who has found Mary, has found all good." Oh!

how many out of all lands, of every state in life, of every age, of each sex, have experienced and yet daily experience in their doubts, in their tribulations, in their dangers and in their necessities, the workings of her loving protection! How many are through her become shining stars in heaven, who, were it not for her, would be wretched firebrands in hell! St. Germain says: "If it were possible for him to ask the saints in heaven, one by one, who helped them to attain felicity? he believes he would receive from all the same answer: 'It is Mary who has helped me to work out my salvation.'"

Hast thou, reader, received graces from this renowned Mistress? Has she assisted thee? Oh, how often! oh, how many graces! Glance at the dangers thou hast undergone, at the tribulations thou hast suffered, the straits in which thou wast placed: think on those moments when in trouble and in tears thou didst cast thyself at her feet; oh, how often on those and the like occasions hast thou tasted the sweets of her love! But was thy gratitude for those favors such as it ought to have been? Hast thou visited her as thy loving benefactress? or perchance hast thou failed to bestow a thought on her after having become the recipient of her graces? If this latter has been the case, then entreat her for pardon; and of pardon you have sore need, for there exists no greater monster than he who is ungrateful for favors received. Promise her to remember those which thou hast received from her—often thank her for them—thank her by word and actions; and be assured that this is the best means of paving the way to the obtainment of new and still greater benefactions.

THIRD POINT.

MARY DISTRIBUTES HER BENEFITS WITH UNBOUNDED MAGNANIMITY.

So exalted is Mary's magnanimity that it surpasses all expectation; she communicates her gifts with superabundance; she gives more, far more than is asked for. "She distributes," it can be said, "much more abundantly than we ever desire or conceive." Thou prayest to her for assistance, for bodily health, and she comes to thy succor in such a manner that, together with bodily health, thou receivest the health of the soul also. Thou prayest to her for strength to overcome a certain vice, and so abundantly does she give thee what thou askest for, that thou canst also obtain the virtue opposite to that very vice. Thou prayest to her to preserve thee from that danger; and she preserves thee from not only it, but from that other danger likewise which thou seest not, and which would befall thee, were it not for her protecting care. Thou repairest to her for assistance in that affair, and she helps thee not only in it but in another also, in regard to which thou standest more in need of her assistance.

Oh! that we were all able to discern the spiritual and the temporal favors which flow to us through her! Oh! how we would then recognize her beneficent right hand in so many things in which it is not now given us to recognize it! Solomon prayed to God for wisdom only; but God, "who is rich unto all who call upon him," restricted himself not to giving him wisdom; he gave him riches, he gave him power, besides; and to these he superadded earthly glory. Just in this manner acts Mary in proportion to her circumstances: and this is what Richard of St. Simon means when he tells us: "Mary's generosity resembles the generosity of her Son: she gives more than is asked for."

True, indeed, she will not grant thy petition instantly; for she also desires that, according to the order of Providence, she should be prayed with importunity. Though she may not answer formally and immediately, yet she will at all moments grant thee those particular graces for which thou hast petitioned her; and thus in her whole economy towards thee as her suppliant, she has in view thy greater utility. How often does it not happen that without being aware of it, we pray to her for temporal favors which would in the end, and if they were obtained, turn to our irreparable disadvantage?

What does she in such a case? She lovingly interprets our desires, subordinates our requests one to another, and then in the light of her affectionate wisdom and foresight, grants us other and better gifts instead of those which, in the blindness of our fleshy prisons, we had perhaps often solicited. For her holy and fond providence towards us, instanced in the observations just made, we shall never in this life be able to return her sufficient thanks. Be, moreover, convinced that her magnanimity is always greater than our confidence. She gives more than we hope to obtain—more, according to the multitude, and more, according to the worth, of the favors. She gives more than she is entreated for.

Happy those souls who turn to her with constancy and perseverance!

What then is the reason that in all thy necessities, thou dost not take refuge in this fountain of mercy? why art thou so timid? why so devoid of confidence? wast thou afraid that she would have for thee no graces? that she was unable or unwilling to help thee? In that case, oh, how egregiously thou hast managed to deceive thyself! Flee therefore to her right heartily—she has balm for every wound; and she wishes and rejoices to be able to pour it into thy needy heart. Often say to her with her great servant, Alphonsus Liguori: "I this day recommend myself to thee, I who am so poor in merits and in virtues, and who at the same time am so loaded with faults, committed against divine justice." Oh, Mary, thou hast in thy hands the key to all the divine mercies! Oh, forget not my poverty, and suffer not that I should continue in so great misery! Thou canst help—help accordingly—O Mary! my Mother, my light, my consolation, my refuge, and my hope, I cast myself wholly into thy arms.

FOURTH MEDITATION.

THE PREDILECTION OF THE MOST HOLY TRINITY FOR MARY.

FIRST POINT.

MARY IS THE DAUGHTER OF THE ETERNAL FATHER.

THE Virgin is a child of the eternal Father in a manner far more noble and far more glorious than the manner in which we are his children. He has paternity in relation to us for the great reason that he gave us being, and by his grace elevated us to the supernatural condition of his adopted children. All this he has done for Mary in common with us; and furthermore, she has been chosen in a special manner, as appears from the fact that God with his divine Son has made her in a particular manner the object of his election. Hence she is most intimately united with Jesus Christ; she enters with him by way of relationship unto the hypostatic union; she is as if almost on a level with him, and she assumes in virtue of the divine decrees the next place after him.

Speaking according to the material order of time, she is the daughter of Adam; but according to the plans of divine redemption, she is the first born among pure creatures: "I came out of the mouth of the most High, the first born before all creatures:" Eccl. xxiv. 5 v. From all eternity she has been the delight of the heart of God. "The most High

2

hath known her in advance and prepared her for himself," says St. Bernard, in his second homily on the Mass. On her he looked as on a chosen rainbow which, by the beauty of its brilliancy, should assuage his wrath and announce peace to the human family: he looked upon her as upon a bond which was one day destined to bind Heaven and earth in close and holy alliance. At the creation of the world he contemplated, and found delight in the thought, that he would one day make her queen of the universe. "For her sake," as says St. Bernard, "has the world been created;" since in the distribution of his graces, his favors, his treasures, all he bestows on others he bestowed on her alone, as on one world destined for himself alone. "God created Mary as a world that should belong to himself in a quite peculiar manner," says St. Bernard.

Seeing then that Mary was appointed to be the first born before all creatures, her creation entered into the eternal counsels of God; and all this was of course with the consent of his divine Son, since she was called to participate in one of the greatest of the mysteries of the most Holy Trinity, was elevated to the most close union with God, and was preferred and loved beyond all other creatures. "Who now can conceive in what manner she is a daughter of the eternal Father, the one and only daughter of life?" writes Dionysius, archbishop of Alexandria, "the one and the only one art thou, for thou appearest among the others as a lily among thorns; the one and the only one, because no other is so near to God as art thou."

Rejoice then with Mary on the predilection which the eternal Father entertains for her; but bear in mind that thou also art a child of God. God has favored thee more than he has favored a thousand others; he has elevated thee to the dignity of participating in his graces, his treasures, in never ending and eternal happiness: and all this he has done by making thee one of his adopted children. With how great solicitude hast thou guarded and preserved the character of child of God? Who knows, dost thou thyself know, how often thou hast wantonly trifled with that character, and how much displeasure thou hast thereby given thy good Father who is in heaven? Flee to him for pardon; and entreat this daughter so dear and so faithful to him, to use her influence on thy behalf, and to obtain for thee the grace that henceforward thou mayst never do aught unworthy a name so beautiful as is the name of child of God.

SECOND POINT.

MARY, THE SPOUSE OF THE MOST HOLY SPIRIT.

The illustrious title, "Spouse of the Holy Ghost," belongs to Mary in a sense as wonderful as it is strictly true. Her right to this title is based on the consent which she gave the Holy Spirit to descend on her soul and body, that she might, in virtue of that descent, become Mother; and also that she might, by it and in virtue of it, pass to a state wherein from her virginal body, might be fashioned the members of the Word made Flesh. "The spirit of God himself," says St. Ambrose, "who is the love of the father and the son, came corporally upon her, and made the Queen of heaven and earth his spouse."

"As a light cloud resolves into rain, invisibly penetrates the pores of the earth, and fructifies it without doing it the least damage, so the power of the Most High overshadowed Mary and maintained in all its integrity her most immaculate virginity," (St. Anselm). She resigned her virginal body unto the omnipotent power of God; and this omnipotent power formed in her womb and out of her most pure blood, a supremely perfect body: it created also a rational soul supremely excellent, and united soul and body together, and both with the person of the Eternal Word. Just in this manner did Mary become the spouse of the Holy Ghost. Since the fruit of her immaculate womb is the operation of the Holy Ghost, "what is born of her is of the Holy Ghost." The most pure eyes of this humble virgin—that is, the immaculate purity of her soul, and the very profound humility of her heart—caused the divine spirit to come down on her, and the only begotten Son of God to take up his abode within her.

Well, now imagine to thyself that a poor country maiden, not known beyond her own circle, was chosen for bride by a mighty monarch: oh, how highly would she esteem her happiness! what astonishment, what wide-spread envy would she excite! And still, however, what were that in comparison with the lot that was in store for Mary! Not a prince of this world, but the absolute Lord of all lords, fixed his eye on this creature who lived as if buried in an obscure retreat at Nazareth, and this humble creature he made his bride: "And I will espouse thee to me forever:" Es. ii. 19 v. Oh, the dignities! Oh, the glories of Mary! Rejoice again with her on the predilection which the Holy Ghost conceived for her; but then remember what caught for her the great esteem and love on the part of God! Not the riches and the greatness of this world—not these, but virtue it is which—he esteems; every thing else is nothing in his eyes.

Could not the Holy Ghost have chosen to himself a spouse, born and brought up weighted with gold and silver ornaments? This cannot be doubted; and yet he fixed his choice on a poor and obscure virgin, by reason of her purity and humility, which were great before him.

Imitate Mary if thou wilt be esteemed of God. Endeavor to be as Mary—humble, gentle, and chaste—and doubt not that God will know how to distinguish thee even in obscurity and poverty; and how to give thee signs, and consoling signs, too, of his predilection.

THIRD POINT.

MARY, THE MOTHER OF THE DIVINE SON.

As the most Holy Virgin is the true bride of the Holy Ghost, so also is she the true Mother of the only begotten Son of God; and therefore is she the true Mother of God. The instant she uttered those great words, which expressed her consent to the accomplishment of the unspeakable mystery proposed to her on the part of God by the angel—at that very instant the Eternal Word descended from the bosom of the Father into her most pure womb; he united to himself in unity of person the humanity formed by the operation of the Holy Ghost, and at that instant became man, being then God and man at the same time. "And the word was made Flesh:" John, i. 14 v.

At that moment, and in the most pure bridal chamber of the womb of Mary, was God espoused to human nature; and then also was our blessed Lady elevated to the dignity of Mother of God. Mary visited her cousin Elizabeth who dwelt in one of the mountainous parts of Judea; and it was on occasion of this visit that she received for the first time, and Elizabeth was accordingly the first who gave her, the glorious title of Mother of God: "And how comes it that this favor should be done me, that the Mother of my Lord should come to me? and whence is this to me that the Mother of my Lord should come to me?" Luke i. 43 v. The Apostle Paul also taught this when he said: "God sent his Son born of a woman:" Gal. iv. 4 v. The general council of Ephesus confirmed her in possession of this noble title by framing an article of faith on that special subject; and now, as they did in the past, the faithful invoke her daily: "Holy Mary, Mother of God!"

A creature—Mother of the Creator! A weak young virgin has for offspring the Immense, the Incomparable, the Omnipotent, the Eternal! Carried away by his astonishment, Saint Bernard cannot help incessantly calling this mystery "the miracle of miracles, the most pre-eminent work among the prodigies wrought by

Omnipotence: that a woman should conceive God, was a miracle eclipsing all miracles."

And also what predilection for Mary animated the Son of God? Were it possible that a man of this world could choose his mother, he would doubtless choose her whom he esteemed the most of all. Yet such choice is impossible for any mortal, because human might extends not so far; but the Son of God could make such choice, and even did make it. He himself chose her of whom he willed to be born. He chose unto himself his Mother; and this Mother is Mary. Learn from this to esteem in the highest degree possible this humble virgin, for whom the most Holy Trinity entertained so marked affection and predilection. Our divine Redeemer said one day to St. Margaret of Cortona, that neither the world nor the sacred writings themselves had said enough in regard to the Blessed Virgin. Oh, what an exceedingly high idea we should entertain of her! What is the character of the esteem in which thou hast hitherto held her? What idea can she form of this esteem from thy visits to her images and to her churches, and from thy prayer?

Oh, supremely elevated Virgin! oh, sublime object of the Divine complacence, I felicitate myself with thee in that thou wast loved beyond all others by the Father, the Son, and the Holy Ghost; and I should be very much humbled and put to shame if I could but see how low are my thoughts, and how miserly is the devotion which I entertain towards thee.

Ah, pardon me, O Lady! pardon me my ignorance and my coldness; grant me the grace always to advance more and more in knowledge of thee, because, according to my advancement in knowledge of thee, shall be also my advancement in esteem and love of thee. O Mary, I desire to be numbered among thy most zealous servants; I shall manifest to all the very high esteem in which I hold thee; but do thou on thy part deign to increase in me this esteem, and grant me the strength to manifest it by my actions as often as I shall have an opportunity. Amen.

FIFTH MEDITATION.

MARY'S ELEVATION BEFORE HER APPEARANCE ON EARTH.

FIRST POINT.

MARY IS PROMISED BY GOD.

How great is the honor which God showed to Mary, when he himself was the first to promise her to the world as a pledge of pardon and of peace! He acted after the manner of one who, having a very delightful promise to give, would assign to no one the honor of delivering it, but would charge himself with the delivery thereof. Just of this description was the course which God pursued. Already, at the first instant when he announced to our first parents the future Redeemer, then also did he foretell the victories and the triumphs of that Redeemer's Mother who is our Blessed Lady. "I will put enmities between thee and the woman, and thy seed and her seed; she shall crush thy head and thou shalt lie in wait for her heel:" Gen. iii. 15 v.

The conversation which took place at this mysterious interview, was the same in effect as if God had said to the serpent: "Thou didst vainly glorify thyself on that by means of a woman thou hast brought the human family to destruction; know, however, that I will cause another woman to appear on the scene, who with her immaculate foot shall bruise thy head and crush thy pride. This woman shall make good the losses sustained by her unlucky race, and shall repair the damages that race has suffered at thy hands." "Behold" says Andrias of Jerusalem, "Mary is promised from the beginning of the world, as the one who was to act a principal part in the treaty which was instituted between God and man. She was promised as the Aurora that was to renew the face of all things, and that was to go before or to appear in advance of the Sun of Justice." What honor did not God show to Mary by adopting such a course in her regard? What consolation, what motives to confidence, did he not thereby offer to Adam and Eve and all their posterity? Very probably our first parents knew at least that they were preserved from death in view of her, whether or not they had a very definite idea of the eminence of her prerogatives; and whatever obscurity marked their notions regarding her, they must at all events have been conscious to themselves of entertaining reverence, lively gratitude, and ardent love towards their well-favored daughter; for very probably they at least knew it was on her account that they were preserved from death. If God destroyed them not together with the whole world after the first dire disobedience, the escape all should attribute to Mary in a very especial manner.

Oh, how often must they have raised their minds to this beneficent daughter; how often would they by their yearning have hastened her advent; and then how often too, would they have reminded their children, their grand children, and their more remote descendants, of her as of the one in whom all generations were to be blessed! "And in thy seed shall all the nations of the earth be blessed:" Gen. xxii. 18 v.

In the hope of the great salvation which was in store for the world through the instrumentality of this exalted creature, the Patriarchs, and subsequently all other true believers, found in their common misery at once enlightenment and an incentive to discharge their duties to God. Even this assistance in the troubles of the present life, and even this incentive to serve God, should awaken in thee also the remembrance of Mary. God promised her to the world as a means of repairing the losses we had sustained, and as a sign of mercy in the moment of his anger, like as one who in the heat of battle all at once raises the banner of peace. So did God when he gave Mary.

Salvation is certainly thine, provided thou persistently lift up thy eyes and thy heart to Mary; for it is Mary who is the banner of peace. Hadst thou followed this course, how many a keen pang of regret wouldst thou have saved thyself; and how many sad falls wouldst thou have avoided! But instead of turning to her, thou hast looked to powerless creatures for help; thou hast leaned on them and forgotten Mary; or if thou hast remembered her, cold indeed has been thy invocation of her. Hold this thy past blindness in due horror; pray to the most Holy Virgin for pardon; resolve to be henceforward more solicitous about thy salvation, and more zealous in the service of Mary.

SECOND POINT.

MARY PROCLAIMED BY THE PROPHETS.

As Mary at the same time with her Divine Son was promised to the world by God, so also was she together with him the grand theme of the prophets' predictions. With a view to the great honor of the future Messiah, God willed that the way should be prepared for his advent by means of the old law; and so in like manner did God will that, for the Mother of the Messiah, the same law should clear the way. "Long before" says St. Bernard, "was she promised to the fathers and announced in the prophecies." "Drop down dew," so sighed the people, their faces looking heavenward, "Drop down dew, oh ye Heavens! and ye clouds, rain down the Just One!" And likewise the people addressed the earth, as though it were listening, and implored it to open up and shoot Him forth: "Drop down dew, ye heavens, from above, and let the clouds rain the Just; let the earth be opened and bud forth a Savior." Isa. xlv. 8 v. Oh how often, and in how many different ways, was Mary announced in the prophecies! Jeremias, Ezechias, and Isaias more than any of the prophets, speak of her very frequently; sometimes they employ figures, and sometimes not; but whether they employ them or not, they invariably treat of her in terms which clearly and unmistakably point out that she it is to whom they refer. "Behold a Virgin shall conceive and shall bring forth a Son."

David describes her in the Psalms, Solomon in the Canticle of Canticles: they depict her under the beautiful aspects of her greatness, her dignity, and her power. In the Book of Numbers, in the book of Proverbs, in the history of the emigration of Israel (Exodus), in the history of the creation (Genesis), in the book of Joshua son of Sirac, and in the other books of the old Testament, she is often foretold, pointed out, transparently veiled under images, so that St. Jerome did not hesitate to call her "the prediction of the prophets." And Andreas of Crete denominates her, "the sum and the substance of the decrees of God." Now imagine to thyself what yearning after her must have been produced in the ancient patriarchs by so many prophecies and so many announcements; and imagine also to thyself how ardently must have burned in the hearts of the people the desire of her advent! Such and so vehement was this desire that even the Heathens honored her, although their notions concerning her were in the circumstances necessarily confused; yes, even the Pagans themselves reverenced her, even went so far as to invoke her, and to erect temples in her honor, many, very many centuries before her appearance on earth; and on those temples might be read this most appropriate inscription: "To the Virgin who is about to become a mother."

Of Mary, in a measure as of her Divine Son, can be said that she was the "expectation of nations." In the present state of the world, thou hast no need to occupy thy head with the question of her coming; that question is long since settled. But thou must zealously endeavor to advance in knowledge and love of her; and likewise thou must endeavor to cause her to reign in thy heart by inspiring thee with most pure love of herself.

Oh, how much good would accrue to thee from those noble and earnest endeavors! Among men, desire without successful execution is of little or no account; but with God and his holy Mother the case stands otherwise; in their eyes, mere desire, when it is all that it ought to be, is meritorious and full of worth. "The Lord hath favorably heard the desire of the poor." The archangel Gabriel assured Daniel, that his (Daniel's) prayers were already heard from their very commencement, because he was a "man of desires." So also will the Virgin hear thy petition if thou ardently desire to become one of her true clients, and to serve her with an upright heart.

Awake in thee so ennobling an ambition, and inflame it by meditating on her virtues, by visiting her images, and by performing other exercises of piety and devotion in her honor; and if such be thy course, be assured that thou also shalt be able one day to say that she complies with the pious longings of her own poor suffering children in this valley of tears.

THIRD POINT.

MARY SYMBOLIZED IN THE BEAUTIES OF NATURE.

So zealous was the Holy Ghost for the honor of his well-beloved spouse, that he did not content himself with causing her to be announced so many centuries before her birth; but he wished, moreover, that the most beautiful objects of nature should be as it were but emblems of her.

The holy fathers are lifted into affectionate admiration, when they meet in every page of the inspired writings something that is extraordinary, and that shadows forth in the most striking manner possible her privileges. She is called a cedar, but a cedar of Lebanon; she is called a cypress, but a cypress of Sion; a palm, but a palm of Cades; an olive tree, but one of the most beautiful that ever flourished on any soil; an acorn, but one of the highest that ever grew in water; a lily, but one of those that shoot up among thorns; a rose, but one of those that grew in Jericho; a spikenard, but a spikenard of most delicious fragrance: yea, even is she termed an enclosed garden, in order with one short word to indicate that she comprises in herself the beauty and the charm of all flowers. In like manner is she termed a myrrh of predilection, odoriferous balsam, a pure cinnamon; and all these appellations are given her in order to show that she herself is the most excellent of all creatures. The other images of our Blessed Lady are, I might say, numberless; but every one of them tends to heighten our idea of her perfection.

Accordingly, we find her styled the tent of God; the ark of the covenant; the propitiatory seat of the temple, the blooming rod; the well sealed up; a bush which burns but is not consumed; a dove without spot; a fruitful vine; a field waving with the richness of its produce; the morning star; the aurora; a lighted torch beautiful as the morn, bright as the sun, charming as a many-colored rainbow.

All these things and a thousand others are intended by God to symbolize Mary; that is, they are intended to give a faint idea of her gifts, her virtues, and her privileges: as for example the integrity of her body, the elevation of her mind, the goodness of her heart, the glory of her triumphs, the security enjoyed under her protection. "Now these things were done in a figure." Cor. x. 6 v. But the images have now ceased, and we need no more look for Mary amid the beauties of nature: meditation on her life, on her actions, and on her mysteries, is, in this state of the world, sufficient for all our purposes.

Oh, how perfectly the figures, and the thing prefigured, correspond! She herself appears beautiful as the rainbow, lowly as the spikenard, blindingly white as the lily; she appears as the tent of God, as the distributor of his gifts; as the olive on the field.

Now it remains for thee to meditate on her life; to read the books which treat of her, of her dignity, and of her love. Oh! that thou hadst devoted to the reading of those excellent papers which portray her to thee some time, instead of squandering as thou hast done, so many hours in pouring over the pages of frivolous and dangerous books. Oh, how thou wouldst then feel thy spirit renewed in strength, and thy heart overflowing with pure joys! Oh, Mary! Oh, admirable Virgin! Oh! thou the desire of the Patriarchs, the longing of all the just and the desire of all hearts! I also shall endeavor to love thee daily more and more.

Oh, Mary, I deplore from my heart all the time which I spent in reading the fancies, the phantoms, and the reveries of creatures. Henceforward, I purpose to occupy myself with those books only which treat of thee.

Ah! how can I well find any object greatér, any object more noble, any object more beautiful or more precious, than art thou? Thou wast announced by God himself, foretold by the prophets, and symbolized in every thing that is most precious in the universe. Oh, Mary! strengthen the weakness of my will; confirm my resolution; fill me with love for thee; and then shall I remain faithful to thee forever. Amen.

SIXTH MEDITATION.

MARY'S GRANDEUR IN HER IMMACULATE CONCEPTION.

FIRST POINT.

MARY CONCEIVED WITHOUT SIN.

Among the descendants of Adam, Mary was the only one who was conceived without sin.

We all commence our existence in sin; we are all at that moment children of wrath, all objects of the hatred of God. His greatest friends, the patriarchs, the prophets, the apostles, the saints—even the precursor of Christ, although sanctified in his mother's womb—all were infected with the primal stain. One only exception was there to this general infection; and this exception was Mary. In her, as far as she was concerned, God frustrated the universal law and preserved her by a miracle of his Omnipotence from the universal stain; "for thee"—so spoke he to this well beloved daughter—"for thee and as far as thou art concerned, is the law of death deprived of all its force; through my favor thou shalt by no means die the death!" "Thou shalt not die: for this law is not made for thee but for all others!" Esther, xv. 13.

On that account it was already believed that Mary was never of the number of those who were defiled with original sin. Great, glorious, and beloved of God, was she at the very instant when she received existence; for never had she in her aught that was antagonistic to love—that aught would be nothing else than sin. Who, moreover, could believe that God who could choose unto himself an ever-beautiful and spotless abode, would have selected one which had been pre-occupied and desecrated by his most cruel enemy? "Ah! no," exclaims St. Anselm; "it would seem meet that this virgin should glow with the greatest purity that could be imagined to be possessed by any being inferior to God!"

The important truth that Mary was conceived without sin, is even an article of our holy faith; and books belonging to times long gone by, and which were used to carry out divine service, inculcated this same doctrine. In those books she is styled "the spotless." From the very earliest times, the holy fathers, too, taught that Mary was conceived without sin. They call her "the immaculate, the all beautiful, the all pure, and the all holy." The Church did every thing in her power to further the devotion and the reverence universally testified to Mary; the faithful, the world over, believed in her and honored her; and finally, after many prayers and entreaties had been addressed to the heavenly throne by the children of our heavenly Father, God through his representative on earth spoke and said: "The common enemy never had any share in this much beloved daughter; she was always free from stain; ever was she all lovable and all beloved."

Oh, what a privilege, what a triumph for Mary! Behold the lily among thorns; behold the ark that floats in security on the waters of the deluge which swallows up all else; behold the bush which ever preserves its greenness and freshness in the midst of the plains; finally behold the woman who crushed the head of the infernal serpent. Rejoice with her, and ponder how much Heaven must rejoice and exult in her possession of such privileges. So great was her horror for sin, that she would rather renounce her dignity as Mother of God than consent to be defiled with even one venial sin. Imagine then to thyself, how dear must have been to her this privilege whereby she was preserved free from original sin!

If thou desirest to be loved by her in an especial manner, if thou desirest to be loved with more than a mother's love, then fly from sin: beware of committing any fault whatever; avoid the occasions and the dangers of sin. Oh! how agreeable to her would such a course make thee! Then wilt thou be in a certain manner like unto herself in purity; and she on her part will not fail to manifest to thee her maternal predilection.

SECOND POINT.

MARY REDEEMED IN THE MOST PERFECT MANNER.

Although Mary was never defiled with the stain of sin, she belongs, however, to the number of the redeemed. Her divine Son redeemed all the children of Adam, and also his most holy Mother. But how much more perfect was the manner of her redemption than the manner of ours! St. Augustine teaches that "there is a two-fold redemption; the one delivers from the abyss those who have fallen into it; and the other anticipates the fall and prevents it." We all were redeemed in the first way; in the second way Mary only was redeemed.

Thus we see that the Virgin was not cured of any spiritual sickness, but she was preserved from being afflicted with spiritual evils. She was not lifted up after having fallen, but she was anticipated and not allowed to fall! "Others," very aptly wrote Cusano, "had a deliverer; the holy Virgin had a preserver." Our divine Savior desired, in virtue of his infinite merits, to make this all important difference in the case of his most holy Mother: "He redeemed her from original sin, according to a new plan of sanctification .... and preserved her by an extraordinary grace." St. Bonaventure's Second Sermon on the Assumption.

The great difference which seems to be in this regard between Mary's pure soul and ours, may be likened to the difference which obtains between a city into which the enemy could never enter, and another city of which he had obtained possession, and in which he had given loose reins to his anger. The first city is preserved uninjured and leaves no traces of struggle; the second is devastated and ruined. Unhappily this last is the case with our souls; even admitting that the enemy be put to flight, yet it is true that he left behind him scarce anything sound: into all the powers of our soul he distilled the poison of his wickedness—he introduced into us disorders and calamities of every sort. But on the other hand Mary was free from all the consequences of guilt, because exempt from the cause which produced them; in her all is sound, all in order, all in harmony.

She is as a sky never veiled with clouds, never troubled with storms, but always serene and delightful: "He placed his body in the sun," as says St. Thomas; that is, in the blessed Virgin who never was obscured by sin.

Rejoice with the most Holy Virgin upon her greatness, and pray for the strength necessary to repair the havoc which the sin of our first father has left behind in thy soul. Oh, what and how great a havoc is this! Oh, to how many struggles art thou not subjected by the mere propensity to evil, which in thee is so very violent! But yet despond not. Even the Saints felt the weight of this propensity, and deplored it in the presence of God! By his holy help, however, they were victorious over it: Mary suffered no injuries, and yet she none the less teaches us the means of repairing those we have suffered. This lesson she gives us in her examples, in her vigilance over herself, in the principles of her faith, in the nourishment of her soul by means of the word of God and of constant prayer. Imitate her as well as thou canst; live by faith; strengthen thyself by its principles; pray assiduously; watch over thy senses; and the Virgin will obtain grace for thee to triumph over thy enemies.

THIRD POINT.

MARY FILLED WITH GRACE.

Not content with having redeemed Mary in the most perfect manner, God wishes, moreover, to behold her filled with grace, even at the very first instant of her existence.

On this subject, the holy fathers in astonishment say that the Lord, at the commencement of her life, desired to pour into her his treasures, and to show forth in her his riches and his power. One of those learned writers styles her "an abyss of grace;" another, "a shoreless sea;" and yet another, "an immeasurable treasure." The world's Redeemer, says St. John Chrysostom, did not trouble himself about having a mother rich in earthly goods, but was solicitous to enrich her with spiritual treasures in the most supreme degree; and why did he so enrich her? "He sanctified his tent." He sanctified it by filling it with the rarest gifts he can bestow; and this gift is his grace. Suarez says, that "at the very first moment of her being she possessed such and so abundant graces, that the like were accorded neither to the angels in heaven nor to the most holy among the saints, not even when the zenith of their sanctity had been attained."

In the first sanctification, the grace of the Virgin transcended the highest grace by which either angels or men attain to perfection: angels even of the lowest order received abundant grace; angels of the highest order received grace in measure unspeakably more abundant. Well now the last and highest grace which was granted to the most exalted of those blessed spirits, pales in presence of that grace which was granted to Mary at the first instant of her immaculate conception; and the same is to be said of the last grace which was granted to the greatest among the saints even in the latest moment of life. This was the view of Suarez; and before him, of St. Vincent Ferrer and St. Lawrence Justinian.

Now, canst thou understand why it is said: that the Lord loves the beginnings of this extremely noble temple of Sion more than he loves all the tents of Jacob even when they are finished? "The Lord loveth the gates of Sion above all the tabernacles of Jacob." Ps. lxxxvi. 2 v.; because on her first coming into existence, she was richer and greater than all the others are when they have attained their highest degree of perfection. In view of such greatness, study to preach more and more the mystery of the Immaculate Conception; and rest assured that thou canst do nothing more agreeable to her, than to invoke her under this title, and thereby to call to mind her most cherished privileges. From this practice will result to thee two great advantages:—the first will be high esteem for divine grace, the least degree of which is more worth than all the treasures of earth; the second will be, that thou wilt merit for thyself her special protection at the hour of thy death. This is the reward which the most reputable masters tell us, she gives to those who are devout to her in this most beautiful mystery.

Oh, Mary! Oh, abyss of treasures and of graces! cast a look on this miserable wretch who is astounded at the most charming of the miracles of the divine love. O royal Mistress! in thee God illustrated his greatness; thou art exempt from all sin; thou art free from the sting of passions; thou art full of grace; and I am so loaded with sins, so violently acted upon by my passions, and make so little account of the grace of my God. Cast an eye on me, and have mercy on me; "Look on me and be merciful to me." Deliver me from all guilt;

help me to overcome my passions; and grant that as I honor thee as immaculate in the first instant of thy life, so in like manner every instant of my life, especially the last instant, may be free from every stain of sin. Amen.

SEVENTH MEDITATION.

MARY'S DIGNITIES IN HER BIRTH.

FIRST POINT.

MARY, CONFIRMED IN GRACE.

In the course of her life the most holy Virgin never committed any sin, not even the slightest; and this her spotless career, was in her the result of a special privilege she had received from God. That she committed no sin is an article of our holy faith; and from her sinlessness to the end, theologians conclude she was confirmed in grace: "Thence it follows," says Suarez, "that it must be admitted that, on occasion of her first sanctification, she was confirmed in good."

Accordingly, Mary was never bereft of divine grace, and never could have been bereft of it; but her inability to sin was not absolute and intrinsic as was her divine Son's. His resulted from the hypostatic union; her's from the fulness of her graces and the special assistance given her by the Holy Ghost. Yes, so great is the perfection in which this privilege was given her beyond all others, that St. Antoninus maintains that she alone of all the children of Adam was without sin: "the real truth of the case is, that she alone, of all the pilgrims, was unable to commit sin."

Already in her mother's womb she was as a charming meadow which, continually irrigated by pure and living waters, never could be parched up; already in the womb she was as an auspicious little cloud which, always clothed with the sun, never could grow dark; already she was as gleaming iron which, placed between two glowing coals, can never lose its heat. Her understanding was ceaselessly illumined by the rays of the divine sun; her heart constantly inflamed with the purest and most sublime love; her soul at all times overflowing with the living waters of grace. She thought on nothing but on God; she yearned after nothing but after God; she loved nothing but God: this was the business of her life—nay, was her very life itself. "This," says St. Thomas of Villanova, "this was the whole life of the Virgin; this the briefest summary of her pilgrimage."

Oh, with what great complacency the Father, the Son, and the Holy Ghost, looked upon this child of heaven who was destined to act so important a part in the accomplishment of the divine mysteries! With what burning love must she have acknowledged the gift and exclaimed: even from my mother's womb the Lord made me feel the impression of his grace, and he remembered my name: "from the bowels of my mother he hath been mindful of my name." Mary never committed any, never even the slightest, sin; and indeed she was unable to commit it.

How many sins, not merely slight but grievous, hast thou committed! How many canst thou not commit at every instant of thy life? Oh, how different is our lot from hers! Yet, do not imagine that on this account, she takes our falls and dangers less to heart. No, the greater our necessities, the greater her sympathy for us. The saying: "He who has suffered not knows nothing of sympathy," is by no means applicable to Mary; and never can tongue express the solicitude wherewith she endeavors to obtain pardon for poor sinners and to secure to them the grace of final perseverance. Likewise, perceivest thou not she has won for herself the admirable title of "refuge of sinners?"

If thou wilt obtain such excellent graces, flee to her; say to her thou art resolved never more to commit any sin; promise her that thou wilt employ all means in order that thou mayst persevere in good; then pray to her with confidence to obtain for thee holy perseverance to the end, which is the gift of all gifts. Mary will cheerfully grant thee thy request; and then thou shalt not have expressions adequate to declare to her thy gratitude.

SECOND POINT.

MARY, BORN WITH RICH ENDOWMENTS.

If the Holy Spirit communicates his gifts to each one, since each one is a temple of God: "because of his Spirit dwelling in you," Rom. viii. 11 v., by how much more and in how much greater fulness must he have communicated them to that heavenly infant who was destined at a future period to bear the Divinity corporally within her? At the creation of the seas God wished all the waters of the rivers to be gathered together: "Let the waters be gathered together into one place." Gen. i. 9 v.; and at Mary's creation he willed that in her should be concentrated all gifts, treasures, and graces, and whatever of brilliant and precious boons had been conferred on all other creatures.

The privileged and sainted creatures are the rivers which receive the heavenly waters in superabundance: Mary is the sea which comprises in herself all these rivers. O! what inestimable jewels did the Lord present her with, as though he had intended to adorn her for her nuptials! The apostle Paul says God distributes his graces: "Now there are diversities of graces." He does not give all to all persons, but one grace to this one and another to that one: "To one indeed by the Spirit is given the word of wisdom; and to another, the word of knowledge according to the same spirit; to another, faith in the same Spirit; to another, the working of miracles; to another, prophecy; to another the discerning of spirits; to another, divers kinds of tongues; to another, interpretation of speeches." 1 Cor. xii. 8 v.

But for the servants, not for the Mother was this rule laid down; for her there was no other rule than that of God's own Omnipotence: "God's Omnipotence is the measure of Mary's privileges." (Suarez.) God bestowed on her all gifts; he enriched her and filled her with treasures to an extent as great as was demanded by the most sublime dignity to which she was chosen. "On Mary He conferred the fulness of all goodness," exclaims St. Bernard in transports of admiration; and not content with this, the holy doctor adds, that all wonders are centred in her: "Every thing in her is a miracle." Oh, how lovely must this heavenly child have appeared in the eyes of God and of angels! What must the angels have said when they beheld her like unto the rising dawn, having her being in so much resplendence and adorned with so many precious jewels?

Doubtless will they have recognized her as the Mother of her Savior, and honored her and rendered her with emulation all sorts of homage.

Unite thy acts of honor and praise to those of the angels! Admire, and marvel at, the heavenly infant; and then reflect that on thee also God has conferred his gifts! He caused thee to be born in the bosom of the true faith! By holy baptism he made thee a living temple of the Holy Ghost! He made thee a child of his by adoption; he intended that thou shouldst be an heir to his heavenly kingdom; he overloaded thee with graces and treasures. How hast thou esteemed those boons? Hast thou made less account of them than of thy natural and human gifts—talents, wealth, riches, high position—forgetting that these latter also came into thy possession through the generosity and goodness of the Lord? And in consequence of thy forgetfulness, hast thou not neglected to render him the due tribute of thanksgiving for these his great favors unto thee?

Acknowledge thy twofold delusion; be grateful to thy benefactor for all the gifts thou hast received from him; but constantly bear in mind that spiritual favors are more precious than worldly and natural favors, by as much as Heaven transcends earth in intrinsic worth.

THIRD POINT.

MARY, BORN RICH IN MERITS.

Her privilege of confirmation in grace, and the fulness of her gifts, by no means operated as an impediment to her acquisition of merits.

"Mary," says St. Augustine, "could accumulate merits for herself; but to commit sin, she was not able." Already at the very first moment of her existence, endowed with the perfect use of reason, and enabled by supernatural assistance to love God, she instantly and with the completest perfection recurred to her Creator and Benefactor, by loving him with her whole soul, by adoring him, and by thanking him for the so great predilection and the so many privileges of which she had been the chosen recipient at his bountiful hands. Never was there, except Mary, a pure creature who, from the first moment of conception, loved God and humbled herself before him with the most sincere submission; never was there creature who had consecrated herself to him so perfectly as Mary, by directing to him all her thoughts, desires, and affections.

To say all in a word, there was never a creature who, from the first second of her existence, and for every second of her existence, could affirm of herself what St. Paul declared of himself when the shadow of his years had already grown long: "His grace in me hath not been void." 1 Cor. xv. 10 v. How is it possible to form an idea of the merits she acquired by her very first act whereby she cleaved to God with such profound knowledge of him, and with such perfect surrender of her will to him? What merits upon merits did she acquire during the nine months that she lay in her mother's womb? Suarez assures us that she merited without intermission, from the first minute she began to merit, her advancement in that career, and that she was never arrested nor interrupted in her course. "She merited in a fort"—Suarez.

Now, in order to find out the merit of the second act of her life, multiply by two the merit of her first act; in order to know the merit of her third act, multiply by three that of her second act; multiply by four that of her third, and so on to the moment of her birth, and this process will enable thee to conceive how multitudinous were her virtues on her entrance into the world. Offer the holy child thy felicitations on those her merits, and say to her that she outstripped all the daughters of Jerusalem: "thou hast surpassed them all." And, indeed, so great is the distance between her and them that in consideration thereof we must exclaim: "her like was never seen, neither among her contemporaries nor among those who came after her."

Admire such great riches at so infantine an age; and weigh well the fact that she acquired them by the right and holy use of the graces and gifts she had received from God. What use hast thou made of those he has conferred on thee? Hast thou employed, according to the will of the donor, the means so numerous placed at thy disposal for thy own sanctification and the succor of thy neighbor? Strict the account which God will require of thee in this matter; and indeed the greater has been his generosity to thee, the greater will be his strictness in exacting that account. The servant mentioned in the Gospel, was condemned to be punished, merely because he did no business with the talent he had received. Arrest the evil whilst time yet remains to thee; lay aside thy supineness, and let thy aspirations henceforward have a nobler goal. A jeweller who discovers he has misused his means in purchasing spurious for genuine stock, is ever after more on his guard, and leaves no stone unturned to repair the loss.

Act thou in like manner: "gather to thyself treasures in heaven;" this is the inspiration which the divine Master gives to all; and to facilitate thy following it, cast thyself down by Mary's cradle and say to her: "O wondrous child! thou who, on entering into this valley of tears, wast enriched with so many treasures that thou wast made the admiration of angels and the joy of men, turn those thy sweet eyes to me a sinner; for light, strength, and consolation accompany their glance whithersoever it be directed. I have lost the grace of my God; I have abused his gifts; not merits for heaven, but demerits have I laid up for myself—ah, exemplify in me the goodness of thy heart! Have me from this day in thy holy keeping, so that I may never again lose the grace of God; guide me, that I may henceforward make a more holy use of his gifts; grant me new strength that I may spend myself in repairing the losses I have already suffered. Act thus, O Mary! out of love for that God who caused thee to be so great and so holy when thou wast born." Amen.

EIGHTH MEDITATION.

MARY'S DIGNITY APPEARING IN THE SIGNIFICATION OF HER NAME.

FIRST POINT.

MARY! — LADY!

SHOULD God out of special favor impose a name on any one, that name would be as a secret document setting forth the offices or the qualities of the person so favored. This observation holds good in a very especial manner with regard to the adorable name of Jesus, and to the name of his most holy Mother.

Mary signifies *Lady*; and who in all truth can be called Lady, with so much right as Mary? If the Son is Lord and owner of all things, it follows that the Mother, also, is Lady and owner. Saint John of Damascus very aptly exclaimed: "Since Mary was the Mother of the Creator, she became the Lady of all things that are created." Hence the supremely glorious titles which the Church and the saints confer on the Lady of the universe! "Queen of Heaven, Empress, Princess, Dispensatrix of the divine treasures, Distributer of graces; most mighty Mediatrix between God and men."

No, on the face of the whole earth there is no rational creature who feels not the efficaciousness of her intercession. All that is not God, is inferior and obedient to her; and at her name, Heaven, Earth, and Hell, bend the knee. In Heaven the Angels stand, and hold themselves in eager readiness to execute her slightest intimations; on earth, men still daily experience her loving power, because in their regard, she wards off evil, and obtains for them what is good. In hell the evil spirits tremble when the name of Mary is invoked; and after the name of Jesus, there is against them no more powerful weapon than the name of Mary. All creatures are subjects of her dominion, because Jesus has subjected them all to her. "The Son subjected all created things to the power of his Mother," as says St. John of Damascus. Oh! how true is it that she merits to be styled Lady.

Oh, how applicable to her is so beautiful a term! "O Mary!" said to her Saint Ildefonsus, full of tenderness and holy joy, "thou art my ruler, my Lady, my Mistress! my Lady, and my Mistress who commands me." Thou also sometimes sayst, even often, that Mary is thy Lady; but dost thou say so, with the same disposition, with the same fidelity, with the same firmness of purpose to serve her, as spoke Saint Ildefonsus? See whether she has no reason to complain of thee.

The Saints faithfully rendered her the tribute of their service, and were proud to have her for their guardian Lady. They daily prayed to her; every Saturday they visited her and offered her their homage; they celebrated her festivals, after zealously preparing for them several days beforehand; they approached the Holy Table in her honor; out of love to her, they assisted the poor with more greatness of soul; and besides the practices mentioned, the saints honored her by other works of virtue which also were acceptable to her. Oh! how many examples are there, wert thou disposed to imitate them, of saints of every age, sex, and condition in life.

What, then, dost thou do in order to attest to this exalted Lady thy readiness to serve her? Dost thou imagine that thine actions are in harmony with thy words? Art thou faithful, art thou constant, in offering her the daily tribute of thy prayers; and art thou mindful to do what thou hast so often promised her that thou wouldst do, on the days consecrated to her? Examine thy conscience, and make a resolution.

SECOND POINT.

MARY! — THE ILLUMINED!

Consider how admirably this second signification also of her name is realized in Mary.

Illumined with every sort of knowledge—every sort, not only of acquired and experimental, but also of infused knowledge—she knew more of natural and supernatural truth, than any created intelligence ever knew, or ever shall know. Her knowledge lacked nothing that was suitable to her condition as Mother of God, as Queen of Angels, as general overseer or stewardess of the whole Church. Saint Gaudentius exclaims: "What is there which can be unknown to that Mother who bore a God in her womb?" What wisdom should remain hidden from that Mother who contained a God within her. Oh, what great reason has the Church to invoke her under the title of "Seat of wisdom!" How justly does St. Bernard style her "Abyss of wisdom!" She had most profound knowledge of the perfections of God, of the designs of his hidden Providence, of the charming artifices of his love, of the unspeakable heights of his happiness. To her mind the Divine perfections were disclosed in a far more perfect way than they were disclosed to the angels and archangels, seraphim and the other dignitaries of the heavenly court.

To knowledge of the divine perfections, she united that of Jesus as God and as man, as Redeemer and as head of the Church; and knowledge likewise of all that related in any manner to this most glorious institution. If to St. John the apostle were revealed the humiliations, contests, victories, and the triumphs of the Church militant, also the exaltation and the joy of the Church triumphant; how can it be well questioned that all those facts were likewise revealed to Mary, who was Teacher of the apostles, and the most solid support as well as the highest protector of the Church? Yes, says St. Bernard, it is credible that Jesus made known and revealed to his most holy Mother things which he either concealed from other persons, or at least did not declare to them so fully as to her. Yet of one thing we may be convinced, he instructed his Mother in virtue of his special predilection for her; and by way of privilege, he initiated her into many things. He conferred on her knowledge of the divine and the heavenly glories. So then was Mary that burning lamp, by means of whose glowing light the Church could at all times celebrate her triumphs over all errors: "Thou alone hast brought to nought all heresies throughout the world."

How much dost thou not need true wisdom? How little dost thou acknowledge God, and the good things he has now prepared for thee! How trifling is thy endeavor to procure thyself instruction in the things relating to thy soul! And yet in knowledge of these things, consists the most necessary wisdom; without this wisdom, all is vanity: "And I preferred her (wisdom) before kingdoms and thrones, and esteemed riches nothing in comparison of her." Wisdom vii. 8 v. Aim most zealously at its acquisition, and belong not to the number of those dupes who have a smattering of everything, except of religion and their own duties. Entreat the Virgin to send thee from on high a ray of that divine light which she possessed in so great fulness—one ray of that divine light which produced in so many contempt of what is earthly, and love of what is heavenly—often say to her, "Seat of Wisdom, pray for me;" and if thou be docile to her instructions, thou wilt experience that "She gives abundantly to all, and refuses none."

THIRD POINT.

"MARY, STAR OF THE SEA."

"Mary!"—This sweetest of names signifies also *Star of the Sea*; and such in fact is Mary. She is star of the sea, because she is the light, the consolation, and the directrix, of those who voyage on the sea of this world. Mary is a very useful star for the purpose of conducting us to our heavenly home; yea, useful even for the purpose of bringing us through the sea of this world, to the grace of her Son, "as to the haven of paradise itself."

The foregoing is the sentiment of St. Bonaventure. Whoever finds himself on the high sea, during a dark and stormy night, has no more cheering consolation, than that derived from looking up to that benificent star which will certainly indicate to him his course, and give to his heart fresh courage and renewed strength. And in like manner, whoever finds himself on the troubled and tempestuous sea of this world, has no dearer guide and support than Mary, to conduct him to the haven of a happy eternity.

Oh! how by means of her loving protection she conducts mariners through a thousand dangers; and the dangers over, the mariners are safe and sound. Temptations, the deceptions of the world, the snares of the evil spirits, cause indeed the sea of this life to be full of rocks; but what has he to dread who confides in her? The star which appeared in the heavens at the birth of our Redeemer, guided the wise men to the cave of Bethlehem where they found Jesus; and however mysterious was that star, a brighter one than that leads all who follow the brighter, to Jesus in heaven. Who can ever tell to how many that star by its light pointed out the way, to how many it afforded protection in dangers? Who can tell, how many it conducted to the throne of its God in heaven? All this is Mary's loving office; in all this she rejoices; of all this she is proud. O admirable star of the sea! thy name is the consolation of those who are oppressed with difficulties, the terror of the evil spirits, and the joy of heaven and earth. It delivers from the yoke of the devil; it possesses so great virtue that "heaven smiles, and the earth rejoices."

Ah! in thy adversities, in thy temptations, in thy dangers, why dost thou not cast a glance at this star? why dost thou not seek it out? why dost thou not call upon it? Listen to how St. Bernard would fain entice thee to follow the advices here given thee!—Whoever thou mayst be, that standest in need of light and consolation, lift up thine eyes to Mary—invoke her: look up to the star—invoke Mary—call upon her in the needs of thy life: call upon her in the straits of death! At every time, and in every place, call upon her, and thou wilt experience how very true it is that she "quickens the weary, and delivers from the yoke of the devil."

Beautiful star of the sea! I honor thee, and I greet thee! "Hail, star of the sea!" To thee do I lift up my eyes in my anxiety to be led by thee through so many rocks, to the haven of salvation. On thee I call for help, now and for evermore; weeping I stretch out my hands to thee, and with humble but confident heart, I promise myself all comfort from thee; for no one who confided in thee, was ever disappointed. Oh Mary! I am a wretched sinner—a wretched sinner chained down by a thousand sins: "Loosen the bonds of the guilty." I am a poor blind person: "give light to the blind!" I am filled with miseries: "remove the evils that afflict me!" I am devoid of all good: "obtain for me all good!" Prove thyself a mother unto the most needy of thy children; "show thyself a mother."

Trace out to him the path to heaven! Make the passage secure, and so direct him, that he shall be beatified with the everlasting vision of Jesus face to face, that he may ceaselessly rejoice in the contemplation of Jesus.

NINTH MEDITATION.

MARY IN THE TEMPLE OF JERUSALEM.

FIRST POINT.

MARY FLEES FROM THE WORLD.

WHILST yet of tender age, Mary heard the voice of the Lord inviting her to take up her abode in his holy habitation: "Attend daughter, and see, and incline thy ear, and forget thy people and thy father's house." Not the world was the place designed for this spotless dove; and hence God promised that she should be brought to a place of security, a place appropriate for those souls who yearn after him.

Oh, how meet it was, that in that temple should be reared up and protected that tender infant who was herself destined to be one day the all-beautifnl temple of the Most High! Her parents carried her thither, and many of the holy fathers give it as their opinion, that she was then but three years old. She remained in the temple until she reached her fourteenth year. "When she was three years of age she was brought by her parents to the temple, and continued in it till her fourteenth year"—St. Bonaventure. Such is the teaching of St. Anselm also, and of other illustrious doctors before and after him.

What must that heavenly child have felt when she saw the providence of God which drew her so early from the turmoil of the world, and placed her in the still solitude of the temple? With her great soul filled with exultation, well may she have cried out: "my spirit doth rejoice in God my Savior." And well may she with David have burst forth into the exclamation: "I rejoice in the things that were said to me; we shall go into the house of the Lord." And when she arrived at the gates of the temple, how tenderly she kissed them; at the same time adoring and praising the divine Majesty for having conferred on her so priceless a boon.

No doubt her heart felt the pang of separation from her parents whom she loved so dearly: but what is there which that soul would not have renounced in order to please God whom she thoroughly loved? For it must be borne in mind that this holy child's age is no measure of her knowledge; far from it indeed. St. Bernard, speaking of Mary, assures us that "at the first moment of her life that child had knowledge and love, as had Adam in the earthly paradise, and as had the angels of Heaven." How highly then must she have esteemed her vocation to the temple! What actions of thanksgiving she must have offered to the Lord!

Happy those souls whom God calls, whilst they are yet young, to serve him in his house: "Blessed are they who dwell in thy house, O Lord." They have the most beautiful pledge of the divine predilection. Withdrawn, at the opening of their career, from the seductions, the dangers, and the snares of the world, such souls leave all those things behind; and this they do, even before they know the poison which those things conceal. The spiritual state is for them a city of peace and of pure joys; and if they are faithful to God, they pass from the haven of this life, over to the haven of a happy eternity. Oh, how many exclaim, "Every good thing came to me with my religious vocation!"

Should God give to thee so beautiful an invitation, accept it immediately; lose no time; put not off from day to day; let thy action correspond with the call; and thou shalt quickly feel how sweet is his yoke, and how light is his burthen. He does not say to thee, "forget thy people and the house of thy father;" remember thou canst sanctify thyself in every state which has in it nothing contrary to the will of God; and as he desires that thou shouldst be holy, so will he not fail to grant thee the graces necessary in order to thy sanctification.

SECOND POINT.

MARY CONSECRATES HERSELF TO GOD.

Mary's first act in the temple was a perfect and irrevocable yielding of herself into the hands of God: "she offered and consecrated herself to the perpetual service of God." Her soul with its powers, her body with its senses, her privileges, her gifts, all that she was and all that she had—the whole, and the whole without reserve, she consecrated to God: she considered herself in all things as his spouse. She gave herself wholly up to him, that he might dispose of her according to his good pleasure: in short she thought of living only entirely for him, and of dying for him: "to him do I wholly live, to him do I wholly die—" Cardinal Hugo.

This consecration kept her in constant union with

her Lord, for to him she referred all her thoughts, feelings, and actions; and he on his part attracted her sweetly, giving her incessantly new lights and new graces. St. Ambrose says that this most intimate union was not broken by sleep, because she could truthfully say that her heart watched and loved even in her sleep: "I sleep, but my heart is awake."

What can he not promise himself by reason of his generosity, who gives himself up to the Lord perfectly and in right down earnest! And when a higher light revealed to her in the sacred pages the incarnation of the eternal word, oh, how the ardor of her desires was then inflamed! Accordingly, as she contemplated the unspeakable mystery, she felt in her bosom an increase of love for him—she yearned after the delight of seeing with her own eyes the woman who was destined to be his Mother—she coveted to become the servant of that Mother; with most earnest entreaties she called upon that time to come quickly: "Let the earth open up, and bud forth the Savior."

Who knows how often from the lips of Mary those words had ascended to God as so many ejaculations of love? Who knows how often God assured her by interior light that the time had already arrived when the Mother of the Savior was in the world! Already had he done great things to Mary, and he was now preparing her for the profound mystery: and yet in the midst of so many heavenly illuminations Mary considered herself unworthy to be a maid-servant to the Mother of God. For one thing only was she solicitous, viz., to offer herself to him constantly and in the wholeness of her heart, humbly hoping that he might choose to accept at her hands any, even the very lowest of services.

Oh, what weighty lessons for us in those facts! Mary's consecration of herself was complete and perfect: can so much be said of thine? In a passing moment of zeal it is easy for one to flatter himself that he has offered himself as a perfect holocaust to God; but should he put us to the test, requiring us to tear ourselves away from certain persons, certain situations, and certain places; should he deprive us of health, and let humiliations loose upon us; in each of the trials mentioned we should soon evidence that our offering was neither complete nor perfect. Were we thus tested, how many objections would arise in the very bottom of our hearts!

Then endeavor now to offer thyself to him without reserve; say to him he may dispose of thee as he pleases; and since all things are his, let him send thee prosperity or adversity, consolation or affliction, his assistance will enable thee to be satisfied. Oh, how precious in the sight of God would be such an oblation; and how highly prized would it be by the most Holy Virgin!

THIRD POINT.

MARY SERVED GOD WITH SINGULAR FIDELITY.

That tender child immediately put her hand to the work of conforming in the most perfect manner to all the regulations of the temple. In it was certainly to be found what is to be met with in houses, in which are placed young persons to receive their training and education. In the temple were superiors whom it was necessary to obey, rules which it was necessary to comply with, and duties which it was necessary to fulfil. How assiduously and punctiliously must she not have performed the prescribed exercises; with what eager submission must she not have obeyed the slightest intimation!

St. Bonaventure says that, with conscientiousness almost tainted with scrupulosity, Mary executed in the temple all the orders of the high priest, and that she daily prayed to God to the end that he might give her this spirit of obedience. St. Jerome relates that "Mary was assiduous at prayer and study, the first to assist at the vigils, the best versed in the knowledge of the law; in humility, the most advanced; in the singing of the psalms of David, the most delightful to be heard; in purity, the most pure; and in every virtue, the most perfect;" that she was the first to be present at the vigils, the best instructed in the knowledge of the divine Law, in humility the most practised, the most excellent in singing the psalms of David, the most glowing in love, the most pure in purity, the most perfect in every virtue. "It was so that she was the first at the vigils, the most humble in humility, the most distinguished in rendering the songs of David, the most renowned in love, the purest in purity, the most thoroughly perfect in every virtue." St. Bonaventure.

What a loving and edifying spectacle was it not, to behold this tender maiden whom the angels emulously waited upon, setting an example of promptness to her companions in performing the common duties, and anticipating the wishes of those who held the place of

God in her regard! How edifying to witness the cheerfulness with which she busied herself with the most lowly household work, how she was unto all a perfect model of humility and obedience! Happy the one who understands that God cannot be better served than by obeying those who hold his place: "He that heareth you heareth me."

Thus did she increase in wisdom and age and grace with God and men. Accordingly as she advanced in years, she increased in knowledge of heavenly things, and in perfection before God and men; as the sun from the moment of his rising, till midday, becomes clearer and clearer, and constantly sheds brighter rays on the universe, even so was Mary never lukewarm in her submission to God; no, she offered her sacrifice with constantly increasing zeal. Many devote themselves to God; but afterwards, instead of advancing in fidelity and love, they become so callous that God can apply to them the words formerly addressed to the Bishop of Laodicæ: "I know thy works; that thou art neither cold nor hot." Apoc. iii. 15 v.

Oh, that thou didst not belong to those unfaithful ones who taste not the consolations of God, and consequently remain poor in help and merits! Whatever be thy age and state, keep faithfully the promises thou hast made to God; cast away thy inertness; conquer thy evil habits; and serve him with a generous and a zealous heart. O how contented wilt thou then feel! "To him that overcometh, I will give the hidden manna." Ap. ii. 17 v. Pray, therefore, to Mary for strength and perseverance in order to overcome.

O amiable virgin! who even in infancy didst consecrate thyself to God, and didst raise thyself to him as sweet-scented incense, infuse into me something of that spirit which animated thee in the consecration which thou didst make of thyself to God! The best of my years are already gone by; and truly have I spent them in coldness and ingratitude. Ah, may the remainder of my life wholly and without reserve belong to my God! Do thou offer me to him; speak with him a word for me; say to him I belong to thee; and when I am presented to him by thy holy hands, he will not reject me. Do as I have requested thee, O Lady! and I promise thee that, beginning from this very moment, I shall henceforward be animated with a new spirit and new zeal in thy service. Amen.

TENTH MEDITATION.

MARY'S EXTERIOR PRIVILEGES.

FIRST POINT.

MARY'S HEAVENLY BEAUTY.

THE body of the most holy Virgin shared in the gifts of her soul; and, to an extremely perfect proportion of parts and to a thoroughly natural complexion, was joined an interior so modest and so virtuous, that it was impossible to behold her without feeling within one a sentiment of admiration, and an impulse of most holy love. Was it not indeed meet that the most beautiful of the children of men, "who is indeed fairer than the sons of men," should have a mother who, in like manner, transcended all others in beauty?

The holy fathers tell us wonderful things relating to the Virgin's beauty. Albert the Great assures us she possessed beauty in the highest degree in which it was communicable to a human body: "the most blessed Virgin was the most beautiful and the best formed; . . . . she had beauty in the highest and most perfect degree that was competent to a human body." With most affectionate warmth does St. Antoninus prove from the inspired writings, from the holy fathers, and from reason, that her beauty was superhuman, and that, compared with it, whatever there is on earth of lovely or charming was as a mere nothing.

But the crowning characteristic of this exalted lady's beauty is that, to the beholder, it served as an incentive to sanctification; and so elevated the majesty and so great the lustre which dwelt upon her, that to look at her was enough to enable one to observe how unchaste images vanished from the mind, and irregular motions subsided in the body:—"Her sanctity was reflected in others, and banished from them all sensual emotions of concupiscence"—Alexander de Hales. Merely to look at her sufficed to cut the affections loose from the world, and to make one feel that they were already turned heavenward.

This is the sentiment of St. Thomas, St. Bonaventure, St. Ambrose, and of many others of the holy fathers. Happy the one who could cast a glance even for an instant at that heavenly countenance! St. Thomas of Villanova says: the faithful hastened from all quarters of the world to get a sight of that great miracle of divine omnipotence; and such and so exalted were the dignity and the lustre which she breathed, and of which she was redolent, that all the fame thereof fell short of the reality, and all expectation was surpassed. "From all parts of the world a multitude of believers flocked to Jerusalem, in order to look upon that great prodigy; and the object itself distanced all idea that had been formed of it by those who came; and the actual sight of it surpassed all their expectation." Fourth Council of Assisium.

Ah, if she was already so beautiful when she yet wandered an exile on earth, how beautiful must she be now that she gloriously reigns Queen in Heaven! Oh, what ravishing beauty! oh, what a sea of splendor!

When, O Mary! when will that delightful moment arrive at which it will be granted me to look upon thy face in Heaven? Reflect, however, that the holy Ghost teaches in what esteem beauty should be held when he said: "Favor is deceitful, and beauty is vain: the woman that feareth the Lord, she shall be praised." Prov. 31. 30 v. Certainly not on account of her beauty was the most Holy Virgin extolled; but that she was not praised by reason of her beauty troubled her not the least; nay, she contemned the praise bestowed for beauty's sake alone; and yet, in her, beauty acted as an incentive to virtue, and lifted up to Heavenly thoughts the hearts of those who beheld it.

Oh, how many men miserably deceive themselves on the subject of beauty! Several make more account of it than of spiritual gifts; they work tooth and nail to acquire it; and what is worse than all else, they lay it under contribution to the detriment and the fall of others and of themselves! If thou art of the number of those who thus act, then open thy eyes immediately, and learn of Mary so to regard and to use beauty, as it ought to be used and regarded.

SECOND POINT.

MARY'S MILD TEMPERAMENT.

One's words and actions are an index to the temperament. A person is said to be of a mild temperament, who gives expression to only affectionate, gentle, mild dispositions, and with them harmonizes the tenor of his life. But in whom, after Jesus, can be met with a temperament so charming as Mary's? Nothing, save gentleness and mildness, issued from her blessed lips. "In Mary's mouth were not the gall and poison of the devil, but the honey and milk of the Holy Ghost." St. Bernard.

The Gospel gives us but few of Mary's words: those she spoke to the angel on occasion of his embassy—those to Elizabeth at the time of the visitation—those to her divine Son, when she discovered him in the temple, and afterwards when she was with him at the wedding feast of Cana. But if those words be deeply pondered upon, what can be met with in them else than humility, gentleness, and the most unselfish affection? St. Jerome tells us, "She was never seen nor heard in anger; in her, every word and movement mirrored forth the most unspeakable gentleness of her heart." "No one ever saw or heard her in anger." Her actions breathe a most affectionate anxiety to do good to all, to console all, to afford help and refreshment to all. Who ever went away from her in their disconsolateness or discontent? To whom did she refuse graces or favors?

The apostles, the disciples, the faithful of primitive times, recurred to her as to the common refuge: a word, a look from her, her bare presence was wholesome balm against all bitterness: "She also was the consolation of the saints and of all the faithful, who flocked to her in multitudes from all directions, and whom she warmed, as a hen does her little chickens, under her wings." St. Thomas, of Villanova.

Oh, how amiable sanctity then appeared in her! Imagine not, however, that this her sweetness of manner has grown less in the Virgin; no, she has but rendered it more sublime—nay, she has made it perfect. In the midst of all her glories she is the most gentle and the most mild of creatures, "mild amongst all;" and so well does she know how to win over the most obstinate souls, that the saints call her the "robber of hearts." St. Ambrose, de Virg. Lib. 2. Cap. 2.

If thou wilt be agreeable to Mary, endeavor to acquire that gentleness and mildness of spirit which in her were so truly amiable. The temperaments of men differ as much as do their countenances; but mildness of disposition must be a characteristic of all the followers of Jesus and of all the clients of Mary: "Learn of me for I am meek and humble of heart." Hast thou already meekness? At least, strive to acquire it. Examine a little whether that harshness in thy expressions, those movements of anger which betray themselves in thy exterior, that ease with which thou growest wrathy, sensitive, and discoverest signs of impatience—ask thyself whether these traits in thy character are becoming in one who should be a well beloved son of this most amiable mother.

O how much better wouldst thou do for others and for thyself, by making all efforts to overcome thy every temptation to anger.

THIRD POINT.

MARY'S REFINED DEPORTMENT.

An agreeable and courteous deportment, when it goes hand in hand with holiness, serves to adorn it and render it more amiable. This deportment Mary possessed in the highest degree; and to it she united such modesty and self-discipline, that she excited the admiration and affection of all who came within her influence. Of her, with much greater right than of Esther, can it be said: "she appeared lovely in the eyes of all." She associated with her neighbors as much as circumstances required; but her bearing towards them was as meek and courteous as it was simple and natural: it was, in fact, a very mirror of her soul. She had in her nothing affected, nothing far-fetched, nothing overwrought: "her bearing had in it nothing of levity; her carriage, nothing of looseness; her voice, nothing of arrogance; so that even the make-up of her body was a type of her mind, and an index to her unimpeachableness."

When did she ever show aversion for the poor? When did she ever betray contempt for the weak? "When was she ever at variance with her relations? When did she feel disgust at the lowly? When did she laugh at the infirmities of the weak? When did she turn her back on the helpless?" On the contrary, she always wore a countenance cheerful to all; her movements ever becomingly grave and directed by grace, ravished all and excited them to the practice of virtue. St. Jerome says: "her whole conversation was so seasoned with love, that it was very evident God was on her lips; and a mere look from her availed as much as the most profound lectures delivered by others on virtue." How agreeable and holy must have been the impression she made on all hearts!

We read that so amiable and so composed was the bearing of the whole person of some of the saints, that in them holiness appeared clothed in new beauty; those of the most stubborn disposition left their presence, not only astounded but perfectly contrite; yea, even went away in the resolve to give themselves to God. An Ignatius of Loyola, a Francis of Sales, a Francis of Chantal, by the amiability of their deportment and the serenity of their countenance, drew souls to God. What impression then must Mary have produced, since we know that she was created to be the most sweet attraction to sinners?

Meditate on the character of her intercourse with her neighbor,—even with the poor, the sick, the needy, the servants. Art thou, perchance, of the number of those of whom the apostle James observes, that they treat the rich and powerful with every consideration and distinction, but entertain nothing else than contempt for the lower class of men! Certainly, such was not Mary's way of acting: by her example she taught us to look upon all as children of the one heavenly Father, and to receive them with affection and tenderness. A surly behavior towards neighbors displeases God and men, rouses minds to anger, and instead of sweetly attracting them to virtue, serves to debar them effectually from its practice. Treat others as thou wouldst desire they should treat thee; and bear in mind that the more gentle and affectionate thy behavior towards all, the greater thy resemblance to the holy Virgin.

O Mary! O most beautiful of all the creatures which ever issued from the hand of God, thou didst unite in thyself the most admirable privileges of nature and of grace; heavenly is thy countenance but not less heavenly thy heart! In thee are found mildness of disposition, suavity of conversation, amiability of deportment! O

Mother, most worthy of being loved! turn to us that countenance which, by its love, won heaven for thee; extinguish in us all inordinate affection for creatures; enkindle in our hearts, O Lady, love of thee and of God; raise our thoughts and aspirations heavenward; obtain for us that mildnesss of disposition and gentleness of deportment, which thou didst so much have at heart; and make us also imitate thee therein, and, by imitation, merit to behold one day thy unspeakable beauties in heaven, and to have a place among the angels and saints who surround thy exalted throne for all eternity! Amen.

ELEVENTH MEDITATION.

MARY'S MARRIAGE TO ST. JOSEPH.

FIRST POINT.

MARY'S MARRIAGE INCREASED HER MERITS.

As the time of the Incarnation of the Word drew near, God so ordained things that Joseph obtained Mary for spouse; and also the divine Majesty inspired Mary not to reject the hand of this just man, assuring her at the same time by direct and interior converse with her heart, that her virginity was not to suffer in the step she was about to take.

Mary obeyed; but how much must this her obedience have cost her? She had by vow obliged herself to the practice of virginity; she was extremely punctilious and zealous in matter of this excellent virtue; she had always eschewed the society and glances of men. Now, on the contrary, she is to commit herself to the guardianship of a man; she is to live with him, and indeed live with him in that most heartfelt affection, unsuspecting innocence, and unqualified confidence, which rightly obtain in the married state; and, nevertheless, she must believe that in following this course, her charming virtue will run no danger of any kind whatever. She is to recognize in Joseph all the rights of her bridegroom; and at the same time she is to convince herself with absolute certainty, that he will be the faithful watchman of her unsullied purity.

Unacquainted with the designs which God had upon her, she could not comprehend the sublime ends he had in view, in wishing her to enter upon the marriage state. She believed, indeed, that the man God had selected for her, was just and faithful; and yet what proof had she that he was such?—no proof before she committed herself to his keeping. Oh, what confidence in God, what abandonment to him did she not need in circumstances such as those in which she was placed, circumstances in which all appearances waged war on her reason.

Consider further that, by marrying, the most holy Virgin made a great sacrifice, and this for another reason also; viz., because she was after her marriage to appear in a condition which, according to the judgment of men, was caused in her, as a similar condition is produced in other wives. And yet was Mary more immaculate than the drifted snow which falls from the summits of high mountains; yet was Mary purer than the angels, thus offering in her condition an instance of virginity coexisting with motherhood,—an instance such as had never before been furnished to the world.

In this holy marriage was fulfilled the prophecy of Isaias: "For the young man shall dwell with the Virgin, and thy children shall dwell in thee. And the bridegroom shall rejoice over the bride." 62 cap. 5 v. Joseph, a spotless virgin, lived with the Queen of virgins in perfect integrity of soul and body; and her espousals served as a veil to conceal the miraculous conception of the world's Redeemer; "to conceal his birth from the devil," as says St. Jerome. Book 1st., Commentaries on Matth., Cap., 1st.

However, this administration of matters was known to God alone; and, accordingly, men looked upon Mary and Joseph as utterly undistinguished from the general class of married persons. Now, add to the sacrifices she had already made, the obedience, the hearty and complete submission, which she always practised towards Joseph as towards her head and husband, her constant dependence on him, her zeal in waiting upon him, and in lightening for him the burthen of the troubles of life. How many occasions she had for multiplying her merits! What a continuous exercise of virtue must have been her married years! In the spiritual life, God sometimes causes circumstances to arise which put our fidelity to the test by their being in opposition to our wishes, even when these are pious and holy. By her example, Mary teaches us, not to reason too refinedly on the dispensations of the Lord. When his will is once made known to us, then it is our duty to execute it cheerfully, and to confide in him, in the conviction that he will be more careful of us than we are of ourselves. Had Mary followed her own inclination, never would she have consented to give Joseph her hand. What would have been the consequences of such a course on her part?

If thou wilt not go astray, be governed by the principles of faith: let thy contentment consist, not in doing that which appears good to thee, but rather in doing that which God gives thee to understand he demands of thee.

SECOND POINT.

MARY'S MARRIAGE BROUGHT HER CONSOLATION.

Sovereignly precious was the manifold assistance which Mary obtained through her most pure espousals. The first was the protection of her reputation: "she was married," says St. Ambrose, "in order that her spotless virginity should be preserved without blemish." How, in fact, would she without the bond of legal matrimony have been able to vindicate her motherhood, and to convince the ill-disposed Pharisees that she had become Mother by a purely divine miracle, and that the offspring she had given birth to, was truly a divine offspring

Incapable of discerning so heavenly a mystery, the synagogue would have beheld in her nothing else than a guilty woman who had grievously sinned against the law, and would, perchance, have sought to inflict on her the punishment decreed against those who so transgressed. God did not will that a shadow of suspicion should blight the good name of his most holy Mother; and hence he so disposed things that her marriage with Joseph at once concealed the mystery, and permitted that Jesus should be considered as his son: "He was looked upon as the son of Joseph."

By this means God made Mary's honor unassailable, and at the same time reserved for his own Providence the work of causing to be recognized as Virgin her whom the Patriarchs yearned after;—her who was typified in so many symbols, and announced by so many prophets—as the Virgin Mother of God. As the first object God had in view in Mary's marriage, was the security of her reputation, so the second design was that she might have for Jesus and herself a faithful guardian in all the difficult and painful eventualities to which, at her then tender age, she found herself exposed.

As the Lord at the close of his life recommended her to John that he might take care of her as a loving son cares for his mother, so in like manner, by means of an angel's embassy, he tranquillizes Joseph, and inspires him with the resolution not to put Mary away. He also instructs him as to the divine character of her conception: "Joseph, son of David, fear not to take unto thee Mary thy wife: for that which is conceived in her is of the Holy Ghost." Matt. 1 ch. 20 v.—Joseph conducted her to Bethlehem, accompanied her to Egypt, returned with her to Nazareth, shared in all her fears and sufferings; and all these things did he do with an affection so solicitous and so pure, that, according to the saying of the holy fathers, the Virgin never yearned after solitude so heartily as she yearned to be in company with Joseph: "Truly a faithful and prudent servant," exclaims St. Bernard, "whom the Lord appointed to be a consolation unto his Mother."

The third assistance which Mary obtained from her marriage, was sustenance for herself and for Jesus. How could a tender Virgin, as Mary was, unacquainted with the world, without means and without friends, have in her own home and outside of it, on her journeys and in the places of her sojourn, been able to procure for herself and her son the nourishment of which they stood in need? In view of this state of things, the Lord entrusted the care of all these concerns to her most chaste spouse who, by his laborious and ceaseless toils, procured the means of subsistence necessary for the Mother and for the Son of God.

Learn of Mary to build thy hopes on God; she accomplished his will and abandoned herself completely to him, and he prepared on the way through which he led her, the helps and consolations in keeping with her wants. He prepares similar consolations and helps for all the souls who, renouncing their own self-will, cast themselves without reserve on him. "He gives much more than we ask for, or conceive;" he confers more than we believe and imagine. Blessed are they who, by their actions, say: "Lord, I look but for that which is pleasing to thee." Oh, how easy and smooth are found those ways to be, which at first sight appear impossible!

In every circumstance of thy life, imitate Mary's fidelity to God and her confidence in him; and be assured that, by so doing, thou shalt enjoy the special succor of thy God; for he forgets no one: "for he takes care of each of you;" and still more affectionately does he treat him who generously flings himself into his arms.

THIRD POINT.

MARY'S MARRIAGE PROMOTED HER HONOR.

Not only did the nuptials of the Virgin prove useful in defending her reputation among the people of Israel, but they (her nuptials) were also admirably calculated to establish the fact of her virginity, and to set it forth in bold relief before the whole world. Joseph is the most trustworthy witness that Jesus was born of Mary, the Virgin. Who could attest a fact of this nature with less suspicion than the bridegroom? Joseph's silence, says St. Jerome, is a palpable evidence of the integrity of Mary's virginity: "This is a testimony for Mary, that Joseph, although thoroughly cognizant of her chastity, yet keeps a most profound secret what had taken place in her; and thus he acts even though he comprehended not the import of what had just so mysteriously transpired."

As the apostle Thomas, by doubting and by his efforts to cast off his doubts, became a true witness of the resurrection of the Lord, so in like manner Joseph, by his doubts, and, subsequently, by the assurance he received of the true state of things through the angel's ministry, became the most trustworthy witness of the virginity and integrity of his most holy spouse. Mary in obedience to God gives her hand to a man, and God uses this man not only for the purpose of guarding her virginity, but of having it proclaimed to the whole world. God acts so that this man gives irrefragable and unimpeachable testimony to her virginity, and by giving such testimony, this man becomes instrumental in having that, her virginity, celebrated throughout all nations and for all future time.

The manifest trustworthiness of Mary's spouse put to shame the adversaries of her glorious privilege in their every attack; and it was competent to the Church to sing thenceforth in peace and security and without any misgivings: "O most glorious of virgins, most exalted of stars, thou nourishest on thy breast him who gave thee thy being!"

O how admirable is the Lord in his decrees! O what great honor redounded to Mary from her marriage with Joseph! The Lord is great: "Great is the Lord." He commanded to glorify every one who would glorify him, and his word will never pass away: "Who honors me, him will I honor." Mary honored him by renouncing her own inclinations, by humble submission, by prompt accomplishment of his will in all things; and God exalts her by just those means which seem adapted to cast her into the veriest abyss of humiliation.

If thou wilt have a share in so excellent a reward, then imitate Mary; place not thy glory in honors, dignities, and elevated positions; place it in obedience, in humility, and in resisting thy inclniations, in resisting even those which though blameless, yet are not precisely according to God's good pleasure; also, let thy glory consist in hearkening to the divine inspirations even when they run counter to thy own pet views.

O most humble Virgin! thou who hast subordinated all thy inclinations to the will of God, and didst cast thyself with unreserved confidence into his arms; ah, inspire me with the lively desire to render myself agreeable to him, and also inspire me with the firm resolution never to do aught else than thy most holy will in all things! Oh, happy me, if I obtain from thee so excellent a grace; then I shall be certain never to go astray; then I shall be secure of heaven! O Mary! do not permit that I suffer myself to be led by my own will when it is not according to God's will; grant me the grace to follow thy footsteps, in order, by my observance of this infallible rule, to render unto him that honor which is a pledge and guarantee of the honor which he by his grace will grant me for all eternity. Amen.

TWELFTH MEDITATION.

THE DIGNITY OF MARY'S DIVINE MATERNITY.

FIRST POINT.

MARY'S MOTHERHOOD—THE ONLY ONE OF ITS KIND.

So many elevations and miracles are comprised in the dignity of her who is Mother of God, that they strikingly distinguish her from all others, in the face of heaven and earth.

St. Bernard says that if God resolved to be born of a woman, that woman should be no other than a virgin; and if a virgin were destined to become a mother, she ought to become mother of no other than of a God: "Truly, such a God ought to be born of no other than of a virgin. And also as far as the virgin is concerned, it was meet that if she should bring forth, she should bring forth only a God."

The honor of the Eternal Father demanded that God should be made man on earth in the same manner as generation takes place in heaven. There, generation was the action of a virginal Father: on earth, in due course of ages, offspring was to be begotten by a virginal Mother. From all eternity, generation takes place and is the action of only one, and one in the clearest sheen of the divinity; in time, a birth takes place, and that birth, the offspring of one in the fullest glow of virginity. In heaven, the person generated has no mother; on earth, the person born has no father.

But what kind of a mother is that who gives birth to a God, and who unites in herself two privileges mutually so antagonistic? She is a Mother, one and alone of her kind in the whole world; she is a mother who has not her like; she was formed by a miracle of the Divine Omnipotence, and was anticipated by grace, in virtue of which she should conceive and bring forth without prejudice to her virginity. "She is," exclaims St. Peter Chrysologus, "that blessed soil which of itself causes the flowers of the field and the lily of the valley to bloom; truly blessed, because she possesses the dignity of Mother, and the honor of Virgin."

Consider, further, that the dignity of the Mother of God is the boon of one, and of only one, for another reason also; because the union implied therein is, after the hypostatic union, the most intimate that a creature can have with God. What union canst thou imagine more close than that which obtained in her womb, between her and the Word made Flesh? During nine whole months, did she give of her substance nourishment to the body of her divine Son; and he gave her spiritual nourishment by the in-dwelling in her of his divinity.

In the course of nature there is no greater union than that which obtains between a mother and a child shut up in her womb; the impressions, the dispositions, are transmitted from the former to the latter; and the parent and the offspring appear to constitute but one and the same being. In the course of grace, there is no union such as that which obtains between Jesus and Mary. The dispositions of the Son were communicated to the soul of the Mother; he shared with her all his sympathies—the two formed, in a moral sense, but one and the same being. "He was in the Virgin," says St. Peter Damian, "by reason of similarity, because he is just what she is."

Mary sinks into insignificance in her own eyes the moment she became Mother of God; and, as a drop of water is lost in the ocean, so will she be, as it were, swallowed in the abyss of the divinity. "But she became the Mother of God, on occasion of the angel's message to her; she was swallowed up in the abyss of the mysteries accomplished in her, and with her whole spirit was plunged into the boundless sea of glory."

From these considerations thou must, for the benefit of thy own soul, draw the conclusion that if the divine maternity constituted Mary an extraordinary Virgin, so the honor, the homage, the love which she merits from us, must also be extraordinary. No mere creature is in such close union with God as his most holy Mother; and hence none has such claim on our confidence as she has, and we can place it in no one with the same right as in her.

Admire the ordinances of the Church, which decree to her special honor and higher worship than to all the other saints; and a worship only inferior to that we render to God. Examine and see whether thou settest apart for her in thy heart that place which is her due: see how unwillingly and inconstantly, how indifferently and unaffectionately, thou dost that which thou performest in her honor. Oh, how badly dost thou act towards her!

SECOND POINT.

MARY'S MOTHERHOOD—THE MOST EXALTED.

The dignity of the divine maternity is so comprehensive and so high, that it resembles a limitless sea the shore of which cannot be discovered, even after much search and examination. Our blessed Lady is so great, says the angelic Doctor, that she participates in the infinite; and in this regard nothing better is possible, "She possesses an almost infinite dignity, by means of the infinite good which is God, and in this respect any thing better is impossible."

In order to create a greater mother, God himself should increase in perfection; but so long as no greater God is to be found than he whom she contained in her womb, so long is no greater mother to be found than the Mother of God. He could, indeed, create a more starry firmament, a greener earth, and a larger world; but a more exalted mother than the virgin he could not create; for "there can be (outside of her) nothing better save God."

What elevation, what renown, for a mere creature? Is there indeed a single privilege which God has not conferred on her simultaneously with this dignity? Mary tells us as much in these words: "He that is mighty hath done great things to me," as if she would say: "The measure of my dignity can be nothing else than the omnipotence of God." St. Eucharius says: "In order to know her, the dignities of the Son must be first known. You ask what kind of a mother is she? Ask first what are the perfections of her Son." St.

Bernardine styles her, the "Miracle of all miracles;" "for this virgin," says he, "must, by a countless multitude of perfections and graces, have been, by way of relationship, elevated to the Divinity."

The most learned and holy men speak after this manner and add, that to wish to comprehend Mary's dignity were the same as to wish to be overwhelmed with her glory: "He who is a searcher of majesty, shall be overwhelmed with glory."

Bow down before glory so great: adore God who elevates her so much; and learn from her elevation how sorely those poor blind persons deceive themselves who, in rendering her the honor to which she is entitled, fear to overstep the due bonds, and impute to excessive zeal the manifestations of love and reverence which the Church offers her.

But as for thee; multiply thy homages, heighten thy zeal for her, spend thyself for her glorification, participate in whatever is useful to promote veneration and devotion to her: and be assured, that after God, no creature deserves to be honored so much as Mary, and that no one can ever honor her so much as God honored her, in choosing her for his Mother.

THIRD POINT.

MARY'S MOTHERHOOD, THE SOURCE OF ALL HER ELEVATIONS.

As the extraordinary honors which belong to Christ, are to be ascribed to the fact that he is the true son of God, so in like manner, the divine maternity is the foundation of all the extraordinary honors which are rightly shown to Mary. The privileges, the graces, and the gifts, which so much elevate and adorn her, are accorded her in view of this high dignity: they are as the morning gift which should accompany her, and could not be conferred upon her, without, at the same time, granting her those distinctions befitting her.

For this reason has God so greatly elevated and distinguished her. The recollection that she is the Virgin of whom he desired to be born after a short time, caused him to forget the universal laws of his strict justice; he set her apart from among all the children of Adam; he anticipated her by consecrating the first moments of her existence. He sanctified her whole life by giving her the greatest fulness of grace; he exalted her in such a manner that, as St. Augustine says, "after God's dignity, no greater dignity than Mary's can be conceived." She is raised above every height which can be named or imagined after God's. For this reason, was she immaculate in her conception; for this reason, was she full of grace from the first moment of her existence; for this reason, she was confirmed in grace; for this reason she was not born before she was sanctified; for this reason, finally, was she made worthy to carry a God in her womb, and to become the Mother of God.

Should this consideration enhance thy esteem of Mary's dignity, let not thy esteem therefor cause thee to fear that her merits will be thereby detracted from. No; for, although she did not merit this dignity as a thing strictly due to her (as say the school men), she merited it, however, congruously; that is to say, she prepared herself for it by co-operation with grace, by the exercise of virtues, and chiefly by her most profound self-abasement, a virtue by which more than by any other, "she attracted," as says St. Bernard, "to her the attention of the Lord." By virginity she pleased; by humility she conceived.

From all this, infer that no practice can be more agreeable to the Virgin and more useful to us, than that which thou repeatest as often as thou sayst with the words of the Angelic Salutation, "Holy Mary, Mother of God!" This prayer is the most agreeable to her, because it recals to her mind the origin of all her dignities: it is the most useful to us because it likewise recalls to her that she has in a certain way to thank us for her dignities—since the fact that we are sinners, is the reason why she is Mother of God. Often say to her with reverence and love, "Holy Mary, Mother of God, pray for us sinners!" and reflect that, as the divine Maternity is unto Mary the well-head of all her dignities, so will devotion to the Mother of God be unto thee a source of all blessings.

Oh! what an abundant source of grace and treasures! Devotion to her will increase the holy fear of God in thy heart, will establish thee in the way of the Lord, will protect thee from the assaults of thy enemies, will sustain thee in all dangers, and will assist thee to enjoy for ever in heaven the fruit of that thy devotion to Mary. Thine is salvation, if thou really possess that devotion.

O great Mother of God! O exalted, elevated Lady! thy dignity is extremely regal, but this fact discourages me not, nor causes me to lose the confidence which lives in my heart. Thou rankest immeasurably above all mere creatures; thou art the only one on earth who has privileges such as thine; thou art the most beautiful work of Omnipotence; thou art united with Jesus, in such a manner that thou comest, as it were, on almost a level with God. This, however, is true—that God, who made thee his Mother, made thee also our Mother, and gave thee a heart which is all tenderness and love. This thought fills me with confidence, and urges me to say to thee: Lady! thou art my Mother: accordingly, let me be, my most loving Mother, ever a docile child of thine! Cause me to make myself constantly more worthy of thy graces and love, by co-operating with thy favors, and by the exercise of the virtues, and chiefly by the exercise of humility! Amen.

THIRTEENTH MEDITATION.

MARY'S WONDERFUL FAITH.

FIRST POINT.

MARY BELIEVED WHAT WAS DIFFICULT TO BE BELIEVED.

To no mere creature were things so profound and so difficult, proposed for belief as to the most Holy Virgin. The angel announces to her a series of miracles and mysteries which put her faith to the test; he proposes to her the unspeakable mystery of the most Holy Trinity, which was so hidden under the law of nature, and so little known under the law of grace. He speaks to her of the person of the Father whose ambassador he was; of the person of the Son whom she was to conceive in her chaste womb; of the person of the Holy Ghost who should come upon her. The angel reveals to her the mystery of the Incarnation, which had been hitherto veiled under sensible images and representations; he says to her that the Eternal Word would clothe himself with human flesh, and appear on earth as God-man for the salvation of the world. The heavenly messenger says to her that she is the virgin prophesied by Isaiah—the virgin who, by an unheard-of miracle, should unite in herself the most exalted Motherhood with unsullied virginity; that the one called Holy by way of eminence that was to be born of her, should be the Son of the Most High God, should re-establish the throne of David, and reign for ever; "and of His kingdom there shall be no end."

How many profound mysteries, going far beyond all created understanding! How many unattainable heights,—and heights as difficult to be believed as they are unattainable! Such are the great things which the angel sets forth with wonderful simplicity. For sign of his divine mission, he only relates what occurred to Elizabeth: "And behold! thy cousin Elizabeth hath also conceived a child in her old age." He stands on no other platform than the omnipotence of God, in order to gain credence for the accomplishment of what he says will come to pass: "Because no word shall be impossible with God." Luke, i. 37 v.

Mary understands not such mysteries; the things which she hears transcend her comprehension. She yet knows that by the word of the angel God speaks to her—that from him goes forth the embassy—and this knowledge suffices for her to bring her understanding into that captivity which is through the obedience of faith.

St. Ambrose, in astonishment, tells us that the high priest Zachary did not believe that Elizabeth, far advanced in years, and barren besides, could become mother of a child. But Zachary believed not; and Mary believed, that a virgin would conceive and bring forth into the world a God made man. The fact that she believed that this would happen, appears from her question to the angel, "How shall this be done?"

Admire such great faith, and consider that God has proposed to thee also, for thy belief, unspeakable and profound things; and now, after he has handed down to thee the most luminous proofs of the truth of his word, and has confirmed those proofs by the exact fulfilment of the prophecies, by the most striking miracles, by the blood of so many martyrs, by the wonderful propagation of the Gospel—in fine, by all that was calculated to pave for thee the way to faith;—hast thou, after God has done all this for thee, subjected thy understanding as much as thou shouldst have subjected it? Hast thou offered to God this tribute of the subjection of thy understanding to him? This is the tribute he now demands of thee: "but without faith it is impossible to please God." Woe to him who refuses to accede to the demands: "He who believeth not shall be condemned."

Have never the hardihood to wish to pry into things which thy understanding shall never be able to grasp: to hold as true what we understand, is by no means faith; and where there is no faith, there, likewise, is no merit. Content thyself with knowing that God is the eternal truth, and that he has conferred on thee a very great grace, to the end that he might cause thee to participate in the immense blessings of revelation.

SECOND POINT.

MARY SUBJECTS HER UNDERSTANDING TO FAITH.

The most holy Virgin hesitated not a moment to accept as true the things which God proposed to her for belief; "Behold the handmaid of the Lord, be it done unto me according to thy word." This is the answer she gave to the pregnant announcement that had just been made to her. She was not disputatious as Moses; she desired no proofs as Gedeon; she required not even time for reflection. The councils of

God are not subjects for discusssions. And if she trembled at the first announcement made by the angel, her dread did not proceed from doubt as to whether God was able to execute his profound designs on her, but proceeded rather from her attachment to her unsullied virginity and from the singular prudence with which she was armed.

Mary believed; and the readiness with which she believed was, as says St. Augustine, so efficacious, that she opened heaven and brought down the eternal Word into her womb. Mary's faith opened heaven, in that she acquiesced in what had been proposed to her. She believed; and her readiness to believe induced her to make the journey straightway to the mountain of Judea, to offer her felicitations to Elizabeth: "And Mary rising up in those days went into the mountainous country with haste, into a city of Judea; and she entered into the house of Zachary and saluted Elizabeth." Luke, i. 39 v.

St. Elizabeth praised Mary even by reason of the readiness and strength of her faith, and ascribed to this faith the accomplishment of the divine promises: "and blessed art thou that hast believed; the things which the Lord has said to thee shall come to pass in thee; what the Lord has said to thee will be accomplished."

To this delighting praise every one of us should be entitled, because to every one God has promised great things. Believest thou this truth with that readiness of faith which manifests itself by works? What hast thou done, and what dost thou do, that to thee can be said: "Blessed art thou, in that thou hast believed?"

But deceive not thyself; so long as the fruits of thy faith appear not, the thought that thou hast promptness of faith is not worth the room it occupies. The tree which blossoms not, nor brings forth fruit, is regarded as dead; and according to the expression of the Holy Ghost, that faith is dead which does not show external works worthy of itself: "Faith without good works is dead."

Together with promptness in thy works, show also promptness in thy faith. Practise with holy joy the lessons of faith: confess thy faith heroically; and by holy actions give the world to understand that thou livest as thou believest. This is the faith that has the strength to make thee blessed: if thou hast it, be not afraid; "What the Lord has said to thee will be accomplished." If thou hast it not, employ every means to obtain it, for a barren faith will profit thee nothing.

THIRD POINT.

STEADFASTNESS OF MARY'S FAITH.

Mary's faith was put to the test; and however severe the test, her faith always appeared strong and heroic. It was as a rock in the middle of the sea; the rock moves not in order to combat against the waves and the storms: the more violently is it assailed, all the more admirable does its strength appear.

A test of Mary's faith was it, that she should adore as the Son of God, and as having the same essence with the Father, that infant who, in a poor stable, was born into the world, and who at his birth was not provided with those conveniences which are never wanting even to the poorest children of men. A test of her faith was it, that she should then flee with him to Egypt in order that he might escape from the wrath of Herod, as if the divine Infant dreaded the persecution of a man, or could not otherwise evade that persecution. A proof of her faith was it, that she should behold him so many years in the obscurity of an humble work-shop, hammer and chisel in hand, without his causing to be seen any public mark of his Divinity. A bitter test of her faith was his passion and death, at the time of whose occurrence even the Eternal Father appeared to have forgotten his only begotten; or, at least, not to have acknowledged him as his Son. "My God, my God, why hast thou forsaken me?"

In such melancholy circumstances as those, what would have been the thoughts of a soul, which had not possessed Mary's steadfastness of faith? Oh, how many storms, how many doubts, would have arisen on those occasions! The Apostle Paul, although brought up in the school of miracles, doubted; Thomas the apostle, doubted; so, many others doubted when their faith was put to somewhat of a severe test. "Scarcely," says St. Thomas of Villanova, "did they preserve a spark of faith."

Yet Mary doubted not; yea, she alone of them all weighed in her heart the mystery with perfect faith and plenary hope. Steadfastly and magnanimously she adored Jesus hanging on the cross, as she adored her God; and she adored him as her God at that time, as well as she adored him when he awaked the dead to new life. Notwithstanding all her adversities, "she stood," writes St. Antonius, "with unwavering faith," which, on the subject of the divinity of Christ, she held fast, as the true mother of all the faithful, because her faith surpasses that of them all.

How dost thou believe in those moments when God puts thy faith to the test, whilst he hides himself or appears to have forgotten thee? Dost thou waver? Dost thou veer around as a ship's sail before the wind? Remember that the sun is still there although the clouds hide it from our view: "I know on whom I rely," said St. Paul in his afflictions, "I know in whom I have believed. I know God cannot go back of his words: I know his right arm is not shortened."

How many doubts and uneasinesses wouldst thou have avoided, hadst thou been firmer in faith, hadst thou sought strength and consolation in faith! In future, follow this guide and do not allow thyself to be overcome, whether by apprehensions or by vain appearances or by fallacious conclusions. Imitate Mary's steadfastness, and entreat her to confirm thy mind, and to bless thy efforts in such a manner that thou mayst one day receive the reward promised to faith.

O most glorious Virgin! who by the firmness of thy faith hast merited to become the light of all believers, send me a ray that will clear my understanding, and never allow the flatteries of the world, nor the terrors of hell to extinguish this most precious gift in my heart. Remove far from me so many enemies who lay snares to deprive me of that gift, and remove likewise so many dangers which threaten it; and should it please God to put me to the hard test of sufferings, grant that my faith may be confirmed in them and may issue from them stronger, even as the flame is fanned by the blowing of the wind. Help me, O Lady! and so strengthen my faith, that it may lead me to the promised reward, that I may be able to look upon Jesus, the author and the finisher of faith, face to face. Amen.

FOURTEENTH MEDITATION.

MARY'S HOPE.

FIRST POINT.

MARY'S HOPE—A SUBLIME HOPE.

HOPE reigned in Mary in the most perfect manner that can possibly be expressed. Hope, for the most part, springs from faith; and the firmer is the latter, the farther does the former reach, and the higher does it ascend. According as the knowledge of God, of his goodness, of his power, and of his fidelity, increases in a soul, the heart also grows greater, and feels itself strengthened and encouraged to hope, and to promise itself that it will receive all good from him. Thus hope may be not inaptly compared to the heat and warmth which accompany the light of the sun.

But who had ever in the world a more firm faith, and a greater knowledge of the world than had Mary? And to whom hath the arm of the Lord been revealed so manifestly? Mary surpassed in faith all the faithful, and in like manner, she surpassed them in unwavering expectation of eternal happiness and of all the other good things which God has promised. A most clear light illumined her understanding in order that she might believe; and an extremely warm desire lifted up her will so that she might hope. Oh, with what great right may those words of David be applied to her: "Thou hast made the

Most High thy habitation!"—"the Most High"—for never did any other creature raise its heart to God so high as to be able in all security and peace to repose in him as in its centre: "In thy words I placed exceeding great confidence."

Consider, moreover, that the most holy Virgin was not acquainted with one of the hindrances which are so violently opposed to this beautiful virtue: she was not clogged by undue attachment to creatures, to the world, nor to herself. Freed from all the ties which shackle the heart, she soared instantly and calmly to God, and rested in God. How easily, how confidently must she in all things have committed to him her loving solicitude! Hope in the midst of so many evils in the present life, is an extremely precious good. It alleviates troubles; it gives new strength to the mind; it divests bitter events of their acerbity, and pours mild balm into wounds of every description.

Wilt thou cherish in thy heart so beautiful a virtue? Wilt thou experience its sweet consolation? First animate thy faith anew, and then live in such a way that thy conscience may have nothing to reproach thee with. The greatest obstacles to hope are the stings of an unclean conscience. If our heart have nothing to reproach us with, then we can, as St. John says, represent to ourselves God, with the sweet confidence that we shall obtain what we desire: "Dearly beloved, if our heart do not reprehend us, we have confidence towards God." 1 John, iii. 21 v.

A son who is aware that he has not forfeited his father's caresses, throws himself frankly and securely into his father's arms. When wilt thou feel in thy heart a hope vigorous and not to be shaken? When thou hast a conscience that is clean and at rest, oh, how easy will it then be for thee to say to the Lord in truth: "In thy words I place exceeding great confidence!"

SECOND POINT.

MARY'S HOPE—A STRONG HOPE.

Mary's hope was put to the severest test. In this virtue, also, she should be the queen of all saints. Oh, how many obstacles presented themselves to her attainment of the good things she had hoped for! obstacles which, according to appearance, were insurmountable. How many difficulties crossed each other: how often did she find herself so enveloped in the darkness of adversity, that not a ray of light could be descried!

But in those circumstances, painful however as they were, Mary faltered not a moment. Possessing greater fortitude than Abraham's, she hoped on in spite of all adversities; "against hope, she believed in hope." Unaware of the mystery that had been accomplished in her, Joseph meditates on putting her away privately: "Whereupon Joseph her husband being a just man, was minded to put her away privately." Matt. i. 19 v. Mary feels this to the quick by reason of her consort's anguish; still, she builds on God in such a way, that she utters not a word regarding her situation: to have uttered such a word would have sufficed to relieve Joseph's trouble, and to restore serenity and gladness to them both.

At the marriage feast of Cana she represents to her Son that the wine was failing, and at the same time requests him to deliver by a miracle the bridal pair from their embarrassment. Jesus who had not yet manifested the infinite power of his Divinity, gives her an answer which had all the appearance of a refusal: and notwithstanding the apparent refusal, Mary is so certain that her request will be granted, that she tells the waiters to hold themselves in readiness at his beck, and thus does she prepare them for the forthcoming miracle.

How many assults must her hope have suffered at the time of the passion? What other heart would have been able to bear up, and would, notwithstanding a series of events which seemed to rob her of all hope, have been still able to hope on? The angel had proclaimed to her the wonderful dignities of Jesus, and his glories sovereignly splendid; well now, on the contrary, she sees him a prey to his most relentless persecutors, a criminal dragged from one tribunal to another, condemned to death, nailed to the wood of the cross, and dying! She sees him abandoned by his dearest friends, abused, blasphemed, and loaded with infamy. How difficult was it under such circumstances to maintain in the heart a lively and firm hope! And, yet, a shadow of distrust never passed over Mary's soul; she never doubted that her Son would triumph over his enemies. She abided in the certainty that he would reign on earth and in heaven; that he who was now departing in ignominy would arise in glory, and subject the whole world to the law of the Gospel: "Against hope has she believed in hope."

Learn of Mary never to lose courage, and never to distrust, how violently soever the events that occur, may be antagonistic to thy hopes. Then, rather, say more heartily than ever, as said Job: "Although he should kill me, I will trust in him: And he shall be my Savior." 13 ch. 15-16 v. Should God offer me also as a sacrifice to appease his justice, yet will I hope in him, and he will be my Savior. Happy that heart whose capabilities are heightened by dangers, and which itself grows in confidence under the discipline of chastisement. Oh, how very pleasing to God is this perseverance, how very much this resignation honors him! He said himself to St. Gertrude that, by reason of her heroism and perseverance in hope, there was no grace which he could refuse her; and he also assured her that her confidence had always been to her a key to the divine treasury.

If thou standest firm in spite of all adversities and of all that which militates against thy trusting in the divine goodness, confidence will be for thee also such another key. In that case, a moment will arrive when God will make thee seize, as with thy hands, the truth of the words, "Never was one confounded who hoped in the Lord."

THIRD POINT.

MARY'S HOPE—A WORKING HOPE.

God requires the co-operation of him who will obtain what he hopes for; in regard to things which may be obtained by industry and labor, he will work no miracle. "Do all that thou canst thyself," used to say Saint Ignatius, "as if thou hadst nothing to promise thyself from God; and hope all from God, as if thou hadst done nothing thyself."

On the journey which the most Holy Virgin undertook to Bethlehem, she hoped that the Lord would have prepared for her the place where she should bring forth the divine Child, and yet she by no means omitted to seek out for herself throughout the whole city an asylum; and when she found none within the city, she continued to look for one beyond its limits, until she came to the cavern destined for her. Still more; she did not wish to oblige God to procure for her in a miraculous manner, that which she could herself obtain without a miracle;—hence she took with her the swaddling-clothes and other poor articles which she needed for the new born babe, whilst she committed to God the care of all other matters.

A terrible trial for her was her flight into Egypt. What could she do in so painful a situation? Nothing else than to obey God, and follow the footsteps of Joseph. Well, now, that she did in the most perfect manner; and she cast herself on the fatherly bosom of Providence, while from the same Providence she promised to herself that protection and that help which she dared not expect from man. Did she stand there with folded arms when she lost Jesus? Did she, perchance, content herself with praying to the Lord to lead him back that she might once more take him in her arms. Certainly not; she went in every direction, she looked for him among relations and friends, she resumed and retraced her journey; she turned back to Jerusalem, and allowed herself no rest till she found him.

At the crucifixion and death of Jesus, she stood unappalled at the foot of the cross; this was the only service which her loving heart was able to render him. After he was shut up in the grave, she could do nothing else save by her desires and her yearnings to hasten his resurrection; and on this account she retired to her chamber, and occupied herself with prayer. She went not with the pious women to look among the dead for him who was among the living, and whom she firmly hoped soon again to embrace, when he would be full of life, full of majesty, and full of glory.

Happy those souls who, after they have done what they can, commit themselves to God, and expect from him alone consolation and help! God takes such souls into his special keeping, and looks upon them with an eye of predilection: "for mercy shall encompass him that trusteth in the Lord!" He puts their steadfastness on trial: he appears for a long time deaf to their prayers; and he acts after this manner, in order to excite their zeal more and more; and then he causes them in the end to rejoice beyond all their expectation.

Learn of Mary to bestir thyself in thy necessities, and then to distrust thyself in such a way as to show that thou expectest help from God only. O most Holy Virgin! to whose advancement in virtue adversities and troubles contributed,—even as the wind causes the fire to burn more brightly,—increase and confirm in me the virtue of hope! To whom shall I address myself with confidence to maintain it, if not to thee, who art the mother of hope? "The mother of holy hope." Yes, "our hope!" The Church so salutes thee, "Hail our hope!" and with this title I also salute thee, and I rejoice that I can venture to call thee "my hope!"

O Mary! stay me right firmly on this anchor of salvation: suffer not that I should lose it in the storms that occur on the boisterous sea of this world; and above all suffer not that, on account of the multitude and enormity of my sins, I should be deluded into diffidence of the infinite mercy of my God. I entreat thee that, on the contrary, thou mayst so order matters that from his goodness and thy maternal heart, I may continue to promise myself every assistance for this present life, and for the life which is to come. Amen.

FIFTEENTH MEDITATION.

MARY'S LOVE FOR GOD.

FIRST POINT.

MARY LOVED GOD MORE THAN ALL THE SAINTS LOVED HIM.

So great was the love of God with which Mary was inflamed at the first moment of her existence, when she was filled with grace, that she even then loved him more than did the most holy saints at the close of their lives. St. Bernard adds that her love of God transcended that borne to him by all the saints, whether they be individually or collectively considered. And St. Anselm not satisfied with this, goes still farther and says: "Were we to conceive as united into one love, all the various affections which, from the beginning, actuated creatures, and which now, and will hereafter, actuate them, that one love would be outstripped by that which Mary bore to God."

This Virgin's love for God distanced in greatness all the endearing affections and sweetnesses of all creatures. True, she moved in this world, yet she lived with her heart ever fixed on God; an extremely pure dove, she never bent her affections to creatures; God was the object of her thoughts, God the end of her actions; she saw, she heard, she loved, nothing but her God. This love in her was a flame which daily acquired new strength, and daily found in God fresh objects to feed upon. It increased incalculably at the incarnation of the Eternal Word, at his birth, at the flight into Egypt, on the occasion of losing him, and of finding him again, during the sojourn at Nazareth, at his passion and death, at the resurrection; in short, her love grew greater in all the mysteries, greater in every act she performed.

In this manifold increase of her love she did not pass, as do others, from imperfection to holiness, nor from the state of lukewarmness to that of zeal, but constantly from a degree of ardent love to another degree of love still higher, of love yet more glowing and sublime. Our astonishment is excited by the ardor of the love and by the ecstacies of a Theresa of Jesus, of a Philip Neri, of a Stanislaus Kostka, and of so many other saints, who reached a period when they lived only by love: yet, were the love of all those saints blended together into one love, this one love were, if compared with Mary's, as a flickering flame to a conflagration.

What then must have been the character of her life? How must she have communed with God? How must she have approached Holy Communion, to receive in it her beloved Son? How must she have prayed? With what ardor of spirit? St. Bernard says, that were every creature an apostle Paul, they would not altogether attain to the ravishments of Mary; for the apostle was indeed a vessel of election, but Mary was a vessel of the Divinity: "Were there as many Pauls as there are creatures, even then they could not approach the sublime contemplation of God, which was the Blessed Virgin's privilege; for if Paul was indeed a vessel of election, none the less was Mary a vessel of the Divinity."

If we cannot love God as much as Mary loved him, let us love him at least as much as we ought—that is, with our whole heart: "Thou must love the Lord thy God with thy whole heart." Let us fulfil this commandment; it is the first and the foundation of all the others; let us prefer God to all else, so that we shall never be prepared to displease him or to despise his holy will, whether out of attachment to any good the world can offer us, or out of fear of any evil with which the world can threaten us.

What is the temper of thy heart towards God? Dost thou love him? Dost thou prefer his law to all things else? With what fervor dost thou receive him in holy Communion? How frequently dost thou raise thyself to him by prayer? Entreat the Virgin to enkindle in thy heart a spark of that heavenly love which will cut thee loose from the world, and unite thee closely with God.

SECOND POINT.

MARY'S LOVE FOR GOD—A MIRACULOUS LOVE.

Mary could not, according to the laws of nature, have endured the fire of love that burned in her heart: when love is violent, it consumes the strength and wastes it away to nothing. How many saints felt so happy that they could not forbear exclaiming: "Stay me up with flowers; compass me about with apples; because I languish with love." Cant. ii. 5 v.

Think now within thyself, how the case must have

stood with Mary who loved more than did all others together:—how was she able to hold out under the weight of her affections and to endure the greatness of their intensity? How, asks St Thomas of Villanova, how was it possible for her not to depart this life since she was in the midst of such violent flames, for it was already a constant miracle that she was in a state to endure them and continue to live? The thornbush which Moses saw on mount Horeb, burned without being consumed; and the heart of this venerable Virgin burned with yet greater violence, without suffering the least detriment: "Divine love had inflamed her whole being."

The case of the burning bush was a miracle which lasted but some moments; the miracle of Mary's love covered the whole period of her lifetime. After the ascension of Jesus, who was her treasure and the life of her life, she was in mind and heart wholly in heaven; thenceforward, earth was for her but a place of painful exile; already was Redemption accomplished, the Church established, the Gospel propagated. Mary's sole aim was to unite herself for ever with that God whose Mother, Daughter, and Bride, she was. Oh, who can adequately portray the fire, the warm longings, the ardent desires, of that heart! With what glowing love must she have exclaimed again and again: "When shall I come and appear before the countenance of my God?" Yet, however excellent and sublime those affections, they, nevertheless, kept her in a constant state of martyrdom—of martyrdom, indeed, whose very essence was love, but love not unblended with a certain fear and violence. Had nature's laws taken their course in her, that, her martyrdom, must necessarly have dissolved the bonds of life by little and little. But God's own strength sustained her; God did not permit that the heavenly fire should bring forth its natural results until the moment arrived that should summon her to the crown; and he adopted this course to the end that as her whole life was love, so also her death might be an operation of love.

Great things such as these, certainly, we cannot promise ourselves; but we can easily advance every day in the love of God; yea, we must most earnestly endeavor to do so by co-operating with grace constantly and with ever increasing fidelity, by abandoning ourselves more and more thoroughly to his loving care, by placing ourselves at his free disposal, by offering him the very sacrifices he desires at our hands, by suffering the trials he sends us, and by penetrating ourselves more and more deeply with the knowledge of our nothingness, in order that in us he may be all things and we ourselves nothing.

Oh, were this the course we pursued, how easily would our heart catch the fire of love! How sweet to us would be our detachment from creatures, that we might love the Creator and him alone! Make the attempt to run in this course, and thou wilt say with David: "How good is the God of Israel to them that are right of heart!"

THIRD POINT.

MARY'S LOVE FOR GOD—A LOVE CEASELESSLY IN ACTION.

The uninterrupted duration of Mary's love was its most singular privilege. Her heart was as the altar whereon the fire was constantly kept burning day and night: "Let the fire burn without intermission," always, without a moment's respite; and this distinguishing characteristic of Mary's love was a privilege worthy of the Mother of God, and, as far as is known, a privilege conferred on no other creature. Not as other saints loved him, did Mary love God; that is, she did not love him as they did, by frequently performing acts of love; she loved him by means of one only and continuous act: "The most glorious Virgin loved God in a fort, and this was the result of a special privilege; she also loved him with an act which spanned the whole term of her life on earth."

If the angelic youth, Aloysius, was able to rivet his mind on God in such a way as that he could no longer cease to think of him, what shall we say of the Mother of God who was so distinguished among all creatures and so pre-eminently privileged beyond them? Like unto the royal eagle, she kept her glance steadfastly directed to the divine sun; her heart burned incessantly, amid the most distracting occupations of the day, as well as in the most peaceful repose of night: "The work lessened not the contemplation," says St. Peter Damian, "and the contemplation did not desert the work." Accordingly, whilst her body was taking light sleep, thus enjoying the necessary refreshment, her soul in perfect freedom tended to God: "Her soul then prosecuted its journey towards God;" and indeed prosecuted it by contemplation so sublime that to it the contemplation of which any one else was capable, even in the most perfect state of wakefulness, was not at all comparable. "She applied herself to the exercise of meditation in a more perfect manner during her sleep, than any one else ever did in a state of thorough wakefulness."

This fact will explain to thee the expressions of some of the saints, who maintain that the Seraphim would have desired to come down from their heavenly thrones into Mary's heart, there to learn how to love God. Admire so splendid a privilege, but do not lose sight of her unexampled correspondence therewith, because she on her part did all that was possible for her to keep so charming a fire ceaselessly burning.

Who, indeed, can express the eager watchfulness in which she maintained herself in order to keep her mind constantly recollected, in order to avoid distractions, to behold God in all things? What then do we? Instead of doing as Mary did, we seek occasions of distraction; we suffer our mind to pour itself out on external objects; we run with all our senses after images which stuff mind and heart with earthly follies. Is it, then, anything strange that we are so lukewarm towards God, so indifferent to that which concerns him, and that it is so difficult for us to become recollected at prayer, meditations, the reception of the holy sacraments? Enter into a little self-examination; take the resolution to improve, and entreat the Virgin for her help.

O Mary! O Queen of love! O most beloved and

most loving Lady! cast a glance at this poor heart of mine which feels warmly towards all creatures, but which is so callous towards God; ah, throw into it a spark of that fire which thy Divine Son brought into the world, and with which thou wast so much inflamed! So exceeding great was thy love for him that it caused thee to pine away, and even transcended the love felt by the Seraphim of heaven themselves. Ah, make me, in virtue of thy goodness, love him as much as my condition will allow—with all my powers and with my whole soul. Thou, O Mary! desirest to see God loved; cause me, I entreat thee, to love him; I conjure thee by all that is holy to do so; receive my petition, grant it, and let me truly love that God who loves me so much. Amen.

SIXTEENTH MEDITATION.

MARY'S LOVE FOR MANKIND.

FIRST POINT.

MARY'S LOVE FOR MANKIND MEASURED BY HER LOVE FOR GOD.

THE love which one bears to God, and the love which one conceives for his neighbor, spring from one and the same source. "The affection with which one loves God, and the affection with which one loves the neighbor, are, in their kind, one and the same." Such is the teaching of the angelic Master of the schools.

Accordingly, who loves God truly, cannot forbear loving his neighbor in very truth. This being so, thou canst easily understand the pains which the saints took, the efforts they made, the sacrifices they imposed on themselves—all for the salvation of even a single soul; and thou canst likewise easily understand the most ardent longings wherewith so many holy virgins and matrons were interpenetrated for the salvation of souls,—longings which enabled those holy personages cheerfully to undergo all toils and sufferings with the view to effect the coveted salvation of their neighbors' souls. Indeed, love for their neighbor burned in them as love for God; the stronger the latter, the stronger the former likewise. If thou wilt have an idea of Mary's love for us, then measure her love for God; for "the affection with which one loves God, and with which one loves the neighbor, is, in kind, one and the same."

Mary loved God immeasurably more than did all the saints; and, in like manner, she loves mankind immeasurably more than do all the saints. She exercises her love towards all and towards each and every individual of the human family; her love embraces the entire universe; it embraces all centuries; there is no creature that shares not in her benefactions: "nothing is able to hide itself from the glow of her love." She is like unto the sun which communicates to all its light and its heat, and sheds its salutary influences not only on fruitful fields and blooming meadows, but also on the most slimy valleys and the most barren mountains. Poor and rich, just and sinners, healthy and sickly, believers and unbelievers, all are objects of her love; she prays for all; she exerts herself with God for all; she would be glad to see all blessed, comforted, and safe in heaven. Her chief care, however, her maternal affection has mainly for object the followers of her divine Son who, as St. Paul tells us, "is the Savior of all men, especially of the faithful." 1 Tim. iv. 10 v.

What does she leave undone for those? Oh, what ingenious devices of love does she not employ! St. Bernard knows not how to express himself better in regard to this matter than by saying, that her interior was as if transmuted into love, after God had his indwelling in her for nine months: "Mary's interior was completely changed into love, since therein dwelt, for the space of nine months, the love which proceedeth from God's tabernacle."

Who loves not his neighbor, cannot flatter himself that he loves God: "He who loves not, remains in death." Lovest thou then thy neighbor? Dost thou feel for him in his adversity? Dost thou endeavor to come to his assistance in his necessities? Mayst thou not be of the number of those who think only of self, and care little or nothing for the spiritual and corporal necessities of their brethren or of the number of those who, if such a thought cross their minds, confine their good offices to friends or such persons as chance to be in their company. Not thus acts genuine Christian charity; the genuine charity of the Christian is all sympathy for the miseries of others, and makes no difference between Jew and Greek, between acquaintances and strangers; it sees in them all the likeness of God; it recognizes them all as brethren redeemed by the same most precious Blood; it loves all, and spends itself in the service of all with joy and zeal. Whoever truly loves God, loves his neighbor after this manner.

SECOND POINT.

MARY'S LOVE FOR HER NEIGHBOR, STRENGTHENED BY THE EXAMPLES OF HER SON.

Every day for many years, Mary had before her eyes her divine Son, the most perfect model of love. What he did and suffered, that was for Mary the most powerful incentive to love us. She saw the only begotten Son of God suffering, from love for mankind, privations and ignominies of every kind; she saw him hidden from the eyes of the world, ignored, contemned; she saw with what love he commiserated the members of the human family; how solicitous he was to do them good; with what exertions and zeal, he advanced the interests of their salvation. She was aware that it was for their salvation that he came down on earth from heaven; aware that for it he took flesh in her womb; that for it he subjected himself to a life full of sufferings, and to an ignominious death on the wood of the cross.

What impresssion must these sublime and constant lessons not have made on Mary's tender heart? In what manner and how exceedingly must she not have felt herself fired to do all in her power for those men for whom she saw Jesus suffer so much! Mary watched most closely all the words which issued from his blessed lips, she pondered over all his actions and feelings, and meditated on them in order to imitate him, to be like unto him in all things, and to become the most faithful copy of so perfect an original: "But Mary preserved all these words and pondered over them in her heart."

Of so many virtues that the most holy Virgin admired in Jesus, which, thinkest thou, is she most anxious to imitate? Doubtless, she is anxious to imitate them all; but chiefly charity, which is, as it were, the mother and the queen of all the others: "but the greater of these is charity." Accordingly, this is the virtue which Mary esteemed and loved in the highest degree; and this she made the object of her most heartfelt affection and joy; this moved her to receive all men as children, to sympathize with them, to help them, to love them; this moved her to grant generous pardon to the cruel crucifiers of her divine Son; in one word, this her charity made her our hope, our refuge, our most loving protectress. The examples of Jesus increased Mary's charity as much as was possible for it to increase in the heart of a mere creature.

May her examples strengthen in thee love for thy neighbor! She is all eye to see our miseries, all heart to remove them; endeavor, according to thy power, to do as much, and rest assured thou canst do nothing that will be more agreeable to her than will be this thy imitation of her in her charitable solicitude for the human family. What a wide field opens up before thee, if thou wilt but go over it! How many abandoned souls are there not, who need light, direction, and consolation! How many poor, lacking all sustenance! How many sick, who pine away in misery and sufferings!

An occasion will never be wanting to thee of practising charity towards thy neighbor. Mayst thou know how to put to profit every occasion that presents itself; and if nothing else lies in thy power, set thyself to work with thy whole soul to benefit him by thy prayers. Oh, how much good wouldst thou accomplish by recurring to this most efficacious means; how many graces wouldst thou obtain for thyself and for him; how many souls wouldst thou lead to salvation!

THIRD POINT.

MARY'S CHARITY TOWARDS HER NEIGHBOR, ATTESTED BY THE SACRIFICE OF THE CROSS.

Charity is not so well evidenced by words as by actions; and the more troublesome and difficult are these, the stronger is the love, and the more manifest the proof of its existence.

Dost thou desire to know how Mary attests the love she bears to us? Contemplate her on Calvary at the foot of the cross; look at what she there offers for our salvation; behold what a sacrifice she brings thither for us! "Ye are not redeemed by corruptible silver or gold," can she also say; "your salvation, O men! costs me not earthly riches, but the most painful sacrifice that a mother can offer,—the loss of the dearest, the most amiable, the most holy of all sons! Out of love to you have I offered him up to the divine justice; for your salvation I have allowed myself to be bereft of him by a death most cruel and ignominious; the selfsame sacrifice which my son offered on the altar of the cross, that have I also offered on the altar of my heart."

As God—such is the thought of some of the holy fathers—desired to obtain Mary's consent to the incarnation of the Word, so also God wished to obtain her consent to the sufferings and death of her beloved Jesus; and as she answered to the proposal of the first: "Behold the handmaid of the Lord, be it done unto me according to thy word;" so, in like manner, she gave to the second proposal a reply couched in the same terms.

What a spectacle was it not, to behold a God plunged into a sea of sorrows, expire on a cross for the salvation of men, and to behold at the foot of this cross the most tender of mothers offer up to the divine justice the best beloved of sons for the salvation of those selfsame men! Oh, that is truly a love which is proof against all tests; of such love can it be well affirmed that it is strong as death: "Love is mighty as death."

By giving up his life for us Jesus gave us the greatest proof he could give us of his love: "Greater love than this no man hath, that he give his life for his friends;" and by consenting to the death of Jesus, yea, by her offering up of his life in atonement of our sins, Mary also gave us the greatest proof she could give us of her love for us; because she most cheerfully offered up in sacrifice a life which was immeasurably more precious to her than her own very life itself. Charity towards our neighbors has its own trials, and demands its sacrifices; it is not difficult to do good to others when the cost to us is little or nothing; but it is difficult when our own interest and self-love suffer considerably by the good we perform on their behalf. But a whole and generous heart does not despond, it conquers difficulties, overcomes all opposition, endures troubles and fatigues, and offers, when necessary, even life itself in sacrifice.

Learn how and at what price Mary loved thee, and how she instructs thee as to how thou shouldst love thy neighbor. What a shame would it be, were thou to refuse to do all else save those things which demand no sacrifice! Bear in mind that it does not suffice to love in words: "Let us not love in word and in tongue." Works are demanded; deeds are demanded, "but in deed and in truth." Entreat Mary to warm thy heart.

O Mother of love! thou who didst leave us so many proofs of thy love, and who didst love us so much, that thou didst deliver up for us thy only begotten Son, cause me to know the worth of love, and to make a beginning with the earnest exercise of this heavenly virtue, seeing that it is so precious in the eyes of God, and so necessary to my salvation. Ah, Lady! may the examples of thy adorable Son and thine own, not hereafter serve to procure my rejection and condemnation! Alas, I acknowledge it, I have been hitherto cold and lukewarm in the charity I owed my neighbor; but, henceforward, it shall be no longer so. I resolve with thy help to love him, by advancing his spiritual interests as far as lies in my power, and by assisting him in his corporal necessities. Obtain for me the grace of being able to imitate thy love, and add to thy mercies towards me already so numerous, this one which I now implore, and which is so agreeable to thy heart. Amen.

SEVENTEENTH MEDITATION.

MARY'S HUMILITY.

FIRST POINT.

MARY'S LITTLE ESTEEM OF HERSELF.

THE first step to genuine humility is the knowledge of our nothingness, and the little esteem we entertain of ourselves.

In both these things was Mary truly admirable. As there was no creature, says St Bernard of Sienna, who was so exalted as Mary, so, also, was there no creature who was so little in her own eyes: "As no creature ascended to so high an elevation, so no creature went down so far into the depths of humility." Not that she looked upon herself as a sinner, or that she failed to appreciate the extraordinary privileges with which she was enriched; but because she ascribed all these to the goodness of God, and looked upon herself as a handmaid favored indeed, but favored without having merited to be favored. In her sublime canticle, she speaks only of God and of herself:—of God, in order to exalt him; and of herself, in order to humiliate her: "My soul doth magnify the Lord, and my spirit hath rejoiced in God my Savior."

Who can well conceive the disposition of humility with which she utters those words! She refers all honor to the Lord; she acknowledges his favor for the only purpose of praising him; she forgets herself completely; she thinks of God and is absorbed in him as if she would say: "Thou, O Elizabeth, praisest me by reason of the dignity conferred on me, but I praise the Lord who gave it me and to whom belongs all honor. Thou rejoicest because at the sound of my voice thy child leaped for joy; but I rejoice still more in the consideration that all this resulted from the pure mercies of my Savior, and that all good came to me from the fact that he deigned to cast his eyes on my lowliness. 'For he hath regarded the humility of his handmaid.' This sympathetic look brought all good to me; without it I were nothing: he who considers in me what is in me from myself, finds only an object worthy of the deepest contempt; but he who considers in me what I have received from God, discovers only motives to praise his mercy; for his mercy alone worked great things in me: 'He who is Almighty, hath done great things to me.'"

Mary never lets slip from view her lowliness; she never forgets that she is the humble maid of the Lord; and she will claim no other title. Oh, how great must have been, before the eyes of the Lord, this humble virgin who, clothed in the highest dignity, sees in herself nought but her own nothingness and only studies to humiliate herself! We are all full of miseries and sins, and in all things full of vanity and pride: we have every reason to think humbly of ourselves, to contemn ourselves, and in spite of all this we think we are something. What is the foundation of the esteem we have of ourselves? If we have any distinguishing privilege, does this privilege not come from God? "But what hast thou which thou hast not received?" says St. Paul; and if thou hast received from God all that thou possessest, "why dost thou glory as if thou hadst not received?"

Our self-love it is that deceives and betrays us. What a distance between Mary and us! Pray to her for light in order that thou mayst perceive the horribleness of this vice, and ask her for the disposition necessary to overcome it, for it is certain that the Lord looks only on the humble: "On whom shall I look if not on the poor and lowly in spirit, and on him who trembles at my words?"

SECOND POINT.

MARY CONCEALS HER GIFTS DESIGNEDLY.

It is a peculiarity of humble souls to use every diligence, in order to keep concealed from the eyes of men all the graces and gifts they have received from God. "One conceals," says St. Gregory, "a treasure that has been discovered, and conceals it in order to preserve it;" and the most humble of all creatures kept her treasure hidden with the greatest solicitude.

When did she give the least manifestation of the gifts and the privileges with which she was enriched, or of the high dignity to which she was raised? Indeed, she did quite the contrary; she constantly hid, and with the utmost concern, every thing great that she had, and that could conduce to her honor, and acted as if she possessed it not. She did not allow to betray itself aught of her prudence, of her wisdom, of her sanctity, of the grace to work miracles, which grace also she possessed. From an archangel sent to her in an especial manner, she learns the most exalted mysteries; but, because those exalted mysteries conduce to her honor, they remain concealed in her heart. She speaks to no one a syllable about them, not even to her relative Zachary, the high priest, not even to Elizabeth to whom, as Mary knew, God had revealed them. She contents herself with celebrating in a general manner the praises of the Lord and the greatness of the mercies he had shown in her.

What more? She kept them secret even from Joseph, and on the most trying occasions when she seemed to have every reason to speak, and yet she will rather suffer than with her own lips reveal her dignities. Not yet enough. When her divine Son fed so many thousand men with a few loaves, when he delivered those that were possessed, when he cured the diseased, when he raised the dead to life;—whilst all these miracles were being performed, Mary did not put herself forward in order that she might be known. Amid those flattering circumstances in which mothers, on account of the merit of their children, like to put themselves forward, she never caused it to be remarked that she was his mother or that she had any power over him.

Dost thou know when she caused herself to be recognized as his mother? When he was loaded with humiliations and ignominies, when he ascended Mount Calvary and expired as a malefactor on the cross;—then she gave it to be understood that she was the mother of Jesus; then she made no hesitation amid so many insults, to stand by him amid so many anguishes which accompanied his death.

Learn from this humble Virgin what is the genuine spirit of humility. If God has given thee any grace or shown thee any favors, do not boast of it and proclaim it even to such as are not willing to listen. Think on what St. Gregory said: He who causes himself to be seen whilst the treasure is in his hand, causes himself to be also robbed: "He who bears a treasure publicly on his way desires to be robbed;" that is to say, those who lightly expose the gifts they have received from God, by often talking of them, even when this happens from mere self-complacence and secret pride which, as wormwood, corrupts the most precious works, expose themselves to lose the treasures they possess. Be strictly on thy guard against this wormwood which insinuates itself ever into pious hearts; and give to the Virgin the beautiful homage of imitating her in the concealment of thy gifts, after the manner in which she concealed those which she had received.

THIRD POINT.

MARY EMBRACED HUMILIATION.

The avoiding of the praise which comes to us from the gifts of God, is a great characteristic of humility; but a more glorious feature of it is the peaceful and joyous endurance of the humiliations which we meet without deserving to meet them.

Meditate a little on how the Blessed Virgin accepted the humiliations she experienced on being expelled at Bethlehem. Though the blood was royal that flowed in her veins, she found, because she had fallen to a low estate, no one would give her protection; and she was sent away cruelly by her own: "There was no place for her in the inn." It might be imagined that she should be sensitive on that occasion, since her parturition was near at hand; and yet seest thou how quietly and peacefully she takes her refusal? Far from being angry or from complaining of any one whomsoever, she goes on to the city and seeks shelter in a stable, and was much more content with this asylum than she would have been, had she taken possession of a palace.

Should it happen to thee to be rudely refused or ill-received, remember the humiliation Mary endured on that occasion. The time of the passion was for her a time of constant and most cruel humiliations. Oh, how often must she have been pointed out as the Mother of the malefactor! how often must she have seen herself loaded with insults, mockery, and derisions! "What," said herself to St. Bridget, "what is more contemptuous to a person than to call that person a fool?" And still so little did she fear, still so little did she avoid, those humiliations, that she freely exposed herself to them! "Such, O daughter! was the temper of my humility; this was my joy; this my whole desire."

Those words, also, which Jesus addressed to her in different circumstances, touched her to the quick: and although she thoroughly took in the very exalted motive her divine Son had in addressing her in such terms, yet these terms became unto her an occasion for the exercise of humility. Of this kind were the words which she heard when she found him in the temple after she had searched for him three days in the greatest anxiety:

"How is it that thou sought me? Didst thou not know that I must be about the things that are my father's?" Of this kind were the words which he addressed to her at the marriage feast of Cana, when it would seem as if he approved not her request: "Woman, what is it to me and to thee? My hour is not yet come."

How must these and the like expressions have touched the most sweet maternal heart of Mary! And yet did she endure them! And with what calm of soul! with what admirable serenity of countenance!

Learn of Mary, at least to preserve thy peace amid the humiliations occasioned to thee whether by God or men. Sometimes, humiliations will fall to thy lot without thy deserving them, and even after thou hast faithfully discharged thy duties; so that it will seem to thee that thou meritest praise much rather than reproach. Sometimes, humiliations will be thrown in thy way by good and pious persons who will believe that they do a service to God when they oppose thee, when they set themselves against thy most reasonable desires, and endeavor by every means to lower thy condition. Humiliations of this kind are, indeed, the most irksome: St. Theresa acknowledged of herself that it might be compared to martyrdom. And yet God ordained that she and many others were tried in that crucible.

Should he ever subject thee, also, to such trials, thou must not lose courage; stand firm and console thyself with the thought that Mary, although the most holy of all creatures, yet had humiliations to undergo. Pray to her for the grace of imitating her in the best manner possible. O Queen of all humble souls, I now clearly see that I cannot be agreeable in thy eyes and in the eyes of God, unless I be truly humble in mind and heart! Oh, how far am I from having that spirit of humility which unto thee was the fountain of all thy greatness! I, a miserable wretch devoid of every good, full of sins and vices, extremely ungrateful for the mercies of the Lord, am full of myself, full of vanity, of ambition, of pride. O my mother! deign to heal so many wounds of my poor soul; for the sake of the merits of thy humility grant me true knowledge of my miseries; grant that I may look upon myself and treat myself as I am; that I may humiliate myself among all creatures and willingly accept from the hand of God those humiliations which he may cause to befall me for my greater good. Should it be necessary, in order to please thee, that I should be humbled, then humble me instantly; for I am resolved, cost what it may, to belong wholly to God and to thee. Amen.

EIGHTEENTH MEDITATION.

MARY'S HUMILITY, THE ONLY HUMILITY OF ITS KIND IN THE WORLD.

FIRST POINT.

MARY—HUMBLE IN THE ABUNDANCE OF HER GIFTS.

NEVER was there in the world a creature who knew how to unite so great humility with gifts so numerous as Mary possessed. The holy fathers tell us that God poured forth his gifts without measure into her being; he made her the very creature in whom triumphed his generosity and his glory. Of noble extraction, she possessed mental powers of the highest order; bodily perfections, too, and privileges of every kind she had in most extraordinary degree: beauty, but without ostentation; wisdom, but without presumption; friendliness and courtesy of demeanor, but without levity. The rising aurora, the sun in his mid-day splendor, the silvery moon, the most charming flowers, the most beautiful plants,—all these are symbols which holy writ employs in order to portray her to us.

And as to her interior gifts, who can number them? An understanding clearer than light; an imagination tranquil and pure, that represented to her but heavenly objects; a righteous will conformable in all things with the will of God; a liberty more perfect than that enjoyed by the angels and by Adam when he was yet in the state of innocence. The motions of her interior were always regulated, always in order; her flesh was so holy that it merited to become the flesh of the God-man; no disorderly inclination from within, no undue attraction to what was without; the greatest horror of every sin, of even the slightest; a wonderful power of attracting others to virtue. Imperturbable, calm in her thoughts, in her interior motions, in her actions; an unexampled gentleness in her deportment, and so many other privileges that are more easily imagined than described.

Who in the world was ever like unto her? Who in the world ever approached her? And what was still the character of Mary's humility, notwithstanding that, her great wealth of privileges? What was the character of the thoughts of her mind, of the dispositions of her heart? Oh, how well she knew how to win for herself the panegyric of the Holy Ghost: "If thou wilt separate the precious from the vile, thou shalt be as my mouth!" Lev. xv. 19 v.

She was, indeed, fully aware of the number and the excellence of her gifts; yet she ascribed them all to the generosity of her God and to that alone; the more she saw herself elevated, the more profoundly did she abase herself; and as there was never a soul more richly endowed than she, so never was there a soul more humble also than she. Every humble person may, in a certain regard, be termed a valley of the Lord, according to that saying: "Let every valley be exalted." "Such indeed was Mary," says St. Bonaventure, "as the most humble among the humble, the valley of all valleys."

And what then dost thou? Ah! because thou hast a small tithe of those natural gifts—a title of nobility, some talent or tact in business, an agreeable address in thy intercourse with the world,—thou lookest upon thyself as something great; thou growest vain; thou art puffed up; and, as a consequence of all this, thou despisest others. O miserable that thou art! knowest thou not that this is the way to lose all good? In the eyes of God, there is no monster more disgusting than a proud pauper. God is jealous of his honor, and pursues the vile wretch who robs him of it, with the dreadful punishment of withdrawing from him his gifts, and bereaving him of his mercies: "He hath scattered the proud in the conceit of their heart." Luke, i. 51 v.

Guard thyself well against pride, against self-complacency; and if thou wilt preserve thy gifts and obtain still other and greater ones, render unto God, and to him alone, the honor for them: and this thou shalt do by recognizing him as the only source whence they proceed.

SECOND POINT.

MARY—HUMBLE IN THE FULNESS OF HER GRACES.

As the fulness of graces accorded to Mary was unexampled, so also was the humility, with which she received and utilized such fulness, without example. Of such a kind and so abundant was the grace granted her, that the angel of God knew no better means of expressing it than by styling her by way of eminence the Virgin, "full of grace," "Hail full of grace:" and, likewise, of such a character and so profound was her humility, that it was able to sustain so great a multitude of gifts and to bear to them due proportion: "the deeper a valley, the more water does it contain;" and in like manner the more profound Mary's humility, the more graces did she possess. St. Bernard.

This wonderful combination of so great a treasure on the part of God, with such deep self-abasement on her part,—this combination it is that makes her humility extraordinary. Suppose, says St. John Chrysostom, that at the time of the archangel's communication to Mary, she had been full of grace, but still had not been possessed of that profound humility which induced her to recognize and to proclaim herself to be, in all sincerity, the handmaid of the Lord; would she, in such a supposition, have become the Mother of God? No, answers the saint. Assume, on the other hand, that she had made a sincere protestation of her nothingness, but had not been full of grace; in this case, likewise, she would by no means have been raised to so exalted a dignity.

What the Eternal Word brought into her womb was her capability to ally so great humility with so great graces. God filled her with grace so far as the most sublime dignity to which she was called demanded; and Mary humbled herself as much as was possible for a mere creature. Behold, this it is that transformed her from a handmaid into the Mother of God, and made her a true prodigy of humility for all eternity. "By virginity," says St. Bernard, "she pleased; by humility, she became Mother." But how difficult of practice is this humility in the midst of such prodigious wealth of gifts!

There is nothing great in a soul humbling herself

who is loaded with sins and miseries, for humility in the circumstances of such a soul becomes a necessity; yea, what has she to be vain of? But when a soul knows she is full of grace, and knows it without fear or danger of being deceived; when such a soul thinks so little of herself, and plunges herself into the abyss of her nothingness, and proportions her humility to the fulness of her graces,—this is a marvel of which Mary alone furnishes us an instance.

Contrast thy pride with her humility, and learn the delusion and the danger of those souls who, for a little pleasure they taste in exercises of piety, for a certain tender sentiment of devotion they feel, plume themselves and think themselves superior to others: "I am not as the rest of men." O the poor dupes! Mary, full of sanctifying grace, full of most extraordinary operative graces; exalted above all creatures, abases, humbles, herself below them all; and those other souls are puffed up above their fellows for having what may be termed a mere nothing of Mary's graces!

Deplore their blindness, and keep thyself well on thy guard. God communicated himself to the humble; on these he showers the highest gifts of love in this life, and reserves for them in the next the most brilliant throne: "He looks on the lowliest in heaven and on earth." Happy thou if thou humblest thyself before God and men, in proportion as thou seest thyself sustained by grace!

THIRD POINT.

MARY—HUMBLE IN THE MERIDIAN OF HONORS.

Whoever occupies a lowly and despicable state in life, need take but little pains to walk in true humility. The case stands otherwise with one who enjoys honors, dignities, and fills an exalted station. In these latter circumstances, says St. John Chrysostom, humility is a difficult virtue, and a virtue as precious as it is rare. Now cast a look at the most holy Virgin; to what supremacies, to what dignities, to what honors was she not ordained? Whatever there is on earth of great and splendid, is nothing in comparison with her greatness and splendor.

The Lord desired that heaven and earth should cooperate to her glorification. The angel announces to her her supremacies, and styles her blessed among women: "blessed art thou among women." Elizabeth acknowledges her to be the mother of God, and full of exultation, repeats as if the same words: "blessed art thou among women." Thus, exclaims venerable Bede, thus is Mary glorified by a heavenly spirit and by a holy soul of this world, to show that veneration, praise, and love should be one day rendered her both in heaven and on earth: "The angel and Elizabeth use the same words to extol Mary, in order to show that she should be honored both by angels and men."

Now, reflect that the Virgin knew all those her sublime elevations; she knew she was the mother of God: she knew that in heaven and on earth, by angels and by men, she would be more loved and honored than all other creatures taken together: she knew she was the favored object of God's complacency, and that, in her, men placed their dearest confidence. Well now, what thinks this most humble Virgin, what says she, in reference to her supreme elevation? Just what the poorest of creatures would say and think? She looks not upon the honor nor upon the glory which accrue to her therefrom; she considers only her insignificance in order to humble herself, and the Omnipotence of God with a view to his glorification. "All generations," said she, "shall call me blessed;" but now because the Lord God has wrought in me what I am, "for he who is mighty hath done great things to me," I am only his poor handmaid: "Behold the handmaid of the Lord."

Compare thy humility with Mary's; she rejoices not at the announcement of so great honors, she sets not her eyes on them, she is not moved by them; thou art lifted up by a word of praise, thou rejoicest, exultest on hearing it; Mary thinks on her nothingness, and deems herself unworthy of even nothingness itself. Thou art mindful of thy gifts and lookst upon thyself as insulted when these are not recognized. In the honors conferred upon her, Mary sees but the generosity of her God; in the honors conferred on thee, thou seest the reward of thy own merit. Mary is in no way proud of her honors, and she receives them in order to refer them all to the Lord; thou boastest of the honors paid to thee, and nourishest thy pride therewith. Oh, how far away art thou from Mary's humility! Oh, how hideous a thing is pride in any one who pretends to be a true client of Mary!

Watch more assiduously over the feelings of thy heart; subdue thy evil inclinations with greater earnestness; and entreat Mary for the grace to resemble her closely by imitation of her in the practice of humility, a virtue so dear to her heart, and so meritorious.

O exalted Virgin, who art as humble as thou art great, behold at thy feet a sinner, who is devoid of all good, but full of the desire to walk in the footsteps of thy humility! Ah, may I imitate thee, O Lady! at least in this virtue to which I have just as many motives as there are miseries in me. My self-love blinds me, and renders difficult for me the very virtue which should become easier for me. O Mary! thou lovest the humble, help me to become humble: the grace I entreat of thee is completely after thy own heart; refuse it not to me. Cast one look at me, and turn not away thy eyes from me till I become quite otherwise than I am, and thereby merit for myself the special marks of favor which God gives to those who are humble of heart. Amen.

NINETEENTH MEDITATION.

MARY'S VIRGINAL PURITY, A PURITY WITHOUT EXAMPLE.

FIRST POINT.

MARY'S VIRGINITY—WITHOUT EXAMPLE IN REFERENCE TO TIME.

WHEN Mary, the beautiful Aurora, appeared in the world, virginity was not by any means held in honor among the Hebrews; nay, rather was it despised, whether by reason of the sensuality of that people, or by reason of the hope indulged in by each one of becoming the progenitor of the looked-for Messiah. The Hebrew woman considered it a shame and a curse to have no children, and save by very few persons, the excellence of this heavenly virtue was not recognized, for the Redeemer of the world had not yet made this excellence known. At that time Mary was the first who vowed virginity: "and indeed," as says Albert the Great, "the first, because no one had made such a vow before her." At that time God instructed Mary on the excellence of this sovereignly precious jewel; and, accordingly, without attending to the judgment of men, without one example that strengthened her, she brings and consecrates, the first of all, her intact virginity to God for a constant sacrifice. She appeared as a lily among thorns, as a lily which filled the whole earth with its charming fragrance, whilst the entire world emitted nothing but the fumes of blasphemy: "As the lily among thorns, so is my love in the midst of daughters."

The holy fathers unanimously celebrate her praises for that she was the very first who, in fact, went against the stream, and who raised the white and glorious standard of virginal purity. St. Ambrose congratulates her on this and says: "She raised the standard of holy virginity, and floated the banner of immaculate integrity, which banner has been consecrated to Christ." St. Bonaventure calls her, "the standard bearer of Christ;" St. John Chrysostom calls her, "the first confessor of virginity." St. Bernard ceases not to admire and extol her greatness of heart, because she so perfectly executed an undertaking which no one before her had ever attempted, because it was in antagonism with the universal judgment of men, was in itself difficult of accomplishment, and was, besides, looked upon as disgraceful. "O magnanimous heart!" he exclaims, "more firmly established than the earth, more celebrated than the heavens."

Mary's example is a living condemnation of those souls who pretend to find justification of their weakness in the evil character of the times, and in the corruption of mankind. The judgment of the world, the conduct of the world, is not, and cannot be, the rule of acting to be followed by a Christian soul: and woe to the one who follows such a rule. Who lives, as live the great bulk, ends as end the great bulk.

If the Virgin had troubled herself about the judgments of the world of her time, she would never have made the vow of virginity, and consequently would never have been so dear to God. "Imitate not the multitude in doing evil," says the Lord, in the Book of Exodus. The principles of faith, and the doctrines of the Church are the infallible rules to be observed, if we would not go astray in our judgment of things and in our habits of life. Such principles and doctrines are the lights which God has raised up in the darkness of this world; look upon that light, follow it; and thou shalt be shielded from error and be certain of the friendship of God.

SECOND POINT.

MARY'S VIRGINITY—WITHOUT EXAMPLE, BY REASON OF ITS PERFECTION.

Mary's virginal purity must have been so exalted and so extraordinary before the world, that the unspeakable and adorable union which obtained between God and man in the Word made flesh, could be determined upon. Her's must have been a virginity more precious than that of angels, who were pure not from free choice and in consequence of a vow, but from nature and in virtue of their holiness and glory. Her's must have been a purity worthy of a God who is purity itself; "an extraordinary purity," exclaims St. Bernard, from which the Immaculate should go forth, "to blot out the sins of all others." Her's must have been a purity which was like a constant sacrifice that she offered to the Most High, —a yielding up of her body, which she offered up as a living holocaust, and one agreeable in the eyes of God,

—a consecration of her person, which was to become the sanctuary and the abode of the Lord.

She loved and observed purity with so unselfish a love that she would rather have renounced the dignity of Mother of God than that virtue. The words of the angel, says St. Jerome, which promised a God for a son, could not for a moment shake her resolution. Her determination to vow virginity, was so firm that it was no wise shaken even by the angel who promised her for son the Son of God. With such solicitude did she love and observe virginity, that before giving her consent to the mystery of the Incarnation, she wished to know how that heavenly favor should be communicated to her: "How shall this be done since I know not man?" With such perfection did she love and practise that purity that she prepared within herself a habitation for that God in whose eyes the angels do not begin to be pure enough: "The heavens are not pure in his sight, and he found deficiencies even in his angels."

If, then, the most holy Virgin should send thee a ray of her light, thou shalt better take in the exalted character of this so rare a privilege, than thou canst take it in by meditating and speaking ever so much. The Church styles her "Virgin without her like," "Virgin of all virgins," "Queen of all virgins," and on this subject it declares that it cannot find words sufficient to praise her. Holy and Immaculate Virginity of Mary! I know not with what expressions to praise thee. Happy those souls to whom it is given to pattern after Mary in this virtue so beautiful. In heaven they shall be the most beautiful jewels in her crown, the most charming flowers in her garland.

But "not all take this word." If thou be in the condition to take it, and follow in the wake of the Virgin in offering so noble a sacrifice, then thank the Lord for thy condition as for a very extraordinary grace, and aim at preserving it by means of the closest watchfulness and solicitude; and strive to make thyself more and more worthy of that God "who pastures among lilies," and who desired to be born of a virgin, who is purer than the lily. The treasure is extremely precious; the vessel that contains it, very fragile. Let who fears in that matter, combat and pray, and use every diligence and foresight, to evade the dangers which are innumerable. Always fear thyself and thy weakness; withstand heartily the temptations of the enemy; and then pray to Mary every day for this grace: "Virgin without like, compassionating among all, loose the bonds of the guilty, make us gentle and chaste!" Oh, how acceptable to her will be this thy prayer! Oh, how thou wilt experience her protection!

THIRD POINT.

MARY'S VIRGINITY—WITHOUT EXAMPLE, BY REASON OF ITS GLORY.

The glory of Mary's virginity consists in great part in the fact, that by it she attracted many souls to the practice of so rare and so difficult a virtue. The holy fathers say the Lord so ordered things that Mary was the first who preferred virginity to the marriage state; and that the preference was made to the end that the faithful, after the promulgation of the evangelical counsels, should have at once a stimulus and a model in our Blessed Lady.

And who can tell how pressing was this stimulus, how fruitful of followers was this model! "Virgins shall be brought to the King after her." Behind her came a numerous band of spotless virgins who presented to the heavenly Lamb the stainless white lily of their purity; —magnanimous virgins, who chose rather to lose their lives by allowing their blood to be shed, than to consent to have their purity tarnished. There is no century in the history of the Church, no territory in the Catholic world, which could not boast of having a countless number of such souls who imitated Mary by consecrating themselves to God as a living peace-offering, by observance of perpetual chastity.

St. John Chryostom, St. Ambrose, St. Augustine, give us beautiful word pictures of every part of the world where charity and virginity reigned. In Asia, in Africa, in Europe, the cities and the deserts were full of faithful persons, who on earth mirrored forth the life of the blessed in heaven, and mirrored it forth by leading a life of stainless purity. The observance of this virtue was a distinguishing characteristic of, and wholly peculiar to, that Church which for Lady and Protectress has a Virgin who is purer than light, whiter than snow. Mary by her example, paved the way; and all the multitudes of those happy souls who, "clothed in white garments, follow the lamb whithersoever he goeth," look up to her as their leader, and lay down their crowns at her feet as at the feet of their queen.

Behold here the glory of Mary's virginal purity; it consists in having so many followers and imitators in every age and in every country. Dost thou belong to a society so admirable? Virginity is prescribed by no law: "as to virgins," says the apostle, "I have received no command." But every one who will work out salvation is bound by a very strict command to lead a pure and chaste life. If thou wilt honor Mary, content not thyself by any means with observing the commandments; thou must, moreover, endeavor to daily become more and more spotless; thou must endeavor to observe purity as perfectly as may lie in thy power. How dost thou preserve thy mind from evil thoughts? how thy heart from corrupt inclinations? how thy body from what can tarnish so beautiful a virtue?

O Virgin of all virgins! O teacher! O type of purity! what a beautiful school didst thou on earth open in thyself by thy example. Thou wast the first to consecrate by a vow thy virginity to God, the first to keep thy vow with unexampled perfection, the first to raise aloft the white banner of the immaculate Lamb! Behold behind thee a countless number of virgins, who, armed with thy teachings, lead, in the midst of the corruptions of this world, the lives rather of angels than of human beings. Alas, what can a sinner, who is all filth do on contemplating such a spectacle? Ah, if it be not granted me to walk in the footsteps of so illustrious an assembly and with them to chant the virginal hymn, let it be at least accorded me to hear it sung in heaven, and to covet so ravishing a spectacle! O Mary! I place my heart, my body, my senses, yea, myself wholly and entirely, under thy protection; preserve me from every stain, and make me worthy to celebrate virginal purity for all eternity. Amen.

TWENTIETH MEDITATION.

MARY'S MODESTY.

FIRST POINT.

MARY'S MOST STRICT WATCHFULNESS OVER HER EYES.

CONSIDER the solicitude which Mary exercised in order to preserve the precious treasure of her virginity by holy modesty. It might be imagined that in view of the great privilege she had received from God, she would not have given herself much pains about this virtue; having been conceived in grace, born in grace, confirmed in grace, she was full of the Holy Ghost—what, then, had she to fear? And yet she was more solicitous than any one else to watch over her senses, and especially over her eyes, which are, as it were, the windows of the soul. Oh! with how much greater right than Job could she say: "I have made a covenant with my eyes."

The most beautiful image of Mary's modesty Holy Church has given us from century to century, by representing her to us in all the circumstances of her life with her eyes either fixed on the ground or raised to heaven in prayer; and always with a modesty rather heavenly than human. "So were Mary's eyes; her look was directed only superficially to earthly things, but it all the oftener penetrated heavenly things." Contemplate her on her journeys, in the houses, and in public or in private, or in society, and thou wilt find expressed in her countenance nothing save lessons of reserve. Her countenance was always serene, her look always marked by an agreeable severity; she was always reserved in such a manner that her reserve raised the affections to heavenly things; to see and to be seen, as likewise evil associations, she avoided constantly and with the greatest assiduity. Her joy was solitude and recollection; and yet she by no means fled the company of those of whom mercy was not ashamed, and whose sense of becomingness had not bade them farewell. For this reason she visited Elizabeth, was present at the marriage feast of Cana; she appeared among the multitude to hear the words from the lips of her Divine Son, yet always in such a manner that she reflected in herself as in a mirror the beauties of virginal bashfulness. "In her was reflected the beauty of sanctity, and the comeliness of virtue," as Says St. Paul. The most holy Virgin had not to fear that the lamentation of the prophet was to be verified in her: "My eye hath wasted my soul." Jer. iii. 51 v.: and yet she watched her eyes as if that lamentation might be verified in her.

This lesson is worthy the attention of all, young and old, clergy and laity. Woe to him who indulges his eyes! they will cause his soul to fall, and to die the death of sin. How many, on occasion of an unguarded free look, lost the Lord's grace, and cast themselves into the abyss of beastly crimes! How fell David who was so dear to God, so much in God's confidence, and so pre-eminent in holy works? By an imprudent look. What happened to David, happened to very many others who were already renowned for virtue and holiness.

If thou wilt not go to destruction, it will be necessary for thee to keep thine eyes in check; and remember that it is easier to allow them nothing, than to permit them a little without dwelling unduly on that little. Promise to Mary so beautiful a homage as watchfulness over thine eyes, and shew her by thy actions that her many examples have not been lost upon thee.

SECOND POINT.

MARY'S MOST STRICT MODESTY IN CONVERSATION.

In conversation Mary was very reserved, and she was provident and measured as she was reserved. "In conversation," wrote St. Ambrose, "she was somewhat monosyllabic; in discourse, earnest; in mind, prudent; in confidence, modest." St. Epiphanius confirms this and says: "Mary was friendliness itself; but what she spoke was very little and always wise, whereby she edified all who heard her."

Contemplate her at the moment when the angel of the Lord called her "the full of grace," "the blessed among women," and made known to her her high dignities. What then did Mary? "She was troubled at his saying, and thought with herself what manner of salutation this should be." Extremely perturbed, and besieged by a thousands thoughts, she stood a considerable while motionless. Oh, how easily would another have lost herself in putting curious questions and in exhibiting vain honors! The vow whereby she obliged herself to remain a virgin and to hold secret conferences with God only—the law which she had prescribed herself, to renounce the custom of the world—her attention to, and watchfulness over, herself—produced in her interior, trouble which, in its turn, inspired her with fear and counselled her to say nothing at the commencement.

When, then, the angel explained the mystery of the Incarnation of the Son, she opened her blessed lips and uttered but few and necessary words, whereby, says St. Peter Damian, she mentioned the vow which bound her to the observance of virginity and her obedience to God. And at the wedding of Cana—could she with fewer words have laid open the bridal embarrassment, and have spoken more effectually in their interest? And when Jesus was found in the temple among the doctors, and made known to her the feeling of his heart—could she, on that occasion, have employed more measured and more gentle expressions? And what else are the words she uttered when she visited Elizabeth, than an astonishing lesson of that heavenly discretion of which her soul was full? Could they have been more appropriate, more humble, more holy?

Wilt thou be agreeable to Mary? Be solicitous to imitate her in watching over thy tongue; be reserved in conversation; for the one who without necessity pours out his soul in conversation, easily falls into sin: "In the multitude of words, there shall not want sin." Prov. x. 19 v. Often wilt thou regret having spoken too much, and very seldom that thou hast been silent; and now how many loose words slip unobserved from thee in the course of a single day,—words which are useless, vain, wounding to honor, and offensive? and yet for even every idle word must thou give an account! Keep thy tongue in check, give it not free scope, and pray to the Virgin to watch over it: "Set a watch, O Lord, before my mouth; and a door round about my lips." Ps. cxli. 3 v.

THIRD POINT.

MARY'S MOST STRICT MODESTY IN HER DEMEANOR.

Modesty regulates not merely the eyes and the tongue, but likewise all the movements which a person makes. In this sense the apostle Paul employs the term when he recommends it to all the faithful: "Let your modesty be known to all men." The conclusion is not arrived at with difficulty, that when the exterior is well ordered the interior is fervent; and hence a well ordered exterior is very edifying.

Oh, how truly admirable was Mary in this very particular! Her mere look brought the soul into such peaceful harmony that the soul won sanctity by loving it; her senses and movements were ordered by reason and the will of God. St. Epiphanius thinks that, even in her first years, she was looked upon in all things as a true miracle of modesty, and that she was so considered by reason of her fervor and demeanor. Her carriage had nothing effeminate in it; her step nothing of levity; her whole exterior was an expression of the beauty a d order of her interior: "Her bearing had nothing thoughtless; her gait nothing extravagant; her voice nothing coarse: even the form, the physical part of her being, was an image of her mind, an embodiment, as it were, of her unimpeachableness."

Imagine to thyself that thou seest her at those solemn moments when the angel of the Lord appeared to announce to her the great mystery, or when she journeyed to the mountain of Judea to visit Elizabeth, or when she sat at the table among the guests at the marriage feast of Cana, or when she poured out her soul in prayer to God. What a heavenly spectacle! Imagine to thyself that thou seest her occupied with the commonest duties of life, in her going out and coming in, on the public way, in her attention to work, in care of the infant Jesus. What calm! What perfection! What sedateness and amiability in all her actions and movements!

Ravished by the contemplation of so attractive a spectacle, St. John of Damascus could not refrain from saying that she was a living copy of God; in whose beauty the Creator himself took delight. Stop a little to contemplate the likeness of God, and reproduce it in thyself as well as thou canst. Oh, how much thou standest in need of so doing! What was so pleasing to God, and what his mother observed with so great perfection —look not upon that as a trifle.

Pious souls have generally, even in their exterior, something so becoming that it distinguishes them from the loose bearings of worldly-minded persons. This edifying decency should be the property of all Christians; but the absence of it in spiritual persons is a far more significant evil than its absence in ordinary Christians. Oh, how disgusting is the glance given by a person consecrated to the service of God, when that person is loose in look and conversation, unbecoming and extravagant in bearing! Abominate such an impropriety which is so displeasing in the eyes of God and of men; and pray to Mary to give thee strength to preserve thee from it for the future.

Oh, mirror of self-vigilance and modesty! Most pure Virgin! I am horrified at myself, since I see myself so unlike to thee! Thou, "the full of grace," watched over thy senses so much, and I the full of sins watch over my senses not at all! In look thou wast so cautious; in conversation so prudent; in all thy actions so discreet, that thou became agreeable to God, and the admiration of men; and I was so loose and indiscreet that I excited the displeasure of God and men!

I abominate, O Lady! the liberty I have hitherto allowed my senses; and I promise thee that henceforward I shall watch over myself with greater care. Help me, O Lady! in virtue of thy virginal eyes, of thy blessed tongue, of the dispositions which animated thee in all thy actions; in consideration of these, help me, O Lady! to diffuse in every possible manner the sweet odor of thy Son Jesus. Amen.

TWENTY-FIRST MEDITATION.

MARY'S OBEDIENCE.

FIRST POINT.

MARY'S OBEDIENCE WAS A CONSTANT OBEDIENCE.

By the virtue of obedience man offers to God, as a perfect sacrifice, the most noble and the most precious thing he possesses. This, man does by offering up his own judgment, his will, and everything that depends on it. This complete and perfect sacrifice the most holy Virgin brought to God during the course of her whole life. Her dignity, as Mother of God, had raised her above law and legislators; but her love of obedience throughout subjected her to both.

Already in her first years, in the temple, Mary began to give evidence of her submission and dependence; all orders were so conscientiously fulfilled by her that she became the model of her companions. Even her marriage with St. Joseph was only an operation of her perfect obedience to God. Bound by the vow of purity, wholly captivated by so beautiful a virtue, she would never have thought of giving her hand to a man. She felt strong repugnance to doing so. But scarcely had God given her to understand that such was his will, when she complied with it and obeyed. She was subject to her spouse, the head of the family; she never opposed his arrangements; and though, by reason of her dignity and of special lights she received from the Lord, she was far superior to St Joseph, yet she watched his every nod as if she, more than all others, stood in need of direction and of counsel.

What a delightful spectacle was it not in the eyes of God to see this youthful consort, this most holy, this most exalted of all persons, like an humble maid, hang on every syllable uttered by St. Joseph! Mary took care of her domestic affairs as other married women do; but as in all things she executed the will of her spouse, she had no will of her own. St. Bridget relates that Mary, when a very young maiden, earnestly entreated God for the grace to obey with that spirit of self-renunciation and of the greatest perfection, which was competent to a mere creature; and the saint adds that Mary evinced this spirit to the end of her life. As a child, she evinced it towards her parents; she evinced it towards the high priest in the temple; towards Joseph she evinced it after her marriage; she evinced it in all things, even in the most difficult and painful circumstances of her life.

"Oh, blessed obedience!" exclaims St. John of Damascus, "which repairs all the evils that have grown out of Eve's disobedience. Mary deceived the fallacious serpent and introduced immortality into the world." Oh, what a powerful incentive for thee must be Mary's obedience! If she cheerfully submitted herself who was so exalted, so holy, so much illumined by God, how darest thou refuse to submit to authority,—thou who art so miserable, who art so sinful, so little enlightened? And yet what is the character of thy life? Bear in mind that disobedience brought destruction on the world, and cast ourselves into an abyss of sins and miseries. Another condition would be ours at present, had Adam been obedient in the earthly paradise. His disobedience was repaired merely by the obedience of the Son of God who obeyed unto the death of the cross: "He was obedient unto death, even unto the death of the cross."

Behold, in obedience, the safe way pointed out by Jesus, and followed by Mary; humble submission towards rightly appointed superiors, obedience in every thing not clearly sinful, and, furthermore, obedience in the true spirit of faith, in things of small importance as well as in things of great moment.

SECOND POINT.

MARY'S OBEDIENCE WAS DIFFICULT.

Mary shows herself very noble-hearted in her obedience, by obeying in very difficult and painful circumstances; and even in things in which she was not bound, she obeyed. How difficult and trying was not the obedience which she showed, when Joseph announced to her the divine command to flee to Egypt in the night time, and to flee without a moment's delay. Virgin as she was, so bashful by nature and physically weak,—how much must it have cost her, to set out on a journey so long and necessarily so eventful, and to undertake it in order to flee into an idolatrous land, a land so indisposed to receive a Jewess, for the people of it had an inborn hatred for the Jewish nation. Time fails her to procure the necessaries for flight; she has no protecting directors, no one to point out to her the way, no friends or relations who may assure her that she will not lack lodging and nourishment on the way: she has no idea of even how long she was to remain there. No one but her spouse shares with her the dangers, the difficulties, the fears, which were all enhanced by the darkness of the night, and by the snares of Herod.

How many difficulties! How many troubles! And yet how does Mary act? She does not lose heart, she falters not a moment; she trusts in God and eagerly enters upon the journey. Mary is always prepared for every dispensation of the Lord; and, as says St. Thomas of Villanova, "she reserved to herself not the least freedom, but is subject to God in all things." "God wills it:"—behold the motive which facilitates her every difficulty and renders her heroic in overcoming all obstacles.

How much canst thou learn from obedience, as it was practised by Mary? Consider, further, that her obedience was none the less conspicuous when she was not thereto obliged. What example did she not give by the purification in the temple? According to the strictest interpretation, Mary was not obliged to submit to this ceremony, for the reason that the words of the law made an express exception of her, and also for the reason that her more pure parturition made her in fact a single exception to all child-bearing women whom the law contemplated. This twofold ground on which she could have exempted herself, lessens in no degree her obedience; and she obeys, even at the expense of appearing in the eyes of the world as an unclean woman, like unto other mothers; and as if she needed to be purified from stains with which she had never in the least been sullied. Mary knows that the heroic act of submitting to the ceremony of purification is pleasing to the Lord, and without any more questions she submits to it in the most perfect manner possible.

What dost thou do when thou searchingly examinest whether or not thou art bound to obey? What dost thou do when thou seekest to exempt thyself from commands which tend to break thy pride, or which cannot be observed without trouble and inconvenience? Oh, how far thou removest from the path which Jesus and his most holy Mother pointed out and followed! When the commission given thee is painful or difficult of execution, rely on the Lord; he will stand by thee in an especial manner, and reward thy sacrifices with especial blessing: "An obedient man shall speak of victories." Ever obey in all things that thou knowest to be agreeable to the Lord, and thou shalt be assured of his good will, and shalt rejoice in the protection of the most holy Mother.

THIRD POINT.

MARY'S OBEDIENCE—A SIMPLE OBEDIENCE.

It is the peculiarity of simple and humble souls to obey, without examination, in all things which are commanded; but this obedience supposes that the things commanded are not clearly sinful. Such souls see God in their superiors; they know that the superiors are

God's representatives, and are by him empowered to command. This knowledge suffices to preserve them from misconceptions regarding the instructions they receive; and also it enables them to execute cheerfully and securely whatever is enjoined on them.

Mary's obedience was the result of knowledge of this kind. She obeyed, for instance, without looking at whether the commands laid upon her were easy or difficult of fulfilment, without looking whether they were agreeable or disagreeable. She obeyed by subjecting her own judgment, her own will; and her obedience was accompanied with the certain conviction, that all was right and according to God's own good pleasure. Just imagine that, in Mary's stead, was one of those souls who wish to reason on every order that is laid upon them. Oh, how many pleas and pretexts would they not have devised whereon to base their disobedience! The views that must be taken of the blessed circumstances of Mary's position, especially a glance at her heavenly offspring, would have been more than sufficient to pronounce any of those reasoning souls exempt from the journey to Bethlehem; any of them would have thought within herself that, at the end, not the Son of God should obey Tiberius, but that Tiberius should obey the Son of God.

At the purification, the thought must have quickly occurred to any such soul, that her non-compliance with that usage could not be imputed to her unto sin; nay, further, that it were better not to conform to it, as such conformity would occasion the erroneous notion that Jesus had come into the world in the same manner as all other men. In regard to the flight into Egypt, it would have been no difficult matter for one of the reasoning souls wisely to conclude, that the command which the angel laid upon Joseph, rested upon a mere deception—that it were prudence to await the morrow and sift the whole question a little better: in short, a soul who had reasoned on all the grounds on which obedience in Mary was based, would not have carried out the angel's orders, or would, at best, have carried them out but mechanically and very imperfectly. Not such, however, was Mary's reasoning, and not such was Mary's obedience. She made the most consummate prudence go hand in hand with the greatest simplicity. The calm of her mind was unruffled; the peace of her heart unbroken by violent emotions; her lips uttered no complaint; having once known the will of God as manifested to her by his ambassadors, she accomplished it with all possible serenity and love.

In what manner dost thou obey? Art thou one of those who criticize the orders of their superiors—one of those who scrutinize every word, who disapprove and reject everything that does not fall in with their own views? No; this is not the precious simplicity wherewith Mary obeyed. Remember that the more humble and the more simple thy obedience, the more meritorious and the more pleasing to God will it also be: "With the simple He speaks confidentially." Of simple and humble obedience it is written, "Obedience is better than sacrifice;" for the latter brings to God but the material part of the work, so to say, whilst the former offers to him the precious part which is one's own judgment and one's own will.

O most humble Virgin, whose life was a constant exercise of obedience, deign to facilitate for me the acquisition of a virtue so necessary as obedience! Oh, how many struggles must I go through in order to submit my judgment! How much opposition shall I experience even when the question turns upon the easiest matters! Ah Lady! grant me a small share of that spirit of faith, of simplicity, of generosity—a spirit which was the most charming testimony of thy obedience. Animated with this spirit, it will be easy for me to recognize God in my superiors, to overcome all the opposition of self-love, and to follow more closely that God who was obedient unto death, in order that, with his assistance, I may one day participate in his glories in heaven. Amen.

TWENTY-SECOND MEDITATION.

MARY'S VOLUNTARY POVERTY.

FIRST POINT.

MARY CHOSE POVERTY OUT OF LOVE FOR IT.

OUR Lord in his Sermon on the Mount says: "Blessed are the poor in spirit, for theirs is the Kingdom of Heaven!" It is clear that, by these words, he inculcated and earnestly recommended poverty of spirit. Before, however, he proclaimed this to be a virtue, Mary, fully enlightened by the Holy Ghost, knew its excellence and embraced it from a heavenly impulse. The great Canisius of saintly memory, tells us: "Her parents' means would have enabled her to live comfortably; but her love of poverty induced her to rid herself of all the goods she possessed, save a very small portion, by bestowing them on the poor and on the temple."

Now, our Savior himself was, in the first years of his life, to be poor and in straitened circumstances; and ancient writers,—they, too, of great authority—state that, when Mary read of the infant condition of the expected Messias, she resolved to bind herself by vow to practise poverty, in order that she might be still the more like unto him. The fact of this vow the Blessed Virgin herself deigned to reveal to St. Bridget in those express terms: "At the very dawn of my life, I vowed in my heart never to desire to own any thing in the world." Thus, then, we find her poor with a triple poverty; viz., by actual severance from her goods, by her free choice, and by the vow which she made to God!

But the cavern at Bethlehem was the place in which principally, her heart was more inflamed with love of this beautiful virtue. O what did she not learn when she saw the Word made Flesh, choose a stable for an asylum, a manger for his throne, and two despicable animals for his courtiers, and when she saw that God who is Lord of heaven and earth, become poor for the love of us! Then, more than ever, was she enamored of the most rigid poverty; and the cold cavern and the poor swaddling-clothes are dearer to her than the king's palace and all the purple thereof.

Learn hence what account thou shouldst make of riches. The Son of God declares that the poor in spirit are blessed: he is born in poverty: he lives in poverty and dies in poverty: his most holy Mother chooses poverty, lives and dies in poverty:—what excellent instruction for a Christian soul! Weigh well the fact that detachment of the heart from earthly things, is strictly necessary for every one who would be saved. Even if God does not call thee to follow his Son in the very near distance by renouncing thy possessions, he calls thee to cut off, at least, the affections of thy heart from them, and to live surrounded with them as if thou didst not possess them. Woe to thee if thou lovest them immoderately! St. Philip says: "He who loves wealth and possessions will never become holy!" And on this subject, St. Theresa remarks: "It follows quite evidently from this, that he who yearns after lost treasures, will be also lost!"

Oh, how many are damned by reason of inordinate love of riches! "Woe to you rich!" Examine thyself, and see to it a little whether thou thyself hast not reason to tremble. What value dost thou set upon gold? Art thou disposed to hunt after it with great greed? And when thou hast obtained it, does thy very heart cleave to it? Open thy eyes in time; be extremely on thy guard, for senseless love for the things of earth deprived so many of the eternal goods of heaven,—goods that can never pass away.

SECOND POINT.

POVERTY—THE COMPANION OF MARY'S LIFE.

Run over in thought Mary's life, and in all its circumstances, thou wilt find her lacking not only every comfort, but oftentimes wanting even what was necessary to her maintenance. For spouse, God gives her a holy man; but this holy man is so devoid of the goods of fortune, that he is constrained to earn his bread by the sweat of his brow. When she reached Bethlehem, so very poor does she appear, that not one of the innkeepers of the city will receive her: "There was no place for them in the inn." Driven by necessity to leave the city, she seeks shelter, and her shelter is in a stable exposed to the winds and rains of the season, and absolutely unfurnished with any of the various comforts rendered necessary by her peculiarly delicate situation. And how does she live in Egypt? By the labor of her hands, and the earning of her holy spouse.

Oh, how often will she have seen herself devoid of means to such an extent as that she could scarcely sustain life! Oh, how often will she have experienced the operations of the most rigid poverty in her board, her dwelling, and in all else. Contemplate the glorious mother of God, and learn by her example patiently to endure the privations which God causes thee to meet.

One day, she was invited to a wedding—but to what kind of a wedding? To a wedding feast given by the newly married couple who had no more wine, and that in the very middle of the feast! It was customary to invite to the nuptial feast the friends and social equals of the bridal pair; and if the bridal pair were poor, then, naturally, the circumstances of the guests were also poor. Her divine Son hesitated not to say: "The foxes have holes, and the birds of the air have nests, but the Son of Man has not where to lay his head."

If the Redeemer of the world had not where to lay his head, ought his thrice holy Mother, who was his most perfect follower, be unlike him in this regard? Yes; Mary's poverty extended to all things;—to her clothes, which, according to the narration of St. Epiphanius, were always made "either of wool, or of linen;"—to her dwelling, which was as the dwelling of the poor (the holy house of Loretto is proof of this);—to her board, which was meagre and common: "her nourishment," says St. Ambrose, was "usually the best barley which indeed sustained life, but was not grateful to the palate." Yet more content than the apostle, when she had merely sustenance and clothing, she sought nothing more, and simply desired ever to become more and more like her divine Son who died poor on a cross.

If thou belongest to a religious order, opportunities

will not be wanting thee to practise poverty in one or other of the regards just mentioned. What is the temper of thy mind? what is the character of thy perseverance? how dost thou endure privations in things which agree with thy state, thy health, and thy habits of life? A soul faithful to her calling willingly endures privations, unites them with those which her God and his holy Mother suffered, and rejoices to have a proof that she belongs to those souls to whom is promised the kingdom of heaven. On the other hand, a lukewarm and unfaithful soul falls into anger and fills the house with lamentations: to which of these two dost thou belong?

Examine thyself a little on the exercise of this so precious virtue, and bear well in mind that he who will allow himself to want for nothing, has no love for the virtue of poverty.

THIRD POINT.

MARY'S PUBLIC CONFESSION OF POVERTY.

Mary made no secret of her poverty; she wished to appear poor, and to be looked upon by all as poor. After the birth of her divine offspring, she offered in the temple a pair of turtledoves or pigeons; and this was the offering prescribed for the poor on such occasions. Could she not have purchased, with the gold which she received as a gift from the wise men, a lamb and presented it to the temple? Certainly: but the gold, says St. Bonaventure, quickly passed from her hands into the hands of St. Joseph, and from the hands of St. Joseph into the hands of the poor.

Since she remained completely in her original penury, she rejoiced to be numbered among the poor; and she appeared in the eyes of all, to be what she really was, poor. Take, further, into consideration that Jesus, when on the cross he conceived the idea of giving a stay, so to express it, to his holy mother, committed her to the care of a poor person as was the apostle John; and consider too that, when he so committed her, he could have given her in charge to a more opulent disciple than John;—as to a Joseph of Arimathea, to a Nicodemus, or to another who would have prepared for her a more suitable means of living on in the world. But, St. Augustine says, our Lord did not commit his blessed Mother to the charge of such a person, in order to comply with her own desires and wishes, which desires and wishes were that she should live poor, and be recognized as poor.

The apostles collected alms from the faithful and apportioned them among the widows who stood in need of the charitable offerings of others. Mary was not ashamed, as others are wont to be ashamed, to have a share in what was so apportioned; on the contrary, she wished publicly to belong to the number thus assisted. The venerable Bede, the Abbot Rupert, and some others affirm this.

Let Mary's example encourage thee to appear in the ranks of the poor of Jesus Christ. If thou hast abandoned, from love of him, earthly goods, then act in such way that all may know that thou regrettest it not; and be in no wise ashamed to pass for a true follower of his. Oh, how ill-suited to him who professes evangelical poverty, are worldly adornments, certain extravagances, distinction in garments, and apartments which breathe a spirit not to be reconciled with the nakedness of the cross. Poverty has its own humiliations, because it is contemned by the world; yet those humiliations are its most distinguishing glories. "But indeed I esteem all things to be but loss and count them but as dung, that I may gain Christ." Phil. iii. 8 v. Thus spoke the apostle: and thou wilt joyfully say the same when thou hast the happiness to recognize how precious is the nakedness of the cross.

O Exalted Lady, who pointest out to us, by the glowing examples of thy poverty, the line whereby to attain Heaven! oh, cause that my heart, set free from the vanities of the world, may aim only after unfailing and eternal goods! Thou didst enjoy thyself in the midst of privations; thou didst pride thyself on being known and treated by the world as poor. Ah! Lady, inspire me with at least a little love for so beautiful a virtue, in order that I may, thereby, patiently endure the results of poverty in me, and not blush at the sign of it before the world! All the riches of this earth must pass away forever; I aim after the eternal riches which God holds in readiness for his faithful servants. Mary! help me in thy affection, and then I shall be able to say from my heart "My God and my all!" for in him shall I have all good. Amen.

TWENTY-THIRD MEDITATION.

MARY'S WONDERFUL PATIENCE.

FIRST POINT.

MARY'S PATIENCE—A PATIENCE THAT WAS TRIED IN SEVERAL WAYS.

NEXT to Jesus, no creature suffered so much as did the most holy Virgin. Poverty, contempt, sufferings, were the constant companions of the life of the world's Redeemer; poverty, contempt, sufferings, were the constant companions of his most holy Mother. Who is poor has an opportunity of practising the virtue of patience as in a fortified place: and now recall to thy memory the contents of the foregoing Meditation.

Mary was spouse of one who was, indeed, holy, but yet a poor manual workman; and so poor was he that he was constrained to procure for himself the necessaries of life by the sweat of his brow. How often, therefore, will she have discovered herself in the condition of those working people who must find, in patience, indemnity for lacking what is utterly necessary for their subsistence? Contemplate her in the cave of Bethlehem, in her flight to Egypt, and during her sojourn there, in the workshop at Nazareth; and thou canst not fail to see how she suffers, now hunger, again thirst, now cold, again heat, now from rain, again from winds, now faintness and all privations which the poor can endure. Yet more difficult is it to bear with contempt; and this is a truth which Mary experienced in Bethlehem where she was rejected by all; and not in Bethlehem only, but likewise in all the other places of her sojourn; for everywhere she was, she lived and was treated as a poor person.

Still, all that has been said, is but little in comparison with what has to follow. The most pungent contempt, the most bitter insults and oppositions, weighed her down when the Jewish people began to persecute her adorable Son. Oh, what had not Mary to bear with, even for that very reason that she was the Mother of Jesus! of how much abuse and mockery was she the target! with how much ignominy and barbarity was she laden! Figure to thyself the situation of a woman who is the mother of the most hated and most persecuted of all sons,—mother of a son who is hated and persecuted by people of all classes, by the rich, the poor, the noble, the commonalty, by the learned, and the unlearned, by the clergy and laity—by all alike. In the school of sufferings she graduated in such a way that she became the Queen of Martyrs.

Cast a glance at the sufferings and death of Jesus, and next at Mary's most tender heart; and then see whether there was ever sorrow that would for an instant bear compassion with her sorrow: "Look and see whether there be any sorrow like unto my sorrow." From Simeon's prophecies to the Resurrection, she remained immersed in a sea of most bitter and most agonizing sufferings,—sufferings which were predicted, and predicted under no other figure than that of a sea: "for great as a sea are thy lamentations." O what hard trials! O what a bloody sacrifice! Of her also may we say: "She learned obedience from what she suffered;" she learned patience, for patience is here meant by obedience.

The virtue of patience is necessary to all, whatever their age or state of life; "for patience is needful to you," declares the apostle Paul. But how is patience acquired? By constant exercise. Nature is averse to suffering, and always wrestles with it, always sets her face against it, but is finally overcome by long exercise. Search as long as it may please thee, after other means of acquiring this lovable virtue, and thou wilt at last see that there is no easier path to it than the path of practise thereof.

O how eminently dost thou deceive thyself when, instead of exercising thyself in this virtue, thou evadest every occasion of suffering! Surely not this is the path to obedience. "The life of man on earth is a warfare," and, therefore, combat we must. The occasions of combating will present themselves to thee every day; mayst thou know how to turn them to good account! Amen.

SECOND POINT.

THE MANNER IN WHICH MARY SUFFERED.

Patience, as St. Bonaventure teaches us, consists in suffering in silence. But with suffering in silence, the most holy Virgin did not content herself; she suffered, it is true, in silence: she suffered without the least discomposure of soul. She suffered without being in the slightest degree out of sorts with those who caused her sufferings; she suffered with love because she longed to suffer more, were *the more* pleasing to God. She suffered in silence; but when opened she her blessed lips to complain or repine? When sought she relief for her crushed heart by communicating the knowledge her sufferings to others? In her straits she recurred to God alone. God alone did she wish to be the witness of her sorrows; in God alone, she looked for solace in all her tribulations: "Her habit was to look, not for man but for God himself as the judge of her thoughts." St. Ambrose.

She suffered without the slightest discomposure; her admirable soul enjoyed an imperturbable tranquillity; the shocks and the pressure of adversity were powerless to ruffle the serenity of her mind and the peace of her heart; "In us, justice is not without warfare; but in Mary, justice consisted in perfect peace." She suffered without reluctance. How difficult does it not come to bring into subjection that antipathy which we feel rising within us against the authors of our sufferings! Yes; Mary had all the time before her eyes the doctors of the law, the Pharisees and the Jewish people, all of whom put her Son to death amid contumely and ill-treatment of every kind.

And yet, how did she bear the shameless cruelty of her enemies? "O the wonderful patience and gentleness of Mary!" exclaimed St. Bonaventure; "she never gave way to the slightest impatience in regard to them." Her most gentle heart never harbored the least feeling of resentment or anger; yea, she always prayed the Eternal Father most earnestly that he might pardon the frightful misdeed they had committed; and, likewise, at the very moment when his enemies were offering up the most precious blood of the spotless Lamb, she offered to God that blood to appease his wrath. Hence we find her praying with her divine Son: "Father forgive them."

She suffered with the desire to suffer more; and in this desire she outstripped all the saints, as she outstripped them all in the love of God. St. Theresa of Jesus used to exclaim, "either suffer or die;" St. Magdalen of Pazzi was accustomed to say, "let me suffer, but not die:" and a great number of others rejoiced exceedingly at being able to give in their sufferings a proof to God of their love for him. They desired to suffer still more, and they, time and again, repeated these words: "Yet more, O Lord! yet more!" more crosses, more troubles, more sorrows!

Who will dare doubt that Mary, in her desire to suffer more, were it pleasing to God, far surpassed all those saints? Oh, what admirable, invincible, and heroic patience! And how dost thou bear the little crosses that God sends thee? Dost thou bear them in calmness, or dost thou speak complainingly of God and of his Providence? Dost thou endure them in peace, or art thou thrown into excitement and disconcerted, and dost thou suffer thyself to be carried off and to indulge in unbecoming words and actions? Dost thou repress the feelings of aversion, which spring up in thy heart towards those whom thou considerest or imaginest to be the authors of thy sufferings? or dost thou cherish those feelings whilst thou makest them a subject of complaints and of anger? Wouldst thou be content to suffer yet more, if the *yet more* were pleasing to God? Or dost thou yearn after the advent of that moment when thou canst cast off the cross from thy shoulders; and dost thou not turn every stone in order to free thyself from the yoke of the cross?

"Work as a good warrior," says the Apostle to thee; "Work as a good warrior of Jesus Christ," and it is only by striving that thou shalt be able to acquire so necessary a virtue, and through that virtue to come to the acquisition of that peace which will elevate thee above all contingencies. "In your patience you shall possess your souls."

THIRD POINT.

WHAT MARY MERITED BY HER PATIENCE.

As the Most Holy Virgin was a sea of sorrow, so also was she a sea of merits. Oh, how much merit she acquired by her constant and invincible patience! The merit of patience, says St. Bonaventure, is greater than that of the other virtues, for, in the exercise of the other virtues, nature can help a man who has any leaning towards good; but in suffering, nature certainly assists not at all, for it always feels aversion and opposition to pain. In this sense, says St. John Chrysostom, suffering out of pure love of God, is more estimable than to work miracles, to cure the sick, to resuscitate the dead, and to possess the wisdom of the angels. Suffering is more estimable than all these works, because it is more meritorious: "But patience perfects the works."

Which of those many virtues, wherewith, as with so many jewels, the Virgin was adorned, dost thou imagine did she practise oftenest in the course of her whole life? Patience, certainly. Her entire life was, in fact, nothing else than a series of exercises of patience. "As the rose grows among thorns, so this venerable Virgin grew in the eyes of this world in the midst of tribulations:" such was the revelation made to St Bridget, as we find it in that admirable work written by St. Liguori and entitled "Glories of Mary." Already thou saw her as a little child in the temple, as a spouse at Nazareth, as a wayfarer going to Egypt and returning therefrom, as a woman of a house in her own home,—but always surrounded with a thousand thistles. When the time of the passion and death of her divine Son arrived, the thorns became a two-edged sword which pierced her heart, and more than tortured her soul. After the Ascension, her love for Jesus and her most glowing yearning to be reunited with him, gave another direction to her torture, but did not cause its cessation.

In short, from beginning to end of her being, Mary lived in uninterrupted sufferings. If, now, to suffer out of love for God be the most meritorious thing possible, who can tell how much merit the Virgin must have acquired in so many years of her life through so many and so severe tribulations, through so pure, so unselfish, and so constant a patience? Her patience was extraordinary—extraordinary also was her merit! God alone can fathom this sea. By means of the trials to which he subjected her, God made her Queen of all the martyrs; and he constituted her, through the incomparable merit she acquired, Queen of all the saints.

Oh, what great consolation canst thou derive from this meditation! In thy crosses thou lookest only on their severity and bitterness, and considerest only the violence thou must offer thyself in order to bear them. Yet thou by no means castest a glance at the merits which those crosses worked out for thee. Every exercise of patience has its corresponding degree of glory in heaven. If, then, day after day, thou embracest the opportunity of bearing patiently those inconveniences, adversities, and tribulations of soul and body which the Lord sends thee, thou almost insensibly preparest here on earth for thyself a sovereignly precious crown of merits which will correspond with a most brilliant and eternal crown of glory in heaven. Nerve thyself up, the time is short: "The patient man must suffer till his time come." And what will then take place, "when come emancipation and joy?" In comparison with the glory of heaven, the sufferings of this world are a mere nothing: "For I reckon, that the sufferings of this present time are not worthy to be compared with the glory to come that shall be revealed in us." Rom. viii. 18 v.

In keeping with this apostolic assurance, the seraphic St. Francis used to console himself with this thought, and often used to repeat: "The good I await is so great that all suffering is a pleasure to me." Do even as was wont to do St. Francis, and pray to Mary the Virgin, that she may deign to help thee. O Lady! when I behold thee so composed and so patient amid so many and so severe tribulations, then am I ashamed and I blush at myself, because of my not understanding how to bear smaller and lighter crosses. Ah, that I do not understand how to do this, is all but too true! In every difficulty, in every adversity, I grow discontented and complaining; anger bows me down as a hurricane, sometimes in this direction, sometimes in that; it drives me hither and thither; it strikes me down; and thus does it multiply my sufferings.

'O most compassionate Lady! support my weakness, teach me to know the worth of this so necessary virtue, in order that, in the future, I may not miss so many favorable opportunities to acquire heavenly treasures.

I promise thee that henceforward I shall take pains, and offer violence to myself, in order to struggle against my sensibility and to overcome it, and that I may suffer with patience and love. Extend to me thy merciful hand, to the end that, so supported by thee, I shall celebrate victory over myself. Amen.

TWENTY-FOURTH MEDITATION.

MARY'S RESIGNATION.

FIRST POINT.

MARY'S RESIGNATION—A PERFECT RESIGNATION.

THE most holy Virgin had never, whether in welcome or unwelcome events, another will than that of her God; and never did she desire anything other than the perfect accomplishment of that will. To this temper of her mind, she gave expression in the pregnant words which she addressed to the angel: "Behold the handmaid of the Lord;" and although these expressions had special reference to the incarnation of the Word, yet in them Mary gave God the key of her heart, that he might dispose of her and all that was hers with perfect freedom and according to his own good pleasure.

For this reason she never departed a hair's breadth from the will of the Lord: she always desired that this will should be done in heaven, on earth, in her Jesus, in her Joseph, in the angels, in man, and in all creatures. She was always satisfied with whatever God ordered in relation to herself, her health, the powers of her body and of her mind; whatever befel her, be it grateful, or be it untoward, disturbed not in any way her internal peace. Galilee, Egypt, Nazareth, Bethlehem, were all alike to her as places of sojourn; want or superabundance, work or rest, were, likewise, equally agreeable to her. Oftener than David she repeated; "My heart, O

Lord! is ready, my heart is ready;" order, O Lord! in regard to thy handmaid as it seems good and is pleasing to thee. Thou mayst raise me, thou mayst lower me; my heart surrenders itself to thy will, surrenders wholly and without reserve: "My heart is prepared, O God!"

Also, thou must not believe that this complete committing of herself into the hands of God, rendered her insensible or indifferent as regards sufferings. No; she felt them even in the very bottom of her soul; she felt the trials which God sent directly to herself; she felt those which her most pure spouse underwent; and yet more than she felt all them, did she feel the anguish and the tortures endured by her dear Jesus. "Did she have compassion on Jesus on their account?" asks St. Bernard; and then he exclaims: "By all means she had compassion on him, and very much, too, did she compassionate him; for he could die corporally, but she could not die with him as her heart desired." Yet her feelings and sufferings were of a calm nature, because they were accompanied with the most perfect conformity to the will of her God. Still the most complete and heroic resignation takes not their bitterness from sorrows, although such resignation assuages them; and the reason is, bitterness of sorrows and most perfect resignation are thoroughly compatible. Human life is a compound of happiness and misfortune,—misfortune being the larger element. No one in the world can be wholly exempt from trouble and tribulation—the path of these was trodden by all the saints after Jesus and Mary: "Through many tribulations the faithful entered."

What is the character of thy resignation in regard to the crosses which God has in store for thee? Art thou prepared to accept them with resignation, notwithstanding the opposition of nature? Dost thou endeavor to say in regard to all the events that may happen to thee in the future: "My heart is ready, O God?" Acceptance of those events, and conformity with the will of God—such are the means to render them less oppressing. "Who embraces the cross," says St. Theresa, "does not perceive that it is the cross."

Be assiduous in exercising so beautiful a discipline as the discipline of tribulation. Say to the Lord, "Do with me as thou wilt." Say this to him from thy whole heart and soul, and doubt not that God will take care to come to thee; he will sweeten thy crosses for thee, and will help thee to bear them in such way that thou wilt one day heartily thank him for having sent them to thee.

SECOND POINT.

MARY'S RESIGNATION—A CONSTANT RESIGNATION.

Mary's resignation endured till the very last breath of her life. It would seem that, after the ascension of her Divine Son, she had no more need for the exercise of this virtue—the great storm was over, the calm had set in, and yet all was not as would at first sight appear.

Although her divine Son had shed the last drop of his blood for the redemption of the world, still the great bulk of those who, by way of eminence, were called his chosen people, remained in infidelity;—that people who had for chiefs, the patriarchs, the doctors of the law, the prophets,—that people who had received the law from God himself, and to whom he had made so many promises,—remained in darkness of error, crushed by unspeakable tribulations, and far removed from God. What bitter recollections were those for the heart of Mary? what keen sorrow for her to behold that people in so deplorable a condition—that people for whose salvation she would have laid her life down a thousand times! And yet more:—the circumstance that, after the departure of Jesus, she had to remain so long on earth, must have been unto her an occasion for the constant exercise of resignation! Ceaselessly did she yearn after her heavenly country; more inflamed with love than were all the Seraphim together, all the more, just on this account, did she conceive an ardent desire to be quickly united with her beloved in heaven.

Oh! how must this turtle dove have sighed, separated as she was from her good. "My soul refuses to be comforted," cries out David, in a moment of his holy transports; my soul renounces all consolation from creatures, she will accept of no consolation from this earth, she will have her God, and her God alone. With how much greater ardor of feeling must Mary have said: "My heart desires nothing else, it will have nothing else than thee." During all this time, her resignation was extremely perfect and calm: she was ready to remain many centuries longer on earth, were her so remaining pleasing to God. She loved, she yearned, she burned; but, yet, she would not have consented to depart from this world one moment sooner than God willed her to depart.

Let us learn of Mary to resign ourselves to the will of God in all things, at all times, and to the very end of our lives. Is it to be God's will that we shall lie on the same cross on which Mary lay? Be his most holy will done! Is he going to substitute another cross for it, or will he take every cross out of our way? In like manner, may his most holy will be done! Mary is on the road before us. Let us pattern after her perseverance in all things, likewise in those things which concern the spiritual welfare of souls. The callousness of so many Christians, the multitude of so great sins, brings trouble and sorrow to our hearts: let us, on our side, aim at succoring all, by testifying for them great love and royal zeal; and having done this, let us leave the rest in the hands of God.

A good disposition is depression of spirits at the offences given to God, provided that depression be accompanied with resignation and confidence. As to ourselves, we can do nothing better than to apply ourselves to his service with fidelity and perseverance, and then, with unqualified confidence, to submit ourselves to his dispensations, as a child commits itself to the custody of its loving mother.

THIRD POINT.

MARY'S RESIGNATION,—AN HUMBLE RESIGNATION.

Resignation to the divine will is facilitated in proportion as it is accompanied with sincere humility. A soul who knows herself, and looks upon herself in the eyes of God and of men as being what she is—such a soul has no words to utter complaint regarding the dispensations of Providence.

Behold here the cause why the character of Mary's resignation was most perfect. She was the most humble of creatures, and God experienced no opposition on her part in treating her as seemed good to him. He might raise her to the highest dignities—he might visit her with the greatest humiliations. Mary looked upon herself as a poor slave who had no property, no rights, no valid claims to put forth; whatever treatment she received she considered a favor; she knew but duty; she knew but how to unite herself to God in all things, and to content herself with whatever fell to her lot. "Be firmly convinced that I took myself for a guilty person, for a person very contemptible, and for a person unworthy of the grace of God." St. Bonaventure tells us that this is a revelation which the blessed Virgin made to St. Elizabeth.

As Mary, then, was firmly convinced that she wanted nothing and was unworthy the grace of the Lord, of what kind must have been her resignation to the visitations of Providence? How easy to her must have been that resignation! how calm! how humble! The little esteem she conceived of herself in her own heart, went hand in hand with the exercise of her humility; and hence, without being astonished or surprised, she received those visitations from whatever quarter they came,—and she received them by praising God for everything, by being unchangeable in sufferings and joy, in humiliations and honors. The evil-minded rage of the Pharisees, the inflictions of the death penalty contemplated by the Hebrew people, the treason of Judas, the injustice of Pilate, the cruel and ignominious crucifixion of her divine Son—all these plunged her into a sea of sorrows: "I am fallen into the depths of the sea." And how did she behave throughout all these ordeals? As one who has no voice to utter complaints: "like the lamb before the shearer," since she ever held for a certainty that she would be rightly treated, and treated always better than her deserts. So her profound humility was a stay to her most perfect resignation: and her most perfect resignation was, in its turn, a prop to her profound humility.

Were we a little more humble, how happy should we be; were we more humble, how calmly and peacefully we should accept those dispensations which now throw our hearts into commotion, and so throw them, precisely because we lack sincere humility! We complain of the Lord: it seems to us that he causes us to feel his hand upon us more than is just. But why complain? why do things so seem to us? Simply because we have an erroneous notion of ourselves: because we do not think that we merit a treatment so severe. Look, says St. Bernard, at what thou hast merited by thy sins, and the complaint will expire on thy lips. If we know anything of ourselves then we shall have, in the very midst of our tribulations, no other words to repeat than those: "He is the Lord, let him do what is good in his eyes."

Oh, Queen of Martyrs! thou who wast innocent, hast suffered with so great resignation, and shall I, who am deserving of hell, refuse to suffer? Ah, obtain for me even a small share of that resignation of which, from the begining to the end of thy life, thou hast left us such brilliant examples. I do not solicit exemption from sufferings; I do not solicit that they may not approach me; I am well aware that suffering is the most satisfactory sign that one belongs to the happy multitude of those who form thy crown in heaven! I therefore do not refuse to suffer; I only entreat thee for the grace to suffer with humble resignation, with calmness, and in a meritorious manner. O consoler of the afflicted! I entreat thee by the bitterness of thy dolors, infuse into my soul this balm of resignation to the will of God; console me; assist me in all my tribulations, and make them become unto me as so many stepping stones to eternal joys! Amen.

TWENTY-FIFTH MEDITATION.

MARY'S HEROISM IN HER DOLORS.

FIRST POINT.

MARY ASSUMES HEROICALLY THE OFFICE OF CO-REDEMPTRESS.

WHAT greatness of heart, imperturbable firmness, and heroism, did it, indeed, require in order not to give up outright in the face of so many sufferings and sorrows, as the Divine Maternity was destined to have in its train!

Mary must have been acquainted with the nature of those sufferings and sorrows before they came upon her, and, indeed, acquainted with them from the time of the Annunciation; since from that time especially, she was full of heavenly light, and very well versed in the Sacred Scriptures. It, therefore, could not have escaped her that the world's Redeemer was pointed out by the prophets as a Man of Sorrows, and that the life of that virgin who was appointed to be his Mother, could not be very unlike his life. By all means, she well knew what awaited her; and oh, how minutely and how clearly did she know all at that moment when she heard from Simeon's lips that terrible prophecy, "a sword shall pierce thy own soul!" St. Thomas of Villanova says that the holy old man, illumined with light from above, saw the whole grand drama enacted of the future sufferings and death of him who was then the Child Jesus: "Illumined with Divine light, he saw through the blindness and ingratitude of the Jewish people, and the Child's future passion and death:" and all this the old man related to the Virgin Mother: 'I should like not to have to tell thee anything of the sort, yet hear; the time will come when thou shalt feel on the double the pains which thou didst experience in giving birth to thy Son.'"

Poor heart of Mary! What did it not hear and feel at that moment? She heard the whole scenes of humiliations and sorrows which her divine Son had to suffer from his first advent upon earth till he expired upon the cross: and probably his prayer in the garden was also clearly unfolded to her. Yes, from the lips of Simeon she heard all—the treachery of Judas, the apostacy of the disciples, the denial of Peter, the flagellation, the crowning with thorns, the nailing to the cross, and the crucifixion. Oh, what a sight for a mother such as Mary was! Mary herself revealed to St. Mecthildis that, so great was her sorrow of heart, from the moment of Simeon's prophecy forward, all her joys were turned into sorrows: "Those prophetic words of Simeon changed all my joy into sorrow."

And yet did she ever swoon away? or did she ever lose courage? No! Mary knew that God required of her this great sacrifice; and with a heartiness raised above all sufferings, she offers him that sacrifice in spite of all the efforts of an unwilling nature to the contrary. Prostrate before the altar, inflamed with heavenly zeal, holding her divine Son in her arms—in this condition she prays: "Accept, O Almighty Father, accept this sacrifice which I, thy handmaid, offer thee for the salvation of the whole world! Accept, Almighty Father, accept this offering which I, thy handmaid, bring to thee; accept this Son who is thy Son and mine at the same moment; thy Son from Eternity, my Son in time; receive this our common Son; thine has he been from all eternity, and mine is he become in due course of ages."

Such is the affecting and familiar prayer which the holy archbishop, St. Thomas of Villanova, puts into the mouth of our most Blessed Lady. Accept now from my hands this thrice holy morning sacrifice, which will one day offer itself to thee as an evening sacrifice on the altar of the cross. Cast an eye upon the peace-offering which I bring thee and the world: "Accept now from the hands of thy handmaid this thrice holy morning sacrifice which, after some time, will be offered as an evening sacrifice on the altar of the cross. Look, O most gracious Father, at what I offer thee and remember for whom I offer it!" O that magnanimous and invisible heart, O that extremely heroic soul! What woman's countenance would not fall in the midst of such a scene of sorrows? Yet the Virgin was destined to become the co-redemptress of the human race, and she offered up for their salvation her Son upon the cross; and had it been pleasing to God she would have submitted to a thousand tortures in order to work out the same salvation.

Learn heroism of Mary; for heroism is necessary for thee in certain great trials. For what dost thou do when thou knowest that God intends sending thee some heavy cross? Dost thou accept it with magnanimity, or dost thou not endeavor by every means to defer it, and even to evade it altogether? After Jesus, Mary is the most perfect type of souls of whom the Lord demands great sacrifices. What a lesson for thee! The sacrifices to be demanded of thee, can never be compared with those demanded of Mary. Offer thy sacrifices, then, heroically; and should thy mind struggle against thee, and thy courage sink, then address thyself with importunity to the Queen of Martyrs.

SECOND POINT.

MARY'S HEROISM IN NOURISHING HER PEACE-OFFERING.

If Mary was heroic in accepting so onerous a commission, she was not less heroic in its execution. The other women of Israel offered their children to God in the temple, afterwards redeemed them with some pieces of coin, and, finally, took them home with great joy. All this did Mary in regard to Jesus; but ah, how quite differently! with how far superior dispositions! Other mothers saw in their infants the hope of their love; in that sweet little one Mary beheld a peace-offering destined to be brought on the altar of the cross! She well knew how this dear infant was to close his career; she knew that this manner of closing it would be unavoidable; she never could alter an iota regarding his exit from this world; and yet, in the meantime, she must rear him with all maternal solicitude.

Oh, the poor mother! When she saw him going about her, and heard him call her by the sweet name of

Mother, how often then must she have thought on that last word which he was to address to her from the cross! When she pressed him to her bosom, how often must the thought of the thongs have occurred to her which flagellated him through the streets of Jerusalem, and of the hard wood to which he was to be affixed! Whilst she was feeding and dressing him, and taking him hither and thither, how often must she have said within herself: "Ah, this innocent body will one day be a continuous wound; it will be scourged all over, and will be pierced through with nails! Ah, my Son, I must rear thee up in order that thou mayst be offered in sacrifice!"

The expectation and certain foresight of an inevitable evil is often a heavier cross than the evil itself; and this precisely was Mary's situation. This expectation and certain foresight was to her a two-edged sword which ceaselessly penetrated her soul. Mary could not remove that sword, could not go away from it. No! by day and by night, in public and in her own dwelling, whether awake or asleep, in every place, at every time, the suffering of her Jesus, the death of her Jesus, weighed heavily on her soul to afflict it, to torture it,—and to afflict and torture it all the more, the nearer the time of the sacrifice approached: "That sword of sorrow came nearer to the Blessed Virgin every hour, according as the time drew near at which her Son was to suffer."

What great violence must she have constantly offered to herself in order not to to grow weary of her maternal solicitude! What an internal struggle must she have gone through, in order not to allow herself to be overpowered by the frightfully cruel anguish! Happy those souls who, notwithstanding great sacrifices, remain steadfast in the fulfilment of their duties, and continue on that cross to which God has affixed them! Oh, what great merit do they acquire by thus imitating the Queen of Martyrs!

If thy condition be now, or ever will be, that of one affixed to a cross, do not lose courage; remain perseveringly on the cross; disgust, fear, sadness, will seize upon thee, in order to induce thee in every way to come down from the cross; but do not suffer thyself to be overcome. Combat, remain where it is necessary; continue on thy cross till death; the faithful God will assist thee with his grace: "But God is faithful and will not suffer thee to be tempted above thy strength." If thou hast a share in the ignominy and sorrow of Jesus and Mary, thou wilt, likewise, for all eternity have a share in their glory and in their joys: "If we suffer, we shall also be glorified."

THIRD POINT.

MARY OFFERS WITH HEROISM HER SACRIFICE TO GOD.

Mary's heroism increased accordingly as the trials to which she was subjected, increased; and in the offering which she made of her divine Son to the divine Justice, it was that her heroism attained its greatest height. This peace-offering she had already presented in the temple; and already with her holy hands had she offered to the Eternal Father the fruit of her chaste womb, in order that he might accept that fruit as an atonement for the sins of the world. At that moment, the most tender of Mothers became a spectacle of fortitude in the eyes of angels and even before God; and yet the most holy moment of her life, the moment when her greatness of soul should appear unique in the world for ever, was the moment on Calvary when she stood at the foot of the cross during the agony of her adorable Jesus.

Mary! how wert thou able, without dying, to endure so horrible torture? No mother is there, be she ever so holy, who would not give full vent to the sorrows that weigh her down, when she sees her son suffering an unjust and a violent death. Mary, plunged in a sea of affliction, a sea that surrounds her on every side, utters not a word, creates no noise, and by all this, discovers a heroism which is without example: "That she stood, I read," says St. Ambrose: "that she wept, I do not read." Under the keenness of excessive sorrow human nature yields and swoons away; yet Mary by no means swoons away, although her sorrow transcends the anguish of all mothers. With an unspeakable effort of violence to herself, she offers her sacrifice to the divine Justice, she suppresses in her heart all opposition from her tortured soul, and stands mute at the foot of the cross, on which there hangs her dear Jesus pierced through with wounds and covered with confusion! She stood at the cross poring over the boundless goodness of the Lord who, for the redemption of guilty slaves, signs the death warrant against his only begotten Son. She stood pondering on the strict justice of God which pours out its wrath on the immaculate flesh of the divine

Lamb,—wrath which should fall upon sinners. She stood motionless, without fearing the malice of the doctors of the law and of the Pharisees, without fearing the rudeness of the soldiers or the rage of the infuriated populace. She stood, and by standing, gave the whole rising Church a model of heroism and of resoluteness—a course which raised her to the dignity of Queen of all Martyrs.

From some souls God exacts the sacrifice of their darling attachments, of their most precious advantages, of all that they have, even of themselves; and this last sacrifice is very trying to weak natures—it is a sacrifice which, however, is facilitated by grace, and rendered precious by having annexed to it a merit of an extremely rare character. How many magnanimous souls offered that sacrifice, and offer it still every day! No greater consolation for those souls than that they cast a look full of faith at Jesus on the cross, and on Mary at the foot of the cross. Jesus and Mary are the sources whence all that is good is derived; and when we recur to them, we obtain the courage, the strength, and the perseverance, necessary to the complete execution of whatever sacrifice may be required of us.

In Jesus and Mary then take refuge; and twined to Mary say to her: "O Mary, thou who art the richest of all in sorrows, thou who in the bitterest sufferings desponded not, and who, with incomparable courage in thy heart, perfectly executed the most painful of all sacrifices, I sympathize with thee, I admire thee, and I unite my sufferings with thine! Be not angry with me if I dwell on those subjects, I have far other reasons to weep besides. Full of sympathy for thee that I am, permit me to weep with thee. If it can be any consolation to thee to share thy sufferings with me, then give me part in all thou endurest; and then when I am supported by thee, I shall never refuse to suffer. Obtain for me the grace to make with heroism the sacrifices which God demands of me; strengthen my weakness and grant that, as I would share in thy sorrows, I may share with thee the eternal joys of heaven!" Amen.

TWENTY-SIXTH MEDITATION.

THE SPECIAL EVIDENCES WHICH JESUS GAVE TO MARY OF HIS LOVE FOR HER.

FIRST POINT.

THE EVIDENCES WHICH JESUS SHOWED IN ELIZABETH.

JESUS was animated with great love for Mary, since it was his love for her that first opened the vein of grace and of mercy which afterwards flowed in so great abundance unto the salvation of souls. The archangel Gabriel prophesied of John, that in his mother's womb he should be already filled with the Holy Ghost: "Whilst yet in his mother's womb he shall be filled with the Holy Ghost."

And this grace which the Word made flesh conferred on the first fruits of his redemption, he imparted through Mary. Scarce had she appeared at the threshold of Elizabeth's door when the infant John, though shut up in his mother's womb, became conscious of her presence and experienced its beneficent workings: "The child leaped for joy in the womb." Instantly was the unborn infant cleansed from original sin in his mother's womb, adorned with sanctifying grace, filled with the Holy Ghost, enlightened upon the mystery of the Incarnation, and inundated with joy and jubilation. The infant leaped also in acknowledgment of the grace he had received and of the channel through which he had received it. It leaped also because, at the sound of Mary's voice he, although not yet born, rejoiced in the fruits of the redemption. St. Bernard very happily observes that "the soul of the yet unborn infant melted as Mary spoke."

Thus did the Word made man testify his boundless esteem of his most holy mother by causing her to participate in the honor and the joy of the first fruits of our redemption. And through this first conquest, he gave her a title to the other numberless conquests which he would make of sinners for all eternity.

O how appropriate for her is the title, "Charm of sinners!" Consider, besides, that the sanctification of John was not the only grace which his family received on that occasion. Far otherwise; for his sanctification was accompanied by other graces and benefactions. When Mary dispensed graces, she dispensed them with a magnificence and generosity peculiar to her own heart. At Mary's salutation John leaped in his mother's womb; and at the same time, Elizabeth was filled with the holy Ghost, Zachary with joy, and the whole house with grace and blessings.

See in these results the operations of Mary's presence! Happy that soul whom she visits. Oh, how many mercies does not she make that soul partake of! "Happy," should we say, "happy is the man whom thou instructest, O Lady!" She brings with her a grace to the soul whom she visits, she makes such a soul docile to the inspirations of God. She raises the affections of such a soul heavenward; such a soul she enlightens, consoles, and fills with favors and blessings of every kind. Mary delights in being found. She is easily discerned by those who love her: "and yet her desire is that she be sought for in an affectionate manner."

How easy would it be for thee also to rejoice in receiving some charming visits from Mary. With what advantage to thyself thou couldst participate in the beneficent operations of her presence. If thou hast no share in those blessings, with thyself lies the fault; it is a sure sign that thou dost not invite Mary to come to thee, and that thou dost not pray to her as much as thy interest demands. Examine thyself, and see whether, perchance, thy coldness and indifference towards her be not the real and just cause why she visits thee so seldom, and shews herself ungenerous towards thee in the dispensation of her favors.

SECOND POINT.

THE MANIFESTATIONS WHICH JESUS MADE AT CANA, OF HIS LOVE FOR MARY.

What great condescension Jesus evinced for Mary, on occasion of the wedding at Cana! When enjoyment at the feast was at its height the wine gave out; and this mishap covered with confusion the poor bridal pair who were unable to apply the remedy. No sooner does Mary perceive their perplexity than, unsolicited, she turned to Jesus, and with all humility and compassion entreats him to lend a succoring hand in the situation. "Jesus had not yet wrought any miracles, because the time appointed for them had not yet come;" accordingly, he states to his most holy Mother that the time for working miracles had not yet arrived.

And this he says to her in order that the miracle which he then intended to perform, might be all the more patent, and also in order that the power of Mary's intercession might be manifested to us. "My hour is not yet come;" the exact moment of time when I am to work miracles, is not yet in view; but if thou make the request, then, in that case, are no hours appointed; and the hour that is pleasing to thee, is always the appropriate hour.

He then, without further delay, turned to the waiters, and ordered them to fill the pitchers with water; and when they had done so, he immediately changed the water into wine.

Thus did Jesus perform his first miracle at Mary's intercession; and, moreover, he performed it at a time when he seemed to be quite unprepared. Hence, St. John Chrysostom takes occasion to remark: "Although he answered his Mother after the manner he did, yet with a view to honor her, he granted her what she had asked for; and although he gave her such a reply, yet he complied with his Mother's request in order that she might be honored thereby."

Oh, how great, judging from all this, must have been Mary's influence and power over Jesus! How exalted and effectual are the condescension and the love which Jesus entertains for Mary! In the kingdom of grace, Mary was the first fruit of the redemption; in the kingdom of nature, Christ conferred his first favor through Mary. Learn from this latter fact how powerful she is in things relating to the body, as well as in things relating to the soul.

Contemplate in the next place the tenderness of Mary's heart, since her heart was so easily affected by the miseries of others. Had she been requested by the bridal pair, her immediate approval of and compliance with their request would have proved that she had a great fund of charity; but how much greater must her charity now appear, when, neither invited nor entreated, she is, of her own accord, moved to come to the relief of guiltless shame, although a miracle be required therefor of her divine Son! Her tender heart was pained at the sight of the mental sufferings of those strangers; and she could not forbear to seek assistance for them.

O how compassionate then must she be! "For the mother of Jesus," says St. Bernard, "sympathized with them in their confusion, and she so sympathized with them because she was the most merciful and the most gracious!" What else than charity could flow from the fountain of charity; and if she was so merciful and so sympathetic in regard to embarrassments of that sort which were comparatively insignificant, how much more will she be on more difficult and momentous occasions! Be astonished at the graciousness of this Lady, who does not consider it beneath her dignity to stoop so low as to be solicitous for our temporal, even for the least of our temporal, wants. All histories proclaim the fact that she is thus solicitous; and, perhaps, hast not thou thyself the most admirable proofs of her solicitude for thy temporal welfare? May thou be as full of recognition to her, as she was of love for thee.

See well to it that thou be not of the number of those who, in a momentary necessity, are all zeal for Mary, and as soon as the necessity is past, think no more of her benefactions. Be grateful to her by remembering her and thanking her; and doubt not but thou shalt have always in her a loving protectress, who will, at a future time, say to her Divine Son, "He has no wine."

THIRD POINT.

THE MANIFESTATION WHICH JESUS MADE AT NAZARETH OF HIS LOVE FOR MARY.

Meditate and imagine as much as ever thou canst; and yet thou shalt never be able to take in with thy mind the greatness of the love which Jesus bore towards his most holy Mother. All reasonable and well-mannered children love their mothers from natural instinct; but Jesus has so many different grounds for loving Mary that no other child in the world could have such motives.

To her was he indebted for his most holy humanity. He was the fruit of her womb, the fruit of her most pure blood: "Christ's flesh is Mary's flesh." "Thence," says St. Augustine, "thence is the most close union of affection between Jesus and Mary, the closest union of the disposition of their tempers, and of the bent of their mind, and thence also their mutual and quite special confidence." He knew the most tender love which she bore to him as to her God and to her Son. He knew the sufferings, the troubles, the sovereignly painful life to which she had subjected herself for his sake. He saw in her all virtues in the most perfect degree. He saw in her a multitude of graces and privileges; in short, he saw in her the most immaculate, the most humble, the most holy, the greatest creature that ever was or ever will be upon earth.

Who then can say how great is the love which motives so powerful as those, enkindled in the heart of Jesus? "Since the daughter of Jerusalem was adorned with her jewelry the Lord took a liking unto her." St. Bonaventure says that, "when Jesus was a little boy he performed for Mary all those little services which every well bred son is in the habit of performing for his mother." Services of that sort the humble Lord rendered unto his mother; and among the occupations which he had at the house of Nazareth, the saint numbers these, viz., that he remained with his holy mother and kept her company; he travelled with his mother: so dear to him was this incomparable creature.

Imagine now, if thou canst, their affectionate intercourse and their heavenly conversation! Imagine this most close union which reigned between two hearts, constituted as theirs were, so similar in desires and affections! O house of Nazareth! O sanctuary of love! Jesus associated with no one so willingly as with his holy mother. In no other creature did he find so much consolation and rest as in her most pure heart; and as no other creature resembled him so much, so he loved no other creature in the same degree as he loved Mary; and if he sometimes addressed to her a word which would seem to savor of harshness rather than of gentleness, by so doing he proposed to teach us that, in works appertaining to his service, we must cut ourselves loose from our relations, and also to teach us how it is necessary for us to act when great sacrifices are demanded of us. Perfectly did Mary know the designs and objects of her dear Jesus; and yet never did she, on account of her knowledge, fear that she would be less loved.

By his own example, Jesus teaches us to love his most holy Mother. Love her, she despises not thy love; yea, she longs for it, she rewards it, and loves thee in return. However poor, miserable, or contemptible thou mayst be, she will accept thy love; "I am the Mother of beautiful love." Outside of God, what more exalted and more worthy object than Mary canst thou represent to thyself? Tear thy heart away from the creatures of this world. Turn thy affections to Mary. Love her as ardently as thou canst, and be certain that on this earth no greater happiness can befall thee than that of thus loving her.

O most gracious Lady, what grace can thy divine Son refuse thee? None: thou need but say a word and he will withhold nothing from thee. He grants all thy petitions; yes, in thy hands has he placed the treasures of all his mercies, and thee has he constituted the dispenser of all his mercies and graces. Every favor, whether for the soul or for the body, whether for time or for eternity, comes, therefore, from thy hands. Ah! cast a look at me who am attacked by so many enemies and combated by so many passions, and bowed down under the weight of so many perplexities: "To thee do we cry mourning and weeping in this valley of tears!" If thy heart was so tender as to take compassion on those who were slightly embarrassed, how can it refuse to have pity on me, seeing the great necessities and miseries with which I am hemmed in on all sides? O Mary, in thee have I confidence, from thee do I hope for every thing; I hope for pardon of my sins, for final perseverance, for consolations in all my troubles; from thee do I hope to obtain them, and grace to love thee warmly in this life, in order that I may be one day numbered among the blessed, and may then love thee eternally in heaven. Amen.

TWENTY-SEVENTH MEDITATION.

MARY'S CONSOLATIONS ON EARTH.

FIRST POINT.

MARY'S CONSOLATION IN THE SOCIETY OF JOSEPH.

THE assistance of a faithful friend in the eventualities of this life, is a true treasure. The Holy Ghost termed it so, in fact, in order to point out the inestimableness of the services which such a friend can render.

Now represent to thyself to what and to how great consolations of the most holy Virgin, the society of her most pure spouse, Joseph, must have conduced,—Joseph who, chosen of God from among all the just of the old law, was furnished with all the rare privileges which the troublesome office to which he was destined, and to which he was even appointed by the Holy Ghost, demanded. Those privileges were necessary to Joseph, for he held on earth the place of the eternal Father himself. He was chosen to be the faithful foster-father and guardian of his chiefest treasures; these were his Son and his Spouse. In him, Mary found her stay, her protection, her leader, her care-taker; after God, her all. She looked upon him with veneration and loved him with most tender affection. If she were shy in her deportment towards other men, she was, as one of the holy fathers observes, never so joyous as when she was in Joseph's company. With him she shared her sufferings, she followed his counsels; in his fidelity and love she reposed in security and without solicitude.

On his side, Joseph regarded Mary as a heavenly treasure confided to his protection. Oh, who can give expression to the eagerness with which he watched for her welfare, and to the most pure and heartfelt love with which he was animated towards her? He accompanied her as long as she lived; in all her journeyings he procured her sustenance; he protected her in all her dangers; he assisted her in all her necessities, he facilitated all her difficulties; and even on all occasions he was unto her what the trunk is unto the tree, viz., her cherished support: "The Lord appointed him as the consolation of his mother." His virtues, his conversations all heavenly, his glowing love of her and of Jesus, were for Mary a balm of consolation: but ah! a balm ever available, a balm ever ready—available and ready, especially in the dark hour of necessity.

By all means, so much and so greatly did Joseph console her that the holy fathers hesitate not to maintain that she is indebted to him for the guardianship of her inviolate virginity, for the defence of her divine maternity, for her sustenance, for the most zealous and the most loving solicitude which he felt for herself and for all that concerned her. What can Jesus ever refuse to him who so often bore him in his arms, who withdrew him from the wrath of Herod, who procured him nourishment by the sweat of his brow? Can he be refused by that noble Lady who is indebted to him for so much solicitude which he felt in her regard, and which he also felt for the protection of her most transcendent privileges?

Turn thyself with confidence to him; take refuge under his protecting mantle; choose him for thy special defender, and fear nothing whatever. He feels more than fatherly love for us; and all who honor him in an especial manner, he takes under his especial protection. The name of Father was given thee, since the Church was established; and thou hast, as an instrument, conduced to our salvation.

Oh, how many graces does he ceaselessly distribute among those who venerate him! "I do not remember," says St. Theresa, "that I ever asked for anything which he (St. Joseph) has not granted me." Make the experiment, and thou canst be certain that thou also shalt, one day, be able to speak of Joseph, as spoke of him St. Theresa.

SECOND POINT.

MARY'S CONSOLATION IN HER INTERCOURSE WITH JESUS.

Her intercourse with Jesus, which was so confidential and lasted so many years, must have caused Mary to experience great consolation. What heavenly affections must, during that time, have been the life of her heart! In Jesus she beheld every treasure of grace and holiness, and the embodiment of all perfections; in him she saw the Messiah who had been yearned after for so many centuries—that Just One whom the clouds were to rain down, and whom the earth was to bud forth. In him she beheld the Savior of the world, the Redeemer of men, who would soon open the gates of heaven. In him she saw and adored her God, but a

God who at the same time was her true and her only begotten son—a God who had become man in her virginal womb, and had, out of her, issued forth into the world.

If it is granted us to spend a short while with persons of exalted virtue and holiness, and if this privilege consoles us so much that we cannot tear ourselves away from them, what consolation must Mary have enjoyed in her intercourse with Jesus?—an intercourse which was so continuous and which lasted so great a number of years. Besides this, she acted with him so warmly and so confidentially, just as acts a mother with her own child. She conversed with him; her whole soul was taken up with him; she caressed him and ministered to his wants; she took him around as a little child in her arms; she led him by the hand as a mother leads her little son; she had him under the same roof and sitting at the same table with herself; she listened to his conversations, meditated on his words, and utilized his examples.

"Judge, I entreat thee," says St. Thomas of Villanova, "judge how great must have been the fire of love that was enkindled in her heart by an intercourse of so long duration, by conversations of so frequent recurrence, and by a companionship of so constant a character." What a fire of love must have been enkindled in her, what a store of graces must have been amassed in her, by this her constant dwelling with Jesus! What consolations must she have had amid the annoyances of her life! What unspeakable benedictions! What more could she have wished for on earth:

"Outside of thee, what do I desire on earth?" Thus, must she have oft repeated with the royal Psalmist, "What can I desire outside of thee, my Son and my God?"

If the souls who most love this God were, in the bare contemplation of his love and benevolence, carried off in transports, and if they exclaimed, "my God and my all!"—how then, if that were so, must the case have stood with Mary since she saw him with her own eyes, heard his voice, and enjoyed his confidential intercourse? Happy those souls who can cry out in truth, "My God and my all!" But who are those? They are those who understand how to sever their heart from creatures in order to give it wholly to the Creator; they are those who avoid intercourse with men in the view to seek the society of God. So long as in thy miseries thou hast yearning for consolation in creatures, and lookst to them to sustain thee, do not by any means expect that thou canst enjoy sweet confidence with God, who transports the soul with the purest delight. Break asunder so many useless bonds which, in a deplorable manner, chain down thy affections; seek the Lord with all thy heart, and doubt not that he will cause thee to feel his gracious presence in such a way that thou also canst repeat, "what do I desire on earth besides thee?"

THIRD POINT.

MARY'S CONSOLATIONS IN THE FIRST TRIUMPHS OF FAITH.

If the blessed Virgin saw the humiliations of her dear Son, so, before her blessed departure out of this world, she saw likewise the beginning of his glorification. Jesus had promised that he would send the Holy Ghost to the apostles, and Mary was with them in the upper chamber when the Holy Ghost came down upon them in the form of fiery tongues, and changed them from wolves into lambs. She saw those same apostles who, a little before, abandoned their divine Master from fear of the Jews, present with extraordinary courage a firm front to all obstacles; she saw them publicly preach him who had been crucified; she saw them rejoice and glory, that out of love for him, they suffered injuries and ill treatment of every kind: "and they indeed went from the presence of the council, rejoicing that they were accounted worthy to suffer reproach for the name of Jesus." Acts. v. 41 v.

She beheld the first fruits of their sermons—three thousand men who were converted by St. Peter's first discourse, and five thousand by another of his discourses; and besides, she saw throughout all Jerusalem a great multitude of persons of every age, sex, and condition, embrace the faith, invoke the name of Jesus, and acknowledge and adore him as the true God. She saw strangers who had come from all quarters to Jerusalem, astonished at the wonderful apparition of tongues, and heard them exclaim: "Oh! how great is the power of Jesus of Nazareth, who can impart such eloquence to the tongues of the unlearned!" How must Mary's heart have been exalted in those first victories of faith! Already had the apostles portioned among themselves all the countries of the universe. Their voice had gone forth over the whole world; the Crucified was now acknowledged and adored every day; and the cross, the instrument of his ignominious death, came to be looked upon as the standard of salvation. The people opened their eyes to the light, renounced idolatry, and embraced the faith. Knowledge of all things that were going on, the apostles communicated to Mary as to their mother and teacher; and, at the same time they entreated her for the assistance of her counsel and prayers. And thus was she able, even before her death, to see the edifice of the Church commenced on a solid basis, and also to admire the first fruits of the Church's early glory.

Oh! how will our Blessed Lady have exulted, how often will she have congratulated herself with Jesus, and have cried out, "Let us rejoice for the days on which thou didst humiliate us." The Lord is faithful; he comes to console his beloved; and he defers for a time his coming, yet he fails not to come. Happy those souls who remain faithful to him in the time of their difficulties: "He comes and delays not." But as for thee, try to discern the true grounds of consolation for a Christian soul; these are the sanctification of the name of God, the propagation of the faith, the invocation of our holy mother the Church; and in a word, every thing conducive to the salvation of souls, and promotive of the glory of our Lord.

David used often to say: "the zeal of thy house hath eaten me up." Canst thou say the same? Dost thou feel in thy heart so admirable a glow of love? Awake; cast off thy slumber; let all thy aims be directed to the country above, and recur to all the resources at thy command in order to co-operate, by every possible means, towards so great a work as that of filling thee with zeal for God's glory: and shouldst thou be able to do nothing else, contribute to that work by thy counsel, thy exhortations, thy alms; and if thou do this, how greatly wilt thou be able to promote the salvation of souls!

Oh, Mother of Mercy! I turn to thy goodness with the view that thou mayst obtain for me by thy intercession, the grace which will set me wholly in harmony with thy spirit. Not for earthly goods do I pray to thee; I pray to thee that thou mayst deign to obtain for me in my troubles those consolations, which thou experienced in thy difficulties. Thou hadst the assistance and the love of thy most pure spouse, Joseph. Oh! gain for me his assistance and his protection in all the casualties of my life, and especially at my death. Thy delight consisted in being with Jesus; grant that I also may find my protection and my consolation at his feet and in his most sweet heart. Thou didst exult over the triumphs of our holy faith; let the elevation and glorification of that same faith be also to me a subject of earnest and holy consolation. Oh, what a sovereign and precious balm will that grace become for the wounds of my poor heart!

From thee, O Mary! I await that grace: from thee, I promise it to myself: console him who hopes in thee, and who promises himself that he will receive all good from thee. Amen.

TWENTY-EIGHTH MEDITATION.

THE JOYS WHICH SUCCEEDED MARY'S SORROWS.

FIRST POINT.

MARY'S JOY ON OCCASION OF THE RESURRECTION.

ALTHOUGH the sacred Scriptures do not mention that Jesus appeared to his most holy Mother after his resurrection, St. Ignatius of Loyola says that we cannot doubt it, unless we would have addressed to us the reproach, "are you also without understanding?"

Yes! who accompanied Jesus more faithfully than did she during his passion? Consequently, he appeared to his most holy Mother, and indeed, says St. Antoninus, he appeared to her before appearing to any of the others, because she merited to be the first consoled: "He appeared to Mary his Mother, as to the first and before he appeared to any of the others, in order that she who had suffered more than all the others, should be consoled sooner and more than all the others." In her abandonment she found herself plunged into a certain heavenly disconsolateness, and like an uneasy dove, accelerating, so to speak, the resurrection of her beloved Son.

We cannot doubt, then, that her Jesus, all radiant with heavenly light, and his body and soul reunited, appeared to her: "He appeared to his venerable Mother, with his body and soul reunited." (St. Ignatius of Loyola, in his book of Exercises).

Oh, what a spectacle! What an immense change took place in the sorely afflicted Mother on beholding it! Who can fathom the ravishment of her mind, the jubilation of her heart? Should a mother, after having shed bitter tears, again press to her bosom her son for whom she had wept as for one lost or dead;—it would be a miracle if the joy that inundated her soul, did not deprive her of self-command. How, then, must Mary have felt when she saw Jesus again? not indeed as she saw him before, covered with wounds and with blood—but beautiful, glorious, resplendent,—and as the sun emitting his rays, and as victor over death and hell. On that occasion Jesus embraces her with childlike reliance; he shows her his glorified wounds which speak of triumph. He permits her to kiss them, and says to her: "my humiliations, my ignominies, my sorrows, are at an end." He thanks her for the assistance which she always so faithfully rendered him, and likewise for her constant companionship. And how often, and with what boundless love must he have said to her, "Blessed art thou among women!" Yes, that was unto Mary a blessed hour—an hour at which she could not have controlled herself, had she not received from God great strength and great power for that purpose.

Meditate on the beautiful spectacle of the meeting of Jesus and Mary after the Resurrection; nourish thy mind with that spectacle; and learn from it that, if God casts his beloved ones into the furnace of tribulation, he also rescues them in his own good time. Learn, likewise, from it, that he inebriates them with so great delight that they cannot refrain from exclaiming, "according to the multitude of my sorrows in my heart, thy comforts have given joy to my soul." Ps. xciii. 19 v.

The storm does not last always; the darkness does not continue the whole time; the hour of adversity passes away; to the most bitter winter succeeds the most cheering spring; after the darkest night the sun rises in his greatest effulgence; after the most fearful storm comes the most reposeful and the most gentle calm. If now thou pinest away in tribulations, thou wilt not, if thou suffered from love of our Lord, suffer always; as the wicked do not always enjoy, so the good do not always suffer. A moment of consolation will come; remain with constancy at the foot of the cross; place thy confidence in our Lord, and he will pay to thee, in the most manifest manner, one of those visits which cause all tears and all sorrows to be forgotten.

SECOND POINT.

THE FIRST FRUITS OF THE TRIUMPHS OF JESUS PRESENTED TO MARY.

With the view to make his visit still more agreeable to his most holy Mother, our Lord did not appear alone to her; he was accompanied by his courtiers, the blessed spirits of heaven, and by the holy souls of Limbo who greeted him as their Redeemer. "Immediately came," says St. Vincent Ferrarius, "her adorable Son with all the holy patriarchs to his Mother."

Imagine to thyself how Mary exulted on beholding so charming an assembly,—an assembly which constituted the triumphal procession of Jesus; and also imagine to thyself the exultation of those holy souls when they were made acquainted with and honored the Mother of their Savior and their Lord! In that procession were Adam and Eve to whom, after they had sinned, was promised Mary who was to apply the remedy to the evils which their sin had caused. Assisting at that procession were the patriarchs of ancient times, Abraham, Isaac, and Jacob, who gloried in being her forefathers. Among those, too, who took part in that procession, were women renowned, as Sarah, Rebecca, Judith, Esther, who had the great honor of being her types. Present at it, also were the prophets who had pointed her out in so many forms and represented her under so many figures. In that procession were, likewise, John the Baptist, her cousin Elizabeth, and her beloved parents, Joachim and Anne; present at it, too, was her most dear spouse Joseph, who so much loved her and was in return so much loved by her. Likewise among those who made up that procession, were all the souls of the just who, for so many centuries, had been looking for the advent of the Conqueror of death, that He might break the chains which bound them and throw open the doors of their dark prison.

What transports of joy must Mary have felt on beholding so beautiful a multitude of exulting souls! What pure exultation for her most tender heart to witness the celebration of the victory of Jesus which was also her own victory! Oh, had those holy souls spoken! the soul of poor Adam! the soul of poor Eve! What could portray their feelings and affections?

Meditate a little while on the honor which Jesus wished to show his most holy Mother, and meditate also on the humility of Mary's demeanor in the very midst of those so great attentions that were being paid her.

Thank her for having done such great things, and for having suffered so much for thee, and be glad that she now enjoys her reward. Thank Jesus for having consoled her so soon, and for having consoled her with such great heavenly pomp; and if thou desirest to be a well beloved child of so exalted a mother, endeavor, like Her Son, to present to her a charming multitude of souls whom thou hast won over by thy labors and by thy zeal.

Oh, if thou wert able to say in heaven: "Look, O Lady! look at my multitude; with thy assistance I labored hard to enlist among those who honored thee, my friends, those of my household, all those whom I could gain over to thy service. Look at them now, behold them this minute—thanks to thee—here to honor thee, to praise thee, to laud thee for all eternity!"

What joy for thee, oh, what delightful honor for Mary! If thou couldst in truth so speak to her, what a cordial and affectionate reception thou mightst expect from her! Let thy yearning have for aim so splendid a triumph! To one who loves, everything is easy: she will give thee her assistance at the commencement of an undertaking which is so agreeable to her; and she will afterwards give thee the crown reserved for her special venerators.

THIRD POINT.

JESUS DISCLOSES TO MARY THE MOST SUBLIME MYSTERIES.

Before our divine Lord took his departure from his most beloved Mother, he wished to intensify her joys to the highest pitch; and, with this view, he gave her a new proof of his filial confidence, by revealing to her those heavenly mysteries which could speak to her heart. And what was so dear a Son able to reveal to so amiable a Mother on so delightful an occasion? Probably he told her that, before going up to his heavenly Father, he would remain for some time in the world in order to confirm still more his disciples in the belief of his Resurrection; probably he told her the place in which he would remain in the interval; probably, too, he told her of the frequent visits he would pay her, of the day on which he would bid farewell to this earth and ascend glorious into heaven—of the day on which he would send the Holy Ghost, and of the unspeakable fulness of his gifts which she was to receive even before the apostles were to receive them.

Doubtless, he told her at that interview of the fortune which was in store for the Church, especially in those first centuries; he told her that she would be the mistress, the directress, and the stay of the Church—and all this she was to be, by directing the apostles by her counsel, by lighting up the way for the faithful with her virtues, and by sustaining the great edifice of the Church by her prayers. If, in order that she might do all this, he desired to leave her in the world after him, who can doubt that he disclosed to her more in detail than to St. John the Evangelist, the combats, the victories, and the wants, which the nascent Church was to experience? Saint Antoninus says, that "her Son wished her to remain in the world some time after his Ascension—to remain as teacher and illuminator of the apostles."

The holy fathers tell us that our Lord revealed those and other mysteries which we cannot examine, to his most holy Mother. Yet of all the privileges that had been accorded her, the humble Virgin speaks not a word to any one; she kept all a secret locked up in her own bosom; and, as she did not will to reveal to her spouse, Joseph, the mystery of the Incarnation, until the archangel revealed it to him, so also she did not desire to relate the visit she had received from Jesus, nor the distinguishing privileges and joys which were her's on that occasion. She did not like to speak of those matters until the angels or our Lord himself related them.

Rejoice with her, and thus address her with the Church: "Queen of Heaven, rejoice; for he whom thou hast been worthy to bear, is risen as he has foretold; rejoice and exult, Virgin Mary, for the Lord is truly risen, Alleluiah!" What consolation does Mary grant thee on this day, if thou be capable of receiving it, and how many instructions does she give thee also! Pray to her to make thee share in her joys: "let thy countenance shine upon thy servant;" and also pray to her to teach thee the ways which lead to those joys: "and teach me thy justifications."

Oh, exalted Lady! I rejoice and exult in thy joys; after so many troubles and so much suffering the moment is come when thy heart exults with joy. Thou hast seen thy adorable Jesus immersed in a sea of glorious radiance; thou hast pressed him—him more beautiful than the sun—to thy maternal bosom with more than an abundance of heavenly affection; thou hast admired the glorious evidences of his victory, and thou hast shared in the jubilation of the angels and the saints who loudly greeted thee as their queen.

Ah Lady! grant me a small portion of thy delight—a portion which may give courage to my heart, which may bear me up amid the tribulations of this life, and which may be to me a pledge of that delight which, with thy assistance, I hope to enjoy at thy feet for ever in heaven. And should such be the fruit of my sufferings, let me, after thy example, go through them tranquilly, in order that, rich in merits, I may be able to repeat, one day, with yet greater joy, "Queen of Heaven, I salute thee, Alleluia!" Amen.

TWENTY-NINTH MEDITATION.

MARY, THE MOST PERFECT IMAGE OF JESUS.

FIRST POINT.

MARY, THE MOST PERFECT IMAGE OF JESUS IN POINT OF PERFECTION.

WITH a master hand did God fashion the heart of this humble Virgin, in order that it might receive into it the treasures of the Divinity. Other mothers are like animated models of their children; and for this reason, they make them like unto themselves (the mothers) in countenance and demeanor; but God, acting on a contrary principle, forms this Mother in such manner, that she participates in the qualities of her Son, and becomes his very lively image.

The perfections which are to be met with in Jesus, are to be met with, in due proportion, in Mary also. As God, Jesus possesses his perfections from nature; as a creature, Mary possesses her perfections by grace. Jesus who is goodness itself, contains in him, by his very essence, all the perfections and all the treasures of the Divinity. Mary who in like manner might be styled goodness itself, by participation unites in herself all created perfections, and all the treasures of grace which were bestowed on the rest of rational creatures. Jesus is the incarnate wisdom itself; and so abundantly did Mary participate in this perfection, that she became its seat, and the Church calls her, "Seat of wisdom!" Jesus is mercy itself; and so comprehensive and superabundant a channel of mercy is Mary, that there is no creature who experiences not its workings. One can say in her own words that she is "merciful from generation to generation."

Jesus is the wellhead of grace; but Mary is the precious receptacle which took into her heart that grace, and shut it up therein to the end that she would not keep it greedily to herself, but that she would bear it for the whole world, and make it conduce to the common good of all. "The holy Virgin begot grace itself, nay, the fountain of all grace," as says Richard of St. Victor. Jesus is Omnipotence itself; and Mary possesses almost unlimited power, since all things, even God himself, bend to her will; for whatever she can desire, "He will be very condescending, and will be disposed to hear," as St. Anselm tells us.

Sometimes it happens that the sun illumines a favored spot in such manner as to make it very like himself, so like indeed, that the original and the image can scarcely be discerned one from the other; and God does the very same with Mary, this incomparable creature. He gave her his light, his perfections, himself, in such way that he imparted to her the greatest possible resemblance to him; and this is the reason why the holy Virgin ventured to say to Saint Bridget: "who looks upon me can look upon the Divinity and the humanity as in a mirror."

Oh, how great and wonderful is Mary! Consider that the more thou art united with God, the more also wilt thou participate in those high gifts which will assimilate thee to God. How generously did she not share her gifts with her servants! Cast a glance at Moses in the old law, and at Xavier in the new; and who can throw into words the treasures of goodness, of wisdom, of power, that were granted to those personages? God is wonderful in his saints; and he never allows himself to be outdone by them in generosity. If on earth thou shouldst not attain, through unmerited gifts, to similitude with God, thou shalt, through the gifts of glory, reach that similitude in heaven where "we shall be like unto him." In heaven thou shalt be very like unto thy Lord: yea, thou shalt be all the more beautiful an image of him, the more close thy imitation of him.

SECOND POINT.

MARY, THE MOST FAITHFUL IMAGE OF JESUS AS REGARDS THE VIRTUES.

The similarity between Jesus and Mary appeared still more striking in the virtues which she possessed and practised. Humility of heart! behold the expression of the disposition and of the demeanor of Jesus: "learn of me, for I am meek and humble of heart." Charity also was the expression of his disposition and demeanor: "When he loved his own who were in the world he loved them unto the end." An expression also of his disposition and demeanor was his readiness to offer himself in sacrifice, a readiness which actuated him to such an extent that he died on the cross for us; "in the head of the book it is written of me that I do thy will."

These three virtues—humility, charity, and self-sacrifice,—made up the sum of our Redeemer's life; redolent of them are all his words and actions from the cave of Bethlehem to Mount Calvary.

What else is Mary's life? Contemplate her from the beginning to the end of her course, and thou wilt discover that the disposition, the desires, and the affections of her most sweet heart are quite like those of the heart of Jesus; in all her actions thou wilt discover an unexampled humility, a love which, after that felt by her divine Son, had not its like on earth, and a spirit of self-sacrifice which is proof against every trial, and crowns her as the Queen of all Martyrs. Says the apostle: "But he who adheres to the Lord is one spirit." 1 Cor. vi. 17 v.

As no creature was so intimately united with Jesus as was his most holy mother, so in like manner, there was never a creature who so much resembled him in all things. Accordingly, one and the same spirit animated those most holy hearts; one and the same fire inflamed them; they led and enjoyed one and the same life. The Son mentions humility as the distinguishing characteristic of his disposition, and the Mother ascribes to humility the high degree of her elevation. The Son comes into the world from pure love, and lives and dies out of pure love; the Mother devotes her Son to death from pure love, although he was the life of her life. The Son expires on the cross, and the Mother suffers mortal anguish at the foot of the cross.

This perfect resemblance between the original and the copy, thou shalt be always able easily to discover in regard to all the other virtues; for Mary is in them all the most beautiful likeness of her Son. "She was humble, he was humble; she gentle, he gentle; she gracious, he gracious; she most poor, he the most poor; she most prudent, he the most prudent; she most mild, he the most mild; she temperate and abstemious, he the most temperate and abstemious. To be brief, the Mother was nothing else than a photograph of the Son; the Son was nothing else than a perfect prototype of the Mother." St. Thomas of Villanova.

Enter in spirit into the most holy hearts of Jesus and Mary, in order that in them thou mayst examine and appropriate to thyself the dispositions and affections which should reign in thy heart. Their disposition and mind were nothing else than humility, love for their neighbors, and love of sufferings; and, in the exercise of these virtues, they spent their whole lives. How canst thou doubt that they desire to see those same dispositions in all hearts? that they love, with a love of special predilection, those souls who like them are humble, charitable, patient?

If thou wilt be agreeable to Jesus and Mary, study to be of the number of those souls: occasions cannot fail thee of practising those virtues. What day, indeed, is there that does not offer thee opportunity of exercising one or another of those virtues? Love them as being the choice virtues of Jesus and Mary; choose those virtues with the view to give joy to Jesus and Mary, and doubt not that thy heart, hitherto so miserable, will become a sanctuary in which they will find their delight.

THIRD POINT.

MARY MOST LIKE TO JESUS IN HER TITLES OF HONOR.

In such manner does she avow the resemblance of Mary with Jesus, that the holy Church hesitates not to apply to her titles and honorable names which are exactly suited to express the perfections of her divine Son. Thus, for example, Jesus is called our King, our Teacher, our Lord; and Mary is styled our Queen, our Mistress, and our Lady. Jesus is our advocate: "We have an advocate with the Father, Jesus Christ the Just;" and Mary, too, is our advocate, "happily our intercessor." Jesus is the way that leads to heaven: "I am the way;" Mary is the blessed gate by which we enter: "Blessed Gate of Heaven." Jesus is the author of grace: "for the grace of God our Savior has appeared;" Mary is the mother of grace: "Mother of divine grace!" Jesus is our ambassador, and Mary the most faithful ambassadress of our salvation. Jesus is our hope, our consolation, our refuge, our life; and Mary is termed our life, our refuge, our hope. "Jesus is the light which enlighteneth every man that cometh into this world;" Mary is the star which, by its brilliancy, points out the secure path through the darkness of this world. By reason of the beneficial influence which he exercises on salvation and life, Jesus is likened to the sun; Mary is likened to the moon on account of the constant favors which she bestows on the earth.

To say all in one word, Jesus is our Father, Mary our Mother. In how many ways does that conformity of thoughts and affections which obtained between them, appear even from Mary's titles of honor ;—a conformity which warrants the custom of ascribing to the Mother that which is wholly and peculiarly the Son's. Jesus is always found in Mary, as is the flower on the plant that brought it forth ; and he is never found elsewhere than in Mary, never found otherwise than through Mary: "Christ can be found only in Mary or through Mary." St. Bonaventure.

Now say to thyself: "Mary participates in the perfections of her divine Son: she is animated, as much as a mere creature can be animated, with the same spirit that he has ; she possesses the same virtues, the same dispositions, the same temperament and the same titles of honor that he possesses." Now can there well be greater resemblance than this? Admire the multitude of her dignities, and use thy best efforts to earn for thyself the glorious title of Son of Mary. O if thou couldst in truth say to God: "I am thy mother's son!" But to be such a son, it is necessary for thee to resemble her, as children in the natural order resemble their mothers. We must reproduce in ourselves her self-discipline, her dispositions, her manners ; in short, we must pattern after her.

If Mary cast her eye on thee, could she recognize in thee her self-discipline? Could she indentify thee as a child of hers? Could she discover in thee, at least, some trace of resemblance with herself? Bear in mind that the more perfect is the likeness between parent and child, the more perfect is also the quality of being a child: "the greater the likeness, the nearer the approach to the condition of childhood." St. Thomas.

O Mary! thou wast clothed with the divine sun in such manner that he made thee a most charming picture of himself. With what glowing brilliancy art thou adorned, with how many treasures art thou enriched! Thy heart is the nearest to the heart of Jesus, the most closely united with it, and bears to it the greatest resemblance. I render praise and thanks to that God who deigned out of thee to form his most beautiful image; and at the same time I turn to thee with confidence in order to touch thee with compassion for me. Ah Mother! look down on the poverty of my heart. Obtain for me that spirit of humility, of love, of patience, which is so pleasing to thee and with which thou wast so richly endowed! Also give me a share in thy treasures: then will my heart be not so unlike thine; then will my heart be less hateful, and less unworthy of thy affectionate smiles! Amen.

THIRTIETH MEDITATION.

MARY, A MODEL EASILY TO BE IMITATED.

FIRST POINT.

MARY, IMITABLE IN THE FULFILMENT OF THE DUTIES OF HER STATE.

NOTWITHSTANDING how much the most holy Virgin was privileged and exalted by God, yet her life, exteriorly considered, had in it nothing extraordinary. In her then, there was no peculiarity, no difference which rendered her remarkable beyond other women. She had no distinguishing badge that would have fixed on her the eyes of men; the occupations which are suitable to a wife and mother are the business of Mary. All her thoughts are directed to the domestic economy which she desires to practise in relation to her little family; she administered to the wants of Joseph and Jesus with a love which can be more easily imagined than described; her blessed hands prepared for them their garments and their food with all diligence; she thinks upon the cleanliness and neatness of her house; cheerfully does she perform those humble and low offices which fall to the lot of only a woman of a poor family; she did all the housework which must have been considerable. She prepared the meals for her spouse and for her son, and did them all kinds of useful offices, for she had no servant. St. Bonaventure.

An enemy to that commodious and lazy love which constitutes the darling occupation of so many rich ladies, Mary was ever as was her holy consort, assiduous at manual labor, and was not afraid of any trouble. During the sojourn in Egypt she must have experienced all the discomfort common to poor refugees in a strange land. How many privations must she have endured? How many wants?. Accordingly, thou wouldst have seen her bent on one thing only, that is, to procure for herself by labor the necessary sustenance of life, and to sweeten his sojourn for Joseph by her affectionate attentions. Thou wouldst have seen her always calm and serene, and praising God for every thing that fell out; for she so ministered to the wants of her Son and of Joseph her husband, that she did not desist from the constant contemplation of heavenly things. St. Thomas of Villanova.

As regards what appertained to her own person, she never distinguished herself from the rest of women. Her whole bearing, says St. Cyprian, was completely that of the poor of her time; with the poor, however, she had but very little intercourse, for the reason that she loved solitude and retirement; but if duty, charity or decency, required her to mingle with others, then was her intercourse with all, of a becoming and edifying character. Of herself and of her gifts she never spoke; with great solicitude she kept everything secret that concerned herself; and yet she never once failed to fulfil towards her neighbors all the duties which charity or politeness prescribed. In one word, the faithful discharge of the duties of her state in life, constituted the one and the only constant occupation of the exalted Mother of God.

Oh, what a lesson for those who consider it beneath their dignity to see personally to the management of their domestic concerns! Who indeed is greater than the Mother of God? And who is more busied than she with house concerns, and who is more faithful than she in attention to them. The holy Ghost gives great praise to women of fortitude: "Who shall find a valiant woman? far, and from the uttermost coast is the price of her." Prov. xxxi. 10 v. But what then did she do that was brilliant, and had in it aught of eclat? Nothing else, replies St. Ambrose, than—that she with all diligence performed the duties of her state—that she superintended the business of her house—that she reared up her Child—that she gave orders to her servants—that the remainder of the time she devoted to manual labor: "Her manual works possessed all the artistic excellence that her hands were able to impart to them."

Flatter not thyself that thou canst be pleasing to God unless thou faithfully discharge all thy obligations. O how many esteem not those obligations as they ought to be esteemed! Cheerfully do some occupy themselves with works of piety, but not with the works which God desires of them; and in order to satisfy their piety which is often nothing else than their own opinionativeness, they exempt themselves from their real duties—duties for whose performance they will have one day to render to God a most strict account. Mayst thou never belong to the number of those who so deplorably deceive themselves!

SECOND POINT.

MARY, IMITABLE IN HER RELIGIOUS EXERCISES.

As in the Virgin there was with regard to her duties as wife and Mother nothing extraordinary to be seen, so in like manner, nothing singular was to be remarked of her as far as related to her religious exercises. In fact, what is there in her manner of life to indicate her to be the mother of God? All the requirements of the law she observes as other women observed them; like them she goes to the temple; she obeys to the letter the commandment which ordains the circumcision of the male children, also the commandment which ordains the presentation and purification, although she was not bound to observe any one of these commandments. She conscientiously practises every ordinance, conforms to every ceremony and to every usage relating to the worship of God. In his honor she offers the gifts presented by the poor; and in all other things, she passes unremarked by her neighbors, and as a simple inhabitant residing in a poor locality. Mary's life was already a continuous contemplation, as says Richard of St. Victor; she had, however, her stated times for prayer as had all the women of Israel. Her manual labor, of whatever kind it was, served her as an occasion to raise her thoughts to God; and with the most holy affections she consecrated it to the honor of God, and thus did she then practise what the apostle afterwards enjoins in these words: "Therefore whether you eat or drink, or whatever else you do, do all for the glory of God." 1 Cor. x. 31 v. Mary accompanied and followed him as did the other women, when her divine Son commenced his mission of preaching: "And it came to pass afterwards that he travelled through all the cities and towns, preaching and publishing the Gospel of the Kingdom of God." Luke. viii. 1, 2, v.

St. Thomas of Villanova observes that among those pious women, Mary was the first, the most assiduous and the most faithful in hearing the divine word preached. Blessed was she in that she had heard the divine word, but still more blessed in that she had treasured it up in her heart: "Yea, rather blessed are they who hear the word of God and keep it." After the ascension of her Jesus, she observed all that was commanded by the apostles; although she was their mother and their instructress, she yet shone before all with the example of most faithful obedience. We never read of her that she desired to perform miracles, although certainly her claim and power to perform them were superior to the claim and power of all others. We never read that she desired to preach to the faithful, or to publicly assume the office of superioress or teacher: her place was to be the last of all, and never did she by sign or word give them to understand what great, what unspeakable treasures she carried concealed in her inmost soul.

What, therefore, is there in her which can not be imitated by every Christian soul? In this respect, Mary's life presents us with nothing else than fidelity and perseverance in fulfilment of the duties appertaining to the worship of God. Who is there that, likewise, can not be faithful and persevering in obeying the commandments of the Church, also in performing those other works of devotions which so much strengthen the soul in all the necessities of life? Examine thyself: and see if in regard to the past thou canst say that thou hast imitated Mary? See whether thou hast been sufficiently punctual in obeying the commands of the Church, whether thou wast constant in thy exercises of piety, in meditation, in prayer, in examination of conscience, in spiritual reading, in public reception of the holy sacraments, in devotion to our Lady, in very zealous preparation for her festivals, in worshipping God by performing those so called works of supererogation,—works however which are so useful to thee.

Shouldst thou come to know that thou wast not faithful and constant, then pray to the Lord for pardon; promise him that thou wilt resume thy former fervor, and that thou wilt thereby imitate his most holy Mother. Thou canst render her no more welcome service, and none more profitable to thyself, than that which thou renderest her in thy imitation of her.

THIRD POINT.

MARY, IMITABLE IN THE COURSE WHICH SHE FOLLOWED IN RELATION TO THE VARIOUS EVENTS OF HER LIFE.

Not mere tribulations, and not mere joys, constitute the life of the just upon earth,—that life is a compound of both. "The merciful God," says St. John Chrysostom, "infuses sweetness into the bitterness." The merciful God blends joys also with the tribulations; lest he might depress his servants too much, he does not send them afflictions unmixed with consolations. He does not send them consolations unmixed with afflictions, lest if he did so, they would cleave too much to the world.

This is the usual course that Providence pursues, and he departed not from it even in the case of our blessed Lady. Certainly he thus acts towards all the saints, by giving them neither uninterrupted afflictions nor unintermitted consolations. And, in point of fact, Mary had after her marriage with Joseph the joy to visit Elizabeth, to bear to her the choicest benedictions, and to fill that house with purest delight; but soon after tasting of that joy, Mary was penetrated with the most profound grief, arising from the anguish which her chaste husband suffered when he perceived her blessed and mysterious situation. She was inebriated with delight at the birth of the Word made Flesh; but soon was this delight embittered by reason of the place in which she was constrained to bring him into the world. She was consoled at the adoration of him by the wise men; but soon, however, did Simeon's prophecy so afflict her that a sword pierced her soul. Tribulation followed hard upon tribulation; and in order to evade the snares of Herod, who sought the life of Jesus, she is instantly compelled to abandon in the night time her peaceful place of refuge, and to flee into Egypt. In the course of two years thereafter, she received a command to return to her own country; but the joy her return occasioned her was marred by the fear that Archelaus also, Herod's successor, might seek the life of the holy Infant. For some years she peacefully enjoys in Nazareth the society of her dear Jesus; but on coming back out of Jerusalem she misses him, and then spends three full days immersed in anguish. She felt great consolation when Jesus entered upon his career of preaching; yet just as great was the uneasiness caused her by the persecutions recurred to by the Pharisees and the doctors of the law,—persecutions which culminated in making of him the Man of Sorrows, and of her the Queen of Martyrs. To these her sufferings, succeeded her joy occasioned by the resurrection; and thus her whole life was spent amid ever shifting scenes, till she was taken up into heaven where, in God's own bosom, she will for all eternity blissfully enjoy the reward of her fidelity and love.

Behold here the life of the Queen of all saints; a network of sufferings and joys, and indeed of more sufferings than joys. Be not therefore astonished if thou passest through a path strewn with thorns; and if also thou shouldst undeservedly meet with sorrows and anxieties, and at intervals with a gleam of consolation likewise. This is the road which the First-born of all the elect as well as his holy Mother singled out. And this must be also thy road if thou desirest to be a sheep in the keeping of the heavenly Shepherd. Take courage, look for consolation in those tribulations, and expect tribulations blended with thy consolations; but in consolations and tribulations constantly remain firm in thy faith, and in the way of the Lord. Say with Job, "Till I die I will not depart from my innocence" (Job, xxvii. 5 v.); and in this way shalt thou imitate Mary, and attain to that blessed Kingdom where shall be nothing else than unmixed consolations and eternal joys.

O most holy Virgin! even if I cannot imitate thee in the high perfection of thy virtues, let me imitate thee in the things at least that are easier and are necessary to my salvation. Assist me, O Lady! to the end that by the faithful fulfilment of my duties, I may one day hear from the mouth of thy divine Son, those ravishing words: "Well done! thou good and faithful servant: enter into the joys of thy Lord." Let me be exact and persevering in performing those exercises of piety which are, as it were, the panoply which shields my soul from her enemies. Let me not repine at the divine dispensation, and obtain for me, in adversity and prosperity, that peace and calm of mind, of both of which thou wast a perfect model. If thou givest, O Mary! to most pure and loving hearts such precious gifts, refuse not those gifts to thy servant who is anxious here below to love thee without measure, and who hopes to love thee eternally in heaven. Amen.

THIRTY-FIRST MEDITATION.

MARY'S LIFE AFTER THE ASCENSION OF JESUS.

FIRST POINT.

MARY—THE STRENGTH OF THE FIRST BELIEVERS.

SCARCELY had Jesus expired on the cross when his Blessed Mother girds herself for the task of performing towards the faithful the duties of a most tender mother.

O how much assistance and consolation she rendered to them! In the beginning, she strengthened them by her powerful prayers, by entreating God to convert the sinners and to confirm the good; and it is very credible that the thousands of men who were converted on the occasion of the first sermons of Saint Peter, and that even the conversion of Saul, were the fruit of the yearnings of this loving dove. She strengthened the faithful by the good example of her life, which example was to them a most powerful incentive to embrace the faith, and to walk in the path of virtue. Her look alone disposed to sanctity, and raised the mind more powerfully to heavenly things than discourse and exhortation. She strengthened the faithful, furthermore, by her words, by her counsels, by her more than motherly solicitude. The faithful came in crowds to her from all quarters, and came to her with that filial confidence with which children rush to their mothers' bosom.

St. Thomas of Villanovas ays that "the concourse of the faithful to her was so great from all quarters that all the roads which led to her dwelling were crowded." Every one was anxious to see her, to speak to her, to be consoled and strengthened by her, and she received each one affectionately: she consoled those of them who were afflicted: she gave strength to the wavering, council to those who were in doubt: she confirmed the weak, directed all by her prudence, and inspired them with courage by her affection.

"For these reasons did our Blessed Lord wish her to remain on earth after his ascension into heaven: Christ left the Virgin behind him in order that she might be a mother to the Apostles and the faithful, that she might collect together such as had fallen away, that she might console the afflicted, confirm the wavering, counsel those who were in doubts and difficulties, that she might in all things direct the faithful and instruct them and animate them." Cornelius A. Lapidé. With much greater right than the apostle Paul, could she say that she felt in her heart the afflictions and necessities of all, and that she was all love for each and every one: "Who is weak, and I am not weak? Who is scandalized, and I do not burn?" 2 Cor. xi. 29 v.

Let us look upon our altars at a beautiful and devout image of Mary; let us cast ourselves upon our knees and entreat her with confidence, and we have already done enough to experience in our hearts a heavenly balm, and to go away consoled no matter how bitter our grievances. What then must it have been to see her when she was yet living, to speak to her, and to listen to her words of charity, and to her accents of consolation? Consider also to thy great comfort that thou hadst no occasion to envy those who enjoyed so great a happiness. And why so? Because now that for thy sake she is in heaven, she is for thee that, and more than that, which she would have been for thee on earth. She looks out from heaven upon thee, she hears thy prayers, she approves thy sighs, she compassionates thee and helps thee even as lovingly and with just as much motherly solicitude: "Blessed are they that see not, and yet believe."

Adopt the beautiful habit peculiar to so many holy souls, of often visiting her on her altars and in her images:—there pour out thy whole heart before her; there disclose to her thy fears, thy necessities; say to her with confidence whatever thou couldst say to her if thou saw her in her own proper personality: and doubt not, that by so doing, thou wouldst always go away from her bearing with thee her consolation in thy bosom.

SECOND POINT.

MARY—THE MISTRESS OF THE APOSTLES.

In the Virgin the apostles had a most excellent guide, as well in reference to their spiritual advancement as in regard to the general good of the faithful: "After the Ascension of her son she was the mistress of the apostles as well as of all those who preached the gospel; and as to what concerned their own welfare, she collected them together after the apprehension of Jesus had dispersed them and put them to flight. She sustained and strengthened Peter, and exhorted him to confidence and to the sweet hope of pardon, for he was much dispirited at having denied his divine Lord. She inspired with calm and confidence the hearts of the other disciples, who also had wandered away from the path of duty and were now blushing for their infidelity: and all these she strengthened in the faith of the approaching resurrection: "And she confirmed in the faith of the resurrection of Christ which was now near at hand, all those whose faith was shaken by the death of Christ." Cornelius A. Lapidé.

As the wrath of the Jews at the time of the persecution, exhausted all its power for the purpose of annihilating the Church at her very origin, by casting the apostles and the disciples into prison, then Mary sustained and exhorted them, and gave them by her exhortation as well as by her example such lessons as enabled them to triumph over the persecution: "She instructed the apostles both by word and example in the manner to overcome those persecutions." In one word, she educated them in the ways of the Lord and served as their counsellor in all their doubts, and their consoler in all their bitter trials. In addition to all this, Mary taught the apostles regarding the heavenly mysteries which, because she was more enlightened than they, she knew more clearly and penetrated more thoroughly than did they all together. "Much," says St. Anselm, "was revealed to them by the Virgin: she revealed to them whatever she knew of the mysteries of Christ not only through simple knowledge, but also whatever she knew from facts and her own experience." St. Ambrose adds also; "If Saint John spoke more sublimely than the others, and soared higher than they did, the reason is, his intercourse was longer and more familiar than theirs with Mary who was the depository and the guardian of the heavenly mysteries, since he had at his service the inner sanctuary of the heavenly mysteries."

If Mary on several occasions deigned to communicate from heaven to so many souls who entreated her to do so, the treasures of heavenly wisdom, how lovingly must she have rendered this service to the saints first whom her Jesus recommended to her in a particular manner? Oh how many lights, how many sublime degrees of knowledge must she have obtained from this fountain of wisdom and of love! Dost thou, in this dark valley of the world, stand in need of heavenly light as well for the perservation of thy own soul, as for the direction of the souls confided to thy charge? Commit thyself to Mary as her disciple; pray to her to deign to be a mistress to thee, and thou wilt in one moment learn more from her instruction than thou canst learn for a long time in all the schools of this world. Pray her to grant thee so charming a grace as that of becoming thy mistress—a grace, too, which she has already accorded to so very many of her clients. Oh, to how many did she herself impart instructions on the wisdom of the saints! How often did she deign to come down from heaven with that intention!

Ask her to direct thy footsteps! Say to her, "make my paths straight!" She will enlighten thee, counsel thee, guide and direct thee, in all things. Oh! what great benefit wilt thou derive from her school!

THIRD POINT.

MARY—THE SUPPORT OF THE CHURCH.

When from the cross Jesus delivered the Church as a daughter to Mary, he had the design to give it a Mother who should take his own place, and should serve it as a pillar: "He spoke to the woman," says A. Lapidé, already quoted, "O mother! be henceforward a resolute and courageous woman, that thou mayst in my stead be to the Church a pillar and a foundation stone. Support it by thy strength and by thy constancy, by thy counsels and by thy prayers; dissipate and remove from it clouds and storms. Be its support by thy strength; calm all the storms of temptations, and banish them by thy constancy, by thy counsel, and by thy prayers."

Oh, how Mary executed those offices of love! In her heart she embraced the whole of Christendom; and she protected, supported, and defended it, by rendering it assistance of every kind. In accordance with the divine inspiration she had received, she went from Nazareth to the mountains of Judea to visit St. Elizabeth; and acting on divine inspiration, she undertook yet other journeys. She went to Ephesus; travelled, as some relate, to Antioch; and must have probably gone into other countries likewise, in order more and more to consolidate the edifice of her dear Son. Who can indeed describe her solicitude for the propagation of the Gospel, for the conversion of the pagans, for the increase and well-being of the Church? She was all eye to descry its necessities, all hand to relieve them.

St. Thomas of Villanova says: "By her instruction she gave solidity and assistance to the Church." And St. Cyril goes so far as to say that it is through her that the faithful obtained the grace of baptism: "Through thee, unbelieving men attain to the grace of holy Baptism." Through her were the various churches established in the different parts of the world: "and churches were built over the whole world." For all these things was Mary solicitous; but she took great care not to be seen in them, and not to assume the tone of mistress, and acted throughout with consummate prudence and discretion. Her exceeding great love of retirement and prayer would not have suffered her to abandon for a single moment the solitude of her cell, had not the welfare of her neighbor required her to do so; and thus in going out into the world she sacrificed her own inclinations, and said by her actions to the Lord: "If I am necessary to thy people, I do not refuse to encounter difficult labors."

A beautiful instruction which exhorts thee to renounce repose and the tranquillity of thy mind, in order to take account of thy neighbors' wants, and to discharge towards him the duties of charity. Oh, how well did she understand how to always unite those virtues with the most indefatigable zeal and the most active love! If thou hast distinguishing gifts or fillest elevated positions, learn of the most blessed Virgin how to use them. Mayst thou be not of the number of those busy people who make more show than they do good; mayst thou learn how to be solicitous for the salvation of the souls of others, without however forgetting that of thy own soul; mayst thou understand how to make the most active zeal go hand in hand with the love of recollection! Instruct, preach, direct, reprove, enlighten, and console all; but do these things with that humility and discretion which are the most charming characteristics of the servants of Jesus Christ, and of the children of Mary.

O my sweetest Lady! Were thou yet living on earth, I would by all means go to thee and cast myself at thy feet, in order to lay before thee my necessities and to entreat thee to give me strength; and then thy good heart could not withstand the ardor of my desires, but would rather grant me all the graces I had requested of thee. Ah, why dost thou not give them to me now? I see thee not, but thou seest me; thy voice I do not hear, but thou hearest mine; thou penetratest with a glance the inmost recesses of my heart and knowest all its wants. Console me accordingly, O Lady! for I confide in thee as if I were personally in thy presence. Give me light, give me energy, give me strength, give me grace, give me courage, give me all good because I have need of all. Ah! suffer not that I go away from thee without being consoled by thee! O my sweetest hope! O my sweetest love! Amen.

THIRTY-SECOND MEDITATION.

MARY'S MOST BLESSED DEPARTURE.

FIRST POINT.

MARY'S MOST ARDENT LONGING FOR DEATH.

MARY also was subject to the universal law of death. Her son died, hence she also must imitate him by dying. But while natural horror is excited in all by death, death creates in her an ardent longing; for Mary looked upon it as the means of breaking those bonds which held her as in chains in this valley of tears, and also as the means of leading her to her God, in order that she might contemplate him in his infinite beauty, face to face.

If, with the view that he might enjoy his God in heaven, the apostle Paul yearned after death, represent to thyself how much more ardently must Mary have yearned thereafter. Oh my Lord and my God! must she have often repeated, free my soul from the prison of this body, that I may be the better able to celebrate the praises of thy holy name: "Lead forth my soul out of this prison, that I may praise thy name;" thy just ones await me that thou mayst give me the crown of glory which thou hast promised me: "The just are waiting for me, that thou mayst reward me." The frequent visits of angels, yea, even those of Jesus, no longer sufficed to extinguish her yearning; those visits on the contrary rather intensified it: "When shall I come and appear before the countenance of God?"

The port is the sign of victory and triumph to the shipwrecked mariner; the flag of surrender hoisted by the enemy, is the sign of victory and triumph to the warrior fatigued and worn out by his long campaign; and death was to Mary her sign of victory and triumph. The longer death delayed coming, the more did Mary suffer, because "hope deferred maketh the heart sick."

Who loves warmly, cannot long endure to be at a great distance from the person beloved, and finds neither rest nor peace till he comes back to his beloved. Mary loved indeed with perfect resignation to the will of God; but this resignation in no wise lessened the combat of her inflamed heart. "How terribly was she tortured by love! with what longing did she burn, with what intense ardor did she glow to be with him whom she had seen with her own eyes as he penetrated the heavens in his triumphal chariot, and in whom, as she well knew, so much glory and so much joy were prepared for her." St. Thomas of Villanova.

Sophronimus says: "Her exceedingly great desire to enjoy God in heaven, and her most complete willingness not to enjoy him till it would be pleasing to him to call her, worked out for Mary's heart the merit of martyrdom of love and sorrow."

Happy those souls who suffer and pine away from their longing to be united with God! Hast thou so precious a desire? Oh! didst thou love the Lord in truth, this disposition would of its own accord spring up in thy heart, and in the liveliest manner possible. Perhaps thou hast more than once sighed for death; but why so? It may be from impatience, and in order not to be obliged to bear the cross any longer, and in order to be soon delivered from thy sufferings? O how quite different from Mary's desires are thine!

Purify thy affections; raise thy heart heavenward; let God alone be the object of all our love, the end of all our aspirations. Entreat the holy Virgin to accord to thee a spark of that fire which burned in her bosom, and then be resigned to remain on this earth, as long as it shall please God to have thee remain; be resigned to carry that cross which he wills thee to carry, and to accomplish his divine will in all things. Oh, how agreeable to the Virgin will be so admirable a surrender of thyself!

SECOND POINT.

MARY'S ZEALOUS PREPARATION FOR DEATH.

When Mary was drawing near the term of her pilgrimage, God gave her that special mark of his predilection which he afterwards showed to so many of his beloved. He informed her of the very near approach of her passage to another life. Some saints affirm that he sent the archangel Gabriel to make to her the announcement.

O with what dispositions will he have acquitted himself of this duty! With what great joy will he have invited to enter into eternal joys that Virgin to whom he had on a former occasion announced the incarnation of the divine Word. "Hail full of grace,"—such was probably the manner in which he saluted her again; "O full of grace! thy prayers are heard, thy wishes are accomplished. I come to tell thee that the hour has struck, when thy Jesus desires to have thee in heaven with him, in order that thou mayst enjoy the reward that thou hast so well merited, and by thy presence satisfy the desire of the blessed spirits of heaven who are longingly waiting for thee! Thy prayer is granted; thy yearning is satisfied: according as thou hast desired, thou shalt reach the glorious end; according as thou hast merited, thou shalt receive the crown of heavenly glory!"

What reply will Mary have given on hearing news which she so ardently desired? With what dispositions of renewed zeal and renewed gratitude will she have accepted so charming a piece of intelligence! O how highly did she rejoice on listening to this information! How her spirit exulted in God her Savior? Certainly, Mary did not stand in need of preparing herself for death; her affections tended incessantly heavenward; her heart constantly burned with the most cordial love for God: "Stay me up with flowers; compass me about with apples, because I languish with love" (Cant. ii. 5 v.); as if she would say to her soul: the force of love consumes me; therefore, O my spirit, thou, O my heart! bring forth new fruits of virtues, bring forth new fruits of dispositions and of holy works, in order to help my weakness, and to prepare me more and more for my passage out of this world.

O who can ever imagine the sweet colloquies she held with him, or imagine her glowing desires, to unite herself soon with her God? If, as their end approaches, holy souls prepare themselves for it by ceasing to think, to speak, or to hear of, any thing about earthly matters, because their heart entirely reposes in God, what then will Mary have done?—Mary, the Queen of all the saints. Contemplate a little this most amiable Mother when her death was drawing near; strengthen thy mind by means of this contemplation, and endeavor to imitate her with great industry.

God announced to thee also thy death. He did so in the words, "But the day of the Lord shall come as a thief" (2 Peter. iii. 10 v.), at a time which thou wilt not believe, and when, perhaps more than at any other time, thou wilt be wholly engrossed with worldly pursuits, and wilt imagine that thou hast just attained to the zenith of thy good fortune;—then will the Son of Man, then will the "day of the Lord" come.

Think, therefore, on this time; be well on thy guard that thou mayst not be deceived; and hence, from this moment, hold thyself in readiness to make that all important journey; sever thy heart from all creatures; cleanse thy soul from every sin; strengthen and enrich it with good works, with penance and with prayer. If thou actest in this manner, salvation is thine; and thou shalt imitate in a certain manner the Virgin in her preparation, and by this means thou shalt die the death of the just,—a precious, a holy death: "Precious in the sight of the Lord is the death of his saints."

THIRD POINT.

MARY'S JUBILATION AT HER EXIT.

Imagine to thyself that thou seest the most holy Virgin stretched on her lowly little bed, and ready in an instant to yield up her spirit, and to unite herself for evermore with her adorable Son.

Oh, what a heavenly look was hers! her countenance on which dwelt benevolence and serenity, her eyes turned towards heaven, herself all transported with love. She anxiously awaits the moment when her bonds shall be loosed; she has no sickness that preys upon her, no pain that racks her; love, and indeed love the most strong and the most sublime, steadily deprives her of the force of life. She perceives this, and with the sweetest feeling of joy and exultation repeats: "I rejoiced in the things that were said to me; let us go into the house of the Lord."

Surrounding her stand the holy apostles, who had gone thither by divine inspiration; they contemplate her, and with that affection with which loving sons assist at the death of the most tender of all mothers, they weep at her departure and recommend themselves entirely to her prayers. Mary looks upon them with calmness and serenity; she encourages them, and consoles them; she imparts to them salutary instruction; and, like unto her Son, she blesses them and assures them that from heaven above she will never abandon them, but rather that there, too, she will ever remain their loving mother and most solicitous intercessor: "At the command of her Son the apostles were assembled around her, and they had come for that purpose to the city of Jerusalem from the most distant parts of the world." St. John of Damascus.

But while they were thus assembled, behold there enters Jesus to inebriate Mary's soul with heavenly consolation. He remembered, say the holy fathers, how in his agony Mary with invincible constancy was present with him; and grateful for the services of maternal love which she rendered him, he now comes to reward her for them, and to conduct her blessed soul to heaven. O what a heavenly spectacle! Mary is wholly and solely intent on quitting the earth; with the affectionate confidence of a son, Jesus invites her to come to his kingdom; multitudes of angels and of saints stand by, ready to accompany her soul thither. Mary had no longer control of herself; she raised her eyes to heaven, and falling into an extremely delightful ecstasy of love she departed! "Her eyes turned heavenward, without fever, without pain, without uneasiness, without sickness; yea, with boundless joy and jubilation, she resigned to her son her most blessed spirit." St. Thomas of Villanova.

O that most precious death, O that death worthy the mother of God! Happy those souls to whom it is granted to die in that manner! What a beautiful death after a life spent in the service and love of God! If our conscience has nothing with which to reproach us, if on looking back at the past we see our life has been pure, and cleansed from every stain, how charming in such case, will be our departure also!

With what dispositions wilt thou meet death!

With joy or with sorrow? This depends on thyself. If thy life be Christian and holy, Christian and holy will be thy death also; and if thou dost not accept it with joy, thou wilt still receive it with that serenity and peace of conscience which are distinguishing characteristics of the death of all those of whom it is written: "Blessed are the dead who die in the Lord."

I also, O Mary! shall be obliged to take that unavoidable and terrible step; how then shall I begin to prepare? How shall I meet death? Ah, my Lady! I have so great confidence in thee that I doubt not that, under thy protection, my death will be the death of the just. Of what service to me would all thy graces be, unless thou granted me this grace which is the crown of all the others? Assist me now that I may begin immediately to prepare myself with zeal for a blessed death; and when the decisive moment arrives, then put to flight all my enemies by thy blessed presence! "Preserve us from the enemy!" Sweeten my sufferings, lighten my cares, take my soul itself under thy protection, and bring it to eternal rest. O Mary! thou art so loving that there is no grace however great which any one, who has confidence in thee, cannot promise himself that he will obtain. Amen.

THIRTY-THIRD MEDITATION.

THE CAUSES WHICH MADE MARY'S DEPARTURE SUPREMELY BLESSED.

FIRST POINT.

MARY'S DETACHMENT FROM EVERYTHING EARTHLY.

AFTER sin, nothing makes death so bitter and so terrible, as does attachment to the things of this earth. O what violent reluctance so many experience, when at that hour they feel themselves constrained to tear themselves away from the world! But he who is detached from everything by no means feels this repugnance, because no one needs to offer himself violence when it becomes necessary for him to abandon that which he does not love.

Who was more detached than Mary? As Noah's dove flew over the waters without setting foot on the slime, so Mary never fixed the affections of her most pure heart on any creature. Mary had an extremely tender and deeply feeling heart; she loved with that pure and well ordered disposition which emanates from God and has its end in God. Mary indeed made use of all things that are necessary for the maintenance of life, —for the refreshment of the body, for the recreation of the mind—she used them, however, as means to an end, without in the slightest degree fixing her affections on them; nay, she used them even as steps to raise her heart more and more to the Creator.

Most holy Virgin! let me likewise love my neighbor in such way; and let me also use creatures in this manner.

Who loves in this wise, that is in God and for God, always has a heart free and disengaged from disorderly affections; who uses earthly goods according to this rule, will never be ruled over or ensnared by them. The blessed Virgin was always disposed to follow this rule in her use of creatures; she was exempt from every undue attachment how slight soever; she was alike prepared to live and to die, whichever might be pleasing to God. She awaited but the intimation of her Lord; God was the end she aimed at in her thoughts and aspirations; she looked only upon God, as her end, her centre, her all: "Thou, O Lord! art my protector, my honor, and thou raisest up my heart."

Ah, would that I also, O Lord! could end my days in like manner. "May my soul die the death of the just!" Dost thou desire so beautiful a lot? Struggle to cut away heroically all those ties which bind thee to the things of this earth; leave the earth to him who yearns after it, but set thou thy heart on Heaven. Live as a traveller and a pilgrim who journeys to his home, for in the end thou art at best nothing else: "man passes away as a shadow."

Our life is as a journey, and happy he who ends it without allowing himself to be blinded by the objects which he meets on the way. If thou hast been hitherto one of those poor deceived persons who, on crossing the street, forget the object for which they had set out, then open thy eyes whilst thou hast yet time; begin immediately to detach thyself from everything, for life grows shorter every day, and every day death draws nearer.

SECOND POINT.

MARY'S GOOD WORKS.

Not the honors, the pleasures, and the consolations, enjoyed in this life give consolation in death, but the good works and the virtues which we shall have practised: "for their works follow them."

According to this principle, how precious and gentle must have been Mary's death! Verily was her life nothing else than a tissue of the most sublime virtues and of the most pious works of every description. Some of the holy fathers affirm that, in order to fill her with consolation and joy, her divine Son placed before her eyes the entire array of her good works and of her virtues. She saw the whole of her sixty-two years full of merits; she saw that the least moment of her time had not passed away without profit to her; that even she had made her sleep meritorious; that her eating, her drinking, her manual labor,—that every thing she had to do with, was a fruitful source of merit unto her; she saw that she had prayed, contemplated, and suffered, with the highest perfection possible to a mere creature. She sees her fidelity to God, her co-operation with grace, the works of mercy and of charity which she had performed for her neighbor; and she sees so many vigils, so many fasts, so many prayers, so many sighs, so great love for God,—all of which were truly hers.

O with what holy joy will this spectacle have inundated her soul! Shalt thou at thy death feel like consolation? Shalt thou see thy days full of merits and of holy works? Shall the good use which thou hast made of thy time console thee, or shalt thou be obliged to regret having misspent it in idling and trifling? And yet further must the recollection have consoled Mary of what she had endured at the Passion and death of her dear Jesus; as also her complete resignation to the divine will amid so many storms, her invincible patience amid so many sufferings, the firmness and constancy with which she remained immovable at the foot of the cross, her faith in his resurrection whilst the apostles wavered, her confidence whilst everything appeared calculated to render hope impossible.

How welcome will have been to her the recollection of all these things! If when he found his end approach, the apostle Paul was emboldened to cry out full of consolation and of confidence: "I have fought a good fight; I have finished my course; I have kept the faith. For the rest there is laid up for me a crown of justice, which the Lord the just judge will render to me at that day." 2 Tim. iv. 7 v.

What now must have been Mary's feelings, what must she have said, when she saw that crown near at hand which she had prepared for herself by so many virtues and sufferings! "The crown of justice is laid up for me!" O blessed obedience! blessed patience! blessed resignation to God! The just hopes in the hour of death: "The just hath hoped in his death." Prov. xiv. 32 v.

Wilt thou at thy death enjoy so beautiful a hope? Live the life of the just: amass treasures of good works,—charity towards thy neighbor, almsdeeds, compassion on the poor, frequent and pious reception of the holy sacraments, zealous prayers, visits to churches, propagation of the honor of our Lord, and above all, the sufferings endured from love for Jesus Christ, the crosses borne with patience, the sorrows endured with love.

O with what and with how great joy will all these inundate thy soul! Then wilt thou have a near view of the crown; and thou also shalt repeat: "The crown of justice is laid up for me;" and thou wilt bless the moment when thou didst truly begin to lay up unto thyself treasures for heaven.

THIRD POINT.

MARY'S LOVE FOR JESUS.

If every mother feels an ardent desire to embrace again her beloved son whom she has not seen for so many years, the most holy Virgin must have felt a still more burning desire to again embrace in heaven, and forever, that Son by whom she was so greatly honored and so greatly loved. She loved him as her son; but as a son the most dear, the most amiable, and the most holy of all the children of men. She loved him as her only begotten son, and as a son who was all her own; and indeed all her own, not by accident or by personal choice, but by a most extraordinary grace conferred upon her by that son who loved her so much: "Only she had conceived him; only she had borne him; to her alone did he belong in every relation; from her did he issue, and from her wholly and exclusively; on earth he had no father; in the conception of her son she acknowledged no share; she alone belongs to him and he alone belongs to her." St. Thomas of Villanova.

Not only did she love him as her son, she loved him as her God also, but as that God who, with special predilection, had created her as the first born of all creatures;—as that God who had redeemed her in a manner all wonderful, preserving her from the original stain;—as that God who had poured into her whole being almost endless treasures of graces, who loaded her with privileges and gifts, who had clothed her with the most beautiful distinctions, so that he caused her to be astonished at what he had made her: "He who is mighty hath done great things to me."

Mary loved this God who was to her a most beloved son; and she loved this son who was to her a most loving God. Who then can comprehend the measure of this love? In the world, there is no other mother who has so great an incentive to love an only begotten child, as Mary had to love Jesus. "Yes," says St. Augustine, "the love which any other mother bears to her offspring is, in comparison with the love which Mary bears to hers, as a little flame compared to a conflagration; and if it is the property of love to create a longing for the person beloved, how much must not Mary have yearned to behold her Jesus and to embrace him? How sweet will have been to her the moment which showed her the accomplishment of her wishes near at hand; the moment which should soon unite her forever in heaven with the dear object of all her love!"

O how, and with how much solicitude, will she roll her eyes around in order to descry her beloved! "Did you see him whom my soul loveth?" Ah! on earth there is no joy which is comparable to this, a fact which the blessed Virgin herself revealed to St. Bridget: "so great was the joy that filled my soul, that my soul could scarcely contain itself." St. Liguori's Glories of Mary.

Love God sincerely, and thou wilt at the hour of thy death exult with holy joy; thy love for creatures will only serve the purpose of troubling and unsettling thee; thy love for God will fill thy soul with consolation, and make the moment of thy death appear to thee as the most charming moment of thy whole life.

O most holy Virgin! enkindle in me also a spark of that love which makes death so lovable. Cause that my desire to see Jesus will, at that hour, outstrip my fear to appear before him. O Mary! in the blood of Jesus Christ, and in thy intercession, repose all my hopes. Indeed I am terrified by the disorderly affection I bore to creatures, by my callousness in the performance of good works, especially in my callousness in loving God. O how many grounds have I to fear! yet thy graciousness consoles me.

Enkindle now in my heart a lively and an active love, in order that I may make atonement for the infidelity and coldness of which I have been hitherto guilty: and when I reach the end of my life, ah, then at that moment be mindful of me, O Lady! and console me in such manner that on the announcement to me of the near approach of my departure, I may be able to cry out with joy: "I rejoice in the things that were said to me; we will go into the house of the Lord." Amen.

THIRTY-FOURTH MEDITATION.

THE PRIVILEGES OF MARY'S VIRGINAL BODY.

FIRST POINT.

MARY'S INCORRUPTIBLENESS.

As the Virgin perfectly resembled Jesus in the humiliations of this life, so it was necessary that she should also resemble him in the glorification of the grave.

The most holy Body of Jesus, although disfigured with wounds, was exempt from all corruption: "Thou wilt not give thy holy one to see corruption:" and Mary's most holy members were likewise exempt from all corruption. "How was it possible God would not have desired that those members should be incorruptible?" asks St. Augustine. Why should he not maintain them incorruptible, seeing, as we see, that he had even wished her virginal purity to remain unimpaired in conceiving and bringing forth her Son; seeing, as we see, that he had wished her as Mother to retain her virginal purity in all its integrity? The curse pronounced upon Eve, in no way regarded Mary: "In sorrow shalt thou bring forth." And well in keeping with her noble offspring was it that she should be in no way affected by the other curse also: "To dust thou shalt return."

The immaculate flesh of our divine Redeemer is, likewise, the flesh of his most holy Mother: "Christ's flesh is Mary's flesh;" and if it were suitable to the dignity and the honor of the divine Person that his flesh should be exempted from the general law of corruption,—of corruption which is nothing else than the dissolution of man's physical nature infected with sin—so it was also meet that regard should be had to the dignity and the honor of the Mother with whose flesh he had clothed himself. And how would it have been possible to give in prey to the worms that virginal body which was the throne of God, the bridal chamber of the heavenly bridegroom, the abode in which remained for nine months the Word made Flesh, and remained in all the plenitude of his Divinity? "How could corruption have triumphed over that body which had received into it him who is life itself?" St. John of Damascus.

The ark of the covenant was constructed out of incorruptible wood, and was all gilt with the purest gold; and yet, that ark contained nothing but the tables of the law, and the little vase in which the manna was preserved. O how far more incorruptible, and with how much brighter and more precious gold must have been adorned that blessed ark which contained in it the well-head of grace for the whole world! Whoever could have approached that thrice blessed grave which had enwombed in it so dear a treasure, would have seen on that holy countenance neither wrinkles nor sorrows nor any other sign of death, but would have descried in those heavenly lineaments which now delight all the angels and saints of heaven, that serene earnestness, that superhuman wisdom, that all pure and holy beauty which made her the most amiable of all creatures. What a lovely spectacle to behold that dear relict as she awaited the invitation of her beloved that she might career to heaven! What heavenly fragrance! What angelic harmony! What astonishment, what transports of the saints!

O Mary! if thy mortal frame was so beautiful in the grave, how beautiful will it be above there in the fountain of life! Thou canst not manage to obtain for thyself so beautiful a gift; thy body will be resolved into ashes; thy members, the abodes of sin, will become a prey to rottenness: "To rottenness I said, thou art my father, my mother, and my sister!" but thou canst be exempt from the rottenness of sin, of sin which is the corruption of the soul and of the body: "If you fly the concupiscence of this world," says St. Peter, "thy body will one day obtain an inheritance incorruptible and undefiled, and that fadeth not, reserved for thee in heaven."

Earnestly endeavor to attain to this; flee whatever can corrupt thy mind; above all, beware of those objects which flatter thy sensuality. Be on thy guard; trust not thyself; mortify thy senses; mortify thy flesh: and by doing these things thou wilt, with the help of God, attain to that beautiful incorruptibleness which is a property common to all the blessed.

SECOND POINT.

MARY'S RESURRECTION.

Not content with preserving incorrupt and in the bloom of life Mary's body, our Lord wished to honor it yet more, by causing it to arise full of life and full of glory on the third day from the grave.

In the midst of all the pomp of his royal palace, David remembered that the ark of the covenant was lodged in a private house, and was not shown any honor or veneration; and hence he immediately gave orders that it should be transferred with the greatest solemnity to his royal city; and he went himself to meet it and take it under his charge. According to our manner of seeing things, our divine Redeemer acted in the same manner in regard to the glorification of the heavenly Jerusalem. He was mindful of that blessed repository in which he had corporally dwelt on earth; and full of most anxious desire to give it due honor, he called her with the voice of his omnipotent power to taste life anew: "Arise, my friend, my delight, and come."

The angels wished to see their Queen joyous and exalted; the same was the desire of the patriarchs, the prophets, the saints of the old law, who were themselves thankful for having been delivered from the shadow of death, and transferred to the admirable light of Paradise; her own blessed soul also, impelled by natural love, desired to be united with her body. "Arise, my friend," spoke Jesus, and in an instant her most pure soul, reuniting with her holy members, arose from the grave, more beautiful than the gleaming Aurora, more glowing than the Sun.

O how will the venerable Lady have thanked her divine Son! with what joy and love will she have sung her canticle, "My soul doth magnify the Lord!" O glorious Virgin! the winter of tribulation is past for thee: "for the winter is already gone by," and there commence joys, honors, triumphs, which never will see an end. O Lady! obtain for us that we also may hereafter participate in those joys and triumphs, and that this our body, now racked with sufferings, may, like unto thy body, one day arise immortal, impassible, subtle, full of glory, and arise never more to taste of death.

Mary's resurrection rests on many grounds. One ground, however, which must conduce much to our consolation is this—that she might be able to retain continuously her name of Mother, and that she might be immediately able to fulfil in Heaven her maternal duties towards us, by praying for us, and by appeasing with her presence the wrath of the Father. The name Mary cannot be applied to her soul alone, nor to her body alone, but is applicable to the soul and body joined together in oneness of person; and in order that she might bear this name unceasingly, her adorable Son caused her to arise in a sea of most transcendent splendor. O loving providence of our God! O intercessor extremely agreeable to heaven!

The resurrection of the flesh is an article of faith; we shall all arise, but we shall not all arise in glory: "We shall indeed all rise again, but we shall not all be changed." Some shall rise in glory, and the others in confusion.

How shalt thou rise again? What will be the appearance of thy body on that day—beautiful, glorious, as appeared Mary's body? If thou will it, thy body shall so appear; the manner and way to assure thyself of so beautiful a lot consists in this, that thou now deliver thyself from sin, from sin which is the only thing that can prevent thee from attaining the happy end designed for thee; and if thou be not in grievous sin, then at least leave behind thee that lukewarmness which can bring thee by degrees to lose the life of thy soul by committing mortal sin.

Oh, how many dangers can lukewarmness in the service of God call forth! how many obstacles can it create! Examine thyself, look in what state dost thou now find thyself, and pray to Mary to obtain for thee the grace that thou mayst make those heroic resolutions which thy salvation demands.

THIRD POINT.

MARY'S ASCENSION INTO HEAVEN.

As soon as the most holy Virgin was risen, she was taken up into heaven in most glorious and magnificent triumph.

Who can well picture to himself this triumph? O how miserably deficient an idea of it is obtainable from earthly triumphal processions! Why speak here of the concourse that accompanied the Queen of Saba into Solomon's palace, or that accompanied the victorious Judith into Bethulia? Only imagine to thyself, what a heavenly spectacle it must have been to behold this royal Lady set out in majesty and in the midst of the light of Paradise on her upward journey, her eyes turned to heaven, herself all raised to God, supported by the angels, surrounded by the saints of the whole heavenly court! What a beautiful spectacle to behold her so circumstanced, soaring up from the earth, and entering into the highest heaven, in order to be there crowned as queen, and to be enthroned at the right hand of her divine Son! "Who is this?" will the angels have cried out in amazement; "Who is this who cometh from the desert of the world, and pursues her heavenward course, adorned with so great privileges, that she herself is the joy of God? Who is this that cometh forth from the desert, overflowing with delights?" What voices of unspeakable joy, what songs of praise, of angelic harmony, what canticles of rejoicing and jubilation will have accompanied her during her whole triumphal procession! "Come from Lebanon, thou wilt be crowned!" "Come, O Lady!" will the angels have said to her, "for thou hast brought forth into the world our King and Savior." "Come," will the patriarchs have said to her, "for because thou hast issued from the same parents as we have, thou hast conferred on us so much nobility, and hast imparted to us so much glory!" "Come," will the prophets have said unto her, "because thou wast foretold to us for so many centuries, and we by our prophecies have announced to the world thy then future advent." "Come," will all the saints of both sexes have called out to her from the heavenly Jerusalem, "for thou art our Lady, our Queen! come hither from the earth where thou hast suffered so much, where thou hast practised all the virtues, hast loved so much! Come, O Lady! to wield the sceptre as unrestrained mistress of the universe; come to receive the crown which thy well beloved Son has prepared for thee: 'Come from Lebanon thou shalt be crowned.'"

O how will Mary's heart have exulted amid such delightful harmony, amid the praises and acclamations of the whole heavenly court! But knowest thou when her heart was inundated with more than human joy? When she saw herself in the presence of Jesus who had come to meet her that he himself might conduct her to her glory: "Her Son came accompanied with the assemblage of all the heavenly courtiers, and, to her unspeakable joy and honor, took her up to heaven amid the exultation of the angels and the transports of the powers of the celestial court, and, with his own hands, placed her above the supremely blessed choirs of the angels." St. Thomas of Villanova.

O with what loving embraces was she received! With what accents of jubilation was she greeted! Well might she on that triumphal occasion have said: "I found him whom my soul loveth; I kept him, and I will not let him go." I have found the love of my soul; I will hold him fast, and will no more let him depart from me.

Meditate in the spirit of faith on this delighting spectacle; and console thyself with the thought that, if thou remain faithful to thy God, there will some day be a triumph similar to Mary's reserved for thee! In the meantime, congratulate the exalted Lady: rejoice with her upon her glories and her triumphs; and to thy great consolation, reflect that this Lady, so exceedingly elevated in station, so highly honored by the angels and saints, is, after all, bone of our bone, and blood of our blood.

Yes, reflect that she is our most loving Mother. Let not her dignity nor her majesty in any way deter thee; the affection of her maternal heart always outstrips these. Be encouraged to hope all good things from her; and, full of filial confidence, say to her: O unrestrained ruler of heaven and earth! the celebration of thy victory puts me to shame, but thy graciousness gives me heart and animates me with the hope that I shall obtain all good from thee. O yes! I hope that with thy help I shall live in such a way as that I may hereafter be able to arise glorious with the countless legions of the elect; I hope that with these my eyes I shall behold thee sitting on the exalted throne of thy glory; I hope that for all eternity I shall praise thee and love thee.

O Mary! the goods of the mother are the goods of the children; the children have that right to the inheritance of the mother: O my sweetest Mother! cause that I may never more lose thee, cause that I may never again be bereft of so precious rights; obtain them for me by protecting me from all my enemies, and by preventing me from perishing in any of all the dangers that encompass me. O my Mother! I find myself still among the thistles and thorns of this valley of tears; extend to me thy blessed hand; and bring me to the happy possession of the eternal inheritance. Amen.

THIRTY-FIFTH MEDITATION.

MARY GLORIFIED BY GOD.

FIRST POINT.

MARY—GLORIFIED IN HEAVEN.

How deeply soever thou mayst meditate on the glory to which God has elevated Mary in heaven, never shalt thou be able to form to thyself an adequate idea of that glory.

In this connection the assurance is eminently applicable, "He who is a searcher of majesty shall be overwhelmed with glory." God placed her on an exalted throne at the right hand of her Son; but so bright is this throne that it forms by itself a rank in bliss which is brighter than that of all the saints whose Queen she is: "At thy right hand stands the Queen in golden apparel, surrounded with magnificence of every kind." He clad her with a twofold robe of glory, which heightened the beauty of her soul as well as that of her body, and he adorned her with all the different little crowns which are distributed among the choirs of the remainder of the just. On her head he set a diadem adorned with twelve stars, as a sign of the glorious privileges conferred upon her: "On her head a crown of twelve stars;" and he committed to her as to their queen to whom they owed subjection and obedience, all the legions of angels and saints. "The crown of thy head," speaks St. Amadeus to her, "brought thee, through glory, dominion over heaven."

Represent to thyself how all the choirs of the blessed inhabitants of heaven laid down their crowns at Mary's feet, even as the four-and-twenty elders mentioned in the Apocalypse laid down their crowns before the throne of God. By this act they acknowledged her as their queen, and they avowed that she was more worthy than they of that glory; for in her alone shone forth in transcendent splendor the purity of the angels, the faith of the patriarchs, the hope of the prophets, the love and zeal of the apostles, the constancy of the martyrs, the temperance of the confessors, the prudence of the doctors, the chastity of the virgins. There tabernacled in her the purity of the virgins, the constancy of the martyrs, the devotion of the confessors, the wisdom of the doctors, the contempt of the world which characterized the hermits, and every other gift of mind, and every grace, even such as were bestowed on others in vain.

Oh with what thanksgivings to God must not heaven have then resounded! Oh, what great joy and jubilation reigned throughout the whole heavenly kingdom on the day when Mary was crowned its Queen! "Benediction and glory and wisdom and thanksgiving, honor and power and strength to our God forever and ever." Ap. vii. 12 v. When Solomon wished to honor his mother Bethsabee, he was not satisfied with seating her on a throne near his own, with introducing her to his subjects, and seeing that they paid their homage to her; but he assured her moreover, that he would never refuse her any favor, however great, she might choose to ask: "Ask, O mother! for it were not right that I should turn away my face from thee."

Imagine to thyself now, how, on the day of her glorification, God said much more than this to Mary: imagine also to thyself what honor he showed her, and what power he conferred upon her. The holy fathers say that she has been appointed unrestrained dispensatrix of all treasures, and that a power has been given her which goes beyond all measure; and that, from that day forward, she received such dominion that she approaches the throne of God not as one who petitions, but as one who commands: "not petitioning, but commanding." Rejoice in thy heart upon the glories of the most holy Mother, for those glories are eventually our good fortune also; and bear in mind how faithfully God fulfils his promise to the effect that he also, on his part, will honor whoever honors him: "Whoever honors me, him will I honor!"

Why did he glorify Mary so exceedingly? Because Mary glorified him all the days of her life. Wilt thou attain to a high place in heaven? This is the road which leads to that high place; render to the Lord all the honor that lies in thy power; glorify him by thy manner of life, by thy manner of actions, by thy words; ever seek to give him honor and glory in all things; in all that thou dost, have in view nothing beyond this most noble end. O what a beautiful throne wilt thou, by this means, prepare for thyself above in heaven!

On what wast thou most intent up to the present time? On God's honor, or thine own? Didst thou seek God's pleasure or thine? Examine thy intentions; put right order in them immediately; and bear in mind that, the more thou wilt have glorified God on earth, the brighter will be thy throne for-ever in heaven.

SECOND POINT.

MARY—GLORIFIED ON EARTH.

Mary's glorification on earth consists principally in the great and ceaseless mercies which she shows to men. Unrestrained dispensatrix of the divine treasury, yea, mistress over the heart of God, she with great liberality confers many graces and favors of every kind, and employs the plenitude of her power to our greatest advantage. Behold! this is Mary's most beautiful glorification, "dominion over the world through the agency of mercy." St. Amadeus.

She was already prefigured by that small cloud which the prophet Elias saw arise, which spread itself, covered the whole firmament, and by means of its propitious and abundant showers, re-animated the whole earth with new life.

O what an abundance of graces and favors constantly issue forth from her blessed hands! Look around thee on all sides, and see whether there be a corner of the world so distant as not to share in her benefactions—a corner on which she does not pour forth her benefactions! How many most striking miracles are, through her instrumentality, wrought for the consolation of our miserable humanity; how many wonderful graces for the salvation of souls are received from her! Go enter into her churches, into her sanctuaries, and if thou canst, count the gifts which hang around on all sides, and are there consecrated to her service,—gifts, however, which proclaim but the smallest moiety of the graces which she conferred. Is there, in fact, a single species of scourge from which she has not often delivered the Christian family? Is there a species of grace which she has not obtained for that family? Is there a class of men on whom she has not with full hands poured forth her mercies?

O say now, the whole earth is full of Mary's mercy! And what idea have those her mercies given thee of her? With what a great, exalted, agreeable conception of her, with what veneration and affection for her, did she not inspire the minds of the faithful? What charming honor and love she vindicates to herself by her mercy! When through the prayers and intercession of Esther, the Hebrew people were absolved from the sentence of death which had been pronounced against them, they acknowledged with extraordinary joy her power with Assuerus.

So many miracles daily wrought by Mary, and so many favors daily conferred by her, also convinced the Christian people of the immensity of her power in heaven. And to what great benefit and consolation to themselves, do they acknowledge this her power! Behold what the faithful throughout the whole world have done in order to conciliate her; under how many titles they invoke her, under how many forms they represent her, in how many ways they honor her, and above all, observe how confidently they flee to her in their every necessity!

Thank our Lord for having so greatly exalted his Mother; and bear in mind that thou also shalt have a share in her glorification, if thou imitatest her goodness and generosity, by assisting the poor, by protecting the orphan, by visiting the needy, and aiding them with counsel and works, and by consoling the afflicted. Job rejoices that he was "an eye to the blind, a foot to the lame, a father to the orphans;" and do thou also endeavor to act in like manner, and to so act in honor of Mary, and especially in imitation of her mercy.

Why dost thou misspend thy money and thy industry on so many vanities? Henceforward, make a better use of God's gifts: O how agreeable will it be to the exalted Virgin, when she sees thee spend thyself in works of mercy! She will approve thy course in such manner that she will redouble her affection for thee, and will in the end bring thee to the eternal glory of heaven.

THIRD POINT.

MARY—GLORIFIED UNDER THE EARTH.

By reason of the great power which God conferred on the most holy Virgin over the evil spirits, the evil spirits also glorified her. Oh, how exceedingly they dread her! They fear her as if she were a whole army of princes and powers ready to combat with them: "Terrible as an army in battle array." A well ordered army can already, from the fact that it is well ordered, be styled victorious, because the mere spectacle it presents inspires fear: such an army is Mary. In order to put Hell to flight and to bruise to pieces all its power, she has but to appear: "she weakened him with the beauty of her face." Judith, xvi. 8 v. She needs not to arm herself for the purpose of entering upon the engagement; her bare presence suffices to ensure victory.

For this reason St. Amadeus remarks in delight, that men through affection for her, and that the evil spirits through their fear of her, contribute to her glorification: "Men in their affection, and the evil spirits in their terror, contribute to thy glorification." The evil spirit knows that this singularly privileged creature has, from the very beginning, crushed his head; and that, notwithstanding his futile efforts, she crushes it day after day by making void his snares, and by defending against his assaults the souls who recommend themselves to her. In all things, therefore, he is constrained to carry out her slightest will, and to obey her as a powerful mistress: "For she is," as says St. Bernard, "the ruler of those who are in heaven, on the earth, and under the earth." O how he feels the power of her voice, how he shudders when he hears her name invoked!

This name so dear to us, is for the evil spirits as seething oil which brings them under subjection, and puts them to flight. "Thy name is as oil poured out;" and, therefore, in temptations, in dejection, in dangers, there is not, after the name of Jesus, so powerful a weapon against hell as is the name of Mary. O how many experienced, and yet daily experience, its effectiveness and force! The evil spirits themselves often confessed that they had in heaven no enemy more terrible to them than Mary.

How glorious indeed for the Virgin is this power which she received over hell! What protection, therefore, should we not promise ourselves in every contingency, in every assault! True it is that "he goes about like a roaring lion seeking whom he may devour;" he stands all the time on the lookout, to pounce upon us, to rob us, to prostrate us; but what have we to fear when Mary protects us? Flee under her standard, and depart no more from her side; in all temptations be very careful to call upon her for help, and thou wilt experience how great and how limitless is the power which she enjoys over hell.

O most glorious Queen! thou who wieldest the sceptre over heaven, over the world, and over the abyss, deign to cast from the throne of thy glories a glance upon thy poor servants who now mourn, surrounded as we are with a thousand dangers of falling into eternal perdition. See what trouble hell gives itself in order to tear us from the arms of Jesus; behold the traps which it lays for us; the violent attacks which it makes upon us!

O most mighty Queen! manifest the dominion which thou possessest over the evil spirits! Break their pride, cast them down, subject them to thy yoke, that they may never again be so bold as to approach those whom thou takest under thy protection. "Preserve us from the enemy!" I commit myself to the firm hope that I shall obtain from thee so beautiful a grace. Add to thy glories this glory also, that thou preserve me from their attacks, or in case of my being attacked, grant that I may be victorious:—then shall I sing for all eternity, "I was pressed and cast down so that I should fall, but our Lady sustained me." Amen.

THIRTY-SIXTH MEDITATION.

THE SPECIAL HONOR WHICH WAS SHOWN TO MARY BY THE THREE DIVINE PERSONS.

FIRST POINT.

THE HONOR WHICH GOD THE FATHER SHOWED TO MARY.

NOT content with having glorified the Virgin in the universe at large, God desired, moreover, to show her special honor which should be in proportion to the amount of merit that she acquired from each of the three divine Persons.

Jesus has in heaven a Father, but not a mother; he had on earth a mother, but not a father. He is truly the Son of God, and just as truly the son of Mary. As now the Father delivered up to death his only begotten Son, for the Father's honor and for the salvation of men; so also for the Father's honor and for the salvation of men, did Mary deliver up to death her only begotten son: "To redeem the slave," says St. Bernard, in his admiration, "the Father and Mary gave up their common son."

If the Eternal Word desired to have her consent before he began to live in her womb, so it is very credible that he desired to have her consent on that other occasion also, when he was about to offer up that same life on the cross. And hence the permission which Jesus sought from Mary before beginning his passion, was no mere sufferance on her part, but was rather a hearty consent that he should give up for us that life which belonged to her in a special manner, and so belonged to her because she was his Mother. To the passion and death, then, of her son she gave hearty consent, and gave it with that readiness and fortitude which the Eternal Father and the Eternal Father's love demand from us. "Yea," adds St. Bernard just cited above, "she would willingly have given up her own life in addition to her Son's, if, by so doing, she had been able to render more honor to the divine Father, and more service to the human family."

In the truths just taught us by the holy Doctor, is contained the principle of the special merit which Mary acquired from the Eternal Father. How did he reward her for that merit? By causing her to participate in the application of the merits of this great sacrifice, and by making her an instrument in the execution of the merciful design which he had upon the human race,—and indeed an instrument she was in the sacrifice of Calvary, the greatest of all sacrifices. What did God give Abraham for the cheerfulness with which that patriarch was disposed to sacrifice his only son Isaac as a burnt offering? For this cheerfulness, God made him the pattern of all believers: "By my own self have I sworn, saith the Lord: because thou hast done this thing, and hast not spared thy only begotten son for my sake, I will bless thee, and I will multiply thy seed as the stars of heaven, and as the sand that is by the sea shore; thy seed shall possess the gates of their enemies. And in thy seed shall all the nations of the earth be blessed, because thou hast obeyed my voice." Gen. xxii. 16 v.

And if he gave so much to Abraham, what must he not have given Mary, who far more heroically consecrated this her Son to the honor of the Father, and for our salvation offered up that life which in itself was infinitely more precious not only than that of Isaac, but than that of the whole human family? Because thou hast done those things I will, as a reward for that sacrifice which thou hast offered me, give to thee an innumerable posterity of chosen people; I will give thee a heart which is broader than the sea, a mercy which will enable thee to sympathize with the combined miseries of all men; I will give thee a charity so great that there never will be on the face of the earth a human being who may not find in thee a most loving mother: "I will multiply thy seed as the stars of heaven, and as the sand that is by the sea shore."

The Eternal Father required some sacrifices from thee also. How often did the faithful performance of thy duties give thee an opportunity to offer a sacrifice to God; now, a sacrifice of thy own views, of thy love of comfort; again, of thy avarice; and at another time, of thy self-love? Didst thou make to God the offering which he desired? Or, rather, didst thou not immolate the will and the good pleasure of thy kind Father on the altar of thy own inclinations? Of how many charming promises wilt thou, in this latter case have deplorably robbed thyself?

Compare thy sacrifices to those which Mary made, and see how thou must blush! Lament the niggardliness with which thou hast acted towards God! Be generous in thy regard; and pray to the most holy Virgin for that magnanimity which is the fruitful seed of such great space, and of so many graces.

SECOND POINT.

THE HONOR WHICH GOD THE SON SHOWED TO MARY.

From the divine Son, also, did Mary acquire for herself especial merit; and this merit she acquired by rendering it possible for him to feel our miseries.

God was great and rich in mercy; but, notwithstanding those riches, he could not feel the miseries and annoyances which afflict the children of men. He came to their assistance; he affectionately lightened the burden of their difficulties, but experienced no sadness at these difficulties. "God," says the angelic Doctor, "does not come as one who feels sadness at the miseries of another, but as one who comes to remedy the miseries of another." What did the Virgin do? She clothed the Divine Word with human flesh, and by making him capable of suffering, she makes him capable of compassionating also. She clothed him with human flesh; she imparted to him an exceedingly great sympathy; she also assimilated him in all things to those persons to whom he was by his own self-appointment to show mercy: "Wherefore it behoved him in all things to be made like unto his brethren, that he might become merciful." Heb. ii. 17 v.

What will be her reward for that merit? That he accord to Mary as much power to help us, as Mary communicated to him of tender-heartedness to sympathize with us! She gave to Christ of compassion, and Christ gave to her of his power. At Eve's creation, a rib was taken from Adam and flesh given him instead; that is, strength was taken from him, and weakness communicated to him. At the creation of Christ, quite the contrary took place; weakness was taken from the Virgin and strength imparted to her. To increated mercy was given the feeling of compassion, and to created mercy was given the active power to render assistance. Not power, but weakness, did the Word receive from the Virgin, and for the weakness received he gave her strength in return. This is the conduct of our Lord, who never suffers himself to be outdone in generosity. "Rejoice," says St. Methodus, "rejoice, O Mary! thou hadst the happiness to have for debtor him who gives to every one and receives from no one."

We are all debtors to God for every thing we possess, for all we possess is nothing else but a present from God, made by him to us: but God wishes himself to become a debtor to thee, O Virgin Mary! by assuming flesh and blood in thy womb and by becoming man in it. Learn from this what a generous rewarder is the Lord: "for what you give, you will receive a hundred-fold." Salvation is thine—if thou dost anything for him, if thou exertest thyself for his glorification, if thou hast his holy interest at heart, especially, if thou wilt introduce to his presence a soul whom thou hast gained by thy own efforts.

O then how many graces will he give thee in this

world, how great glory in Heaven! Fear not; Jesus will bear in mind every word thou hast said, every step thou hast made, every desire thou hast entertained, provided it were for his sake thou so acted: for everything that thou shalt have done, so profuse will be thy reward that it will be beyond all thou canst conceive, for God will not suffer himself to be surpassed in generosity.

THIRD POINT.

THE HONOR WHICH THE HOLY GHOST CONFERRED ON MARY.

The especial merit acquired by Mary from the holy Ghost, consists in the magnanimity wherewith she corresponded with his sublime designs in relation to the redemption of the world. The angel announced to her an unspeakable mystery which he himself comprehended not: "The holy Ghost will come upon thee, and the power of the Most High shall overshadow thee."

Mary has need here of all her faith, in order to assent to the truth of what she had heard. What is announced transcends her understanding; her prudence induces her to ask some questions, and so comprehensive and so profound are the explanations that are given her, that they distance all her powers of comprehension:—The Holy One which shall be born of thee shall be called the Son of God. The body which by the operation of the holy Ghost, shall be formed in thy womb, will be formed out of thy most pure blood, will be a body consecrated especially to the use of the Son of God himself who will unite it with himself; and of this flesh will it be said, "this is the Flesh of the Son of God:" from this union of the human soul with the flesh, a human person will not result, but soul and body so united will form one perfect human nature inseparably assumed by the Word, and shall not for a single moment belong to any other person than to the Person of the Word himself.

Mary does not wholly take in so great a mystery, but is yet convinced that the Holy Ghost who desires her consent for the purpose of carrying his designs into execution, has means at hand above her understanding. She submits on the spot; she believes and utters these words, "Be it done." What reward will she receive from her bridegroom for this her greatness of soul? That as she corresponded with his design of the salvation of men, even so he would comply with her desires regarding their sanctification.

"She had," says St. Bernardine of Sienna, "she had, so to say, a certain judicial determination and power over the temporal going forth of the Holy Ghost." The treasures of his greatness he placed in her hands, and made her the dispensatrix of his gifts; all the good the whole world ever possessed, proceeded from this divine spirit, but likewise all passes through the hands of his most beloved bride. He comes down to sanctify souls, but he comes down through the medium of Mary; he comes down to justify sinners and to abide in their hearts, but yet he comes to them through the medium of Mary. He infuses wisdom, counsel, fortitude, the holy fear of God, and his other gifts, but he infuses them through the channel of Mary; and infuses them because she is the well-beloved Mistress of his treasures, and so "that no creature obtains from God any grace whatever for the practice of virtue, otherwise than according to the dispensation of this same Virginal Mother."

The fact that she so cheerfully entered into the designs of the Holy Ghost, was the reason why the Virgin obtained so much power and so much glory. O hadst thou quickly followed the inspirations which this animating spirit so often gave thee! But ah! perhaps thou hast slighted his whisperings; and if thou sometimes obeyed, how didst thou obey them? After much delay, with reluctance, and with a distaste amounting almost to disgust!

Take good care of thyself! for the grace of the Holy Ghost admits of no negligence. If he causes thee to hear his voice, give ear to it; if he sends thee an inspiration, correspond with it immediately, without evasion and without murmuring; this is the way to participate abundantly in the favor which he bestows. Turn to his most holy bride and say to her: "O most holy Virgin! the offering which thou didst bring to the Eternal Father, the services which thou didst render to the divine Son, the consent which thou didst give to the Holy Ghost, bound thee up in a most perfect and unspeakable manner with all the Three Divine Persons, and in recompense of what thou hast done, thou hast obtained boundless wealth, unlimited power, inestimable and eternal glory. My spirit doth exult, oh Lady! since it sees the adorable Trinity agreeing to give thee grace and honor! O I also could do something to promote thy honor! But ah! I am so devoid of courage, so deaf to the whisperings of God, that I am absolutely good for nothing.

Ah most holy Virgin! be moved with compassion in my regard: give me but a particle of the magnanimity and eagerness with which thou wast animated in accomplishing the will of God, then shall I be in a state to co-operate to his and thy glorification; then shall I abundantly share the rewards which are prepared for faithful and generous souls. Such is my hope—may it be realized!

THIRTY-SEVENTH MEDITATION.

MARY OUR HOPE.

FIRST POINT.

MARY KNOWS ALL OUR WANTS.

THE first condition necessary, in order that we may hope for help from any one, is that such one know our wants. Should he not know them, he will not compassionate us, even as thou thyself wouldst feel no sympathy whatever with one who, be his necessities what they may, would not be known to thee for one in distress.

Yet, fear not; the matter is entirely easy in the case of Mary. In God she sees all our miseries ; no yearning, no breathing escapes her. If he makes known those things to the angels whom he deputes to be our guardians, how can he conceal such things from the Mother to whom he committed the care of thee and of the whole human family?—and it is true to say that he committed that care more to her than he committed the care of the salvation of each person to the guardian angel of each person.

Hence she sees through the deepest secrets of our hearts; she knows also the state of our souls; our dangers, our necessities, our tribulations, are naked and open to her eyes, as is a picture to the eyes of those who look upon it. To her also are applicable the words, "thoughts are manifested to him."

Therefore, by no means doubt whether she see thy tribulations; she sees them and measures all their bitterness: fear not lest she does not hear thy sighs and thy aspirations; she hears them all, and not one of them does she suffer to pass away in vain. With men, forgetfulness of the motives, and a malicious representation of the cause which induces thee to act, may prove highly disadvantageous to thee; but such can never be thy case with Mary. She hears thee always, and even if thou knowest not how to speak, she supplies thy deficiency and supplies it with superabundance.

Richard says that the venerated eyes of Mary are constantly fixed on all, on the sinners, as well as on the just: "The eyes of our Lady look upon the just, and upon the sinners." And the blessed Amadeus maintains that those saints whom Ezechiel saw in his vision and whom he thought to be living and having eyes on all sides, do not with that sharpness of sight see into, and do not with that penetration of understanding examine after, the troubles, the sorrows, and the miseries of men, with which sharpsightedness and penetration of mind Mary finds out those troubles, sorrows, and miseries. The troubles, sorrows, falls, defects, blindness, sickness, great dangers, uncertain issues, all the weal and woe of the whole human family,—the saints mentioned by Ezechiel could not pry into, as could she who brought forth God. To no one is it given to read so deeply in the heart of God the events that occur to us, as it is given to Mary.

Hast thou no motive for saying that she knows thy situation, thy wants, thy afflictions? Whilst thou wast prostrate in confidence at her feet, and prayed to her, who knows how often she by an interior voice gave thee to understand that she saw thy tribulations, and that she promised thee her assistance? How consoling then is it to place our hope in her who, at every time, in every place, on every occasion, hears us and is ever prepared to help us!

Often greet her with those beautiful words, "Hail our Hope!" and never let slip from thy mind the fact that on the sea of this life there is no anchor more to be depended on than is Mary.

SECOND POINT.

MARY ALWAYS COMPASSIONATES.

Mary does not see and know our temporal and spiritual necessities, without her seeing and knowing them being profitable to us; for, with Mary, seeing them, and compassionating them, are one and the same thing.

The reverse is often the case with men: they see but pity not. Open the Gospel, and examine whether she be really compassionate. At the wedding of Cana, she perceived that the wine gave out, and her perception sufficed to move her to such compassion as induced her, without being requested, to employ her intercession on that occasion. "Since she regarded the confusion of others as her own, she could not," says St. Bernard, "look on, she could not demean herself in the same manner as if she had not observed that the wine had failed." Open the pages of history, and thou shalt surely find as many proofs of her mercy as there were miserable persons who repaired to her for her intercession. What sympathy did she not evince for the poor faithful who groaned under the tyranny of the Moors? She could not see those poor believers so tortured and oppressed, and at the same time not hasten to pity and console them.

This is the reason why in one and the same night she appeared to St. Peter of Nola, St. Raymond of Pennafort, to Jacob, king of Arragon, and with their co-operation founded the order for the redemption of captives. The compassion which she feels borders on the incredible: "No saint is to be found who pities our shortcomings so much as does this lady, the most blessed Virgin Mary." St. Antoninus. So far as compassion is concerned, no one approaches her; and should she not always evidence this fact, nay, even should she sometimes appear to hide herself and not to hear us, she does not, for all that, fail to have pity on us and to interest herself in our behalf.

An affectionate mother cannot help being touched by the wants and sorrows of her children. When the blessed Alphonsus Rodriguez was one day much oppressed with grievous temptations, he took refuge in Mary, and made to her this affecting appeal: "Oh, most holy Virgin, didst thou know how much I love thee! Thou dost not love me as much as I love thee." Scarce had he uttered these words when Mary appeared to him, and having reproached him gently for addressing her after that manner, she continued: "My Son, the love which I bear to thee is so great, that the love which thou bearest to me can never be compared to it."

By this reply she would say: believe not that I am insensible to thy sufferings, or that I refuse thee my assistance; shouldst thou not feel the strength thou desirest, yet I pity thee, and I cover thee with the mantle of my protection.

Some souls doubt occasionally that they enjoy Mary's protection, or they believe that she pays them no attention; and the reason is they do not, when they recur to her, experience that sensible relief of which they were in quest. But ah! how miserably such souls deceive themselves. Mary hears and compassionates thee in thy every necessity, although she gives thee no glimpse whatever of her compassion. She thinks more on thee than thou thinkest on thyself; and it often happens that then is she nearest thee when thou imaginest that she is farthest off.

O did we but thoroughly know the compassion, the love, the gentleness, of that maternal heart, with how much more confidence would we have recourse to her in all our necessities! how much greater graces should we receive from her! Pray to her for the grace that she make known to thee a little of the goodness of her heart, and be firmly convinced that this grace will be for thee a true balm in all thy afflictions.

THIRD POINT.

MARY HELPS AT THE RIGHT TIME.

In consequence of the corruption of our nature, there are in this world many evils which cannot be avoided. After the first man's sin God cursed the earth, and condemned it to bring forth thorns and thistles: "Cursed is the earth, thorns and thistles shall it bring forth." Gen. iii. 17 v.; and those thorns and thistles accompany our life from the day we come into the world, until the day we go out of it. Troubles, sorrows, death, are the common inheritance of all; but this fact does not prevent our blessed Lady from knowing how, amid such evils, to infuse into us a balm so salutary that it makes them more bearable, softens them, and keeps us from sinking under their otherwise crushing weight.

In the sacred pages Mary is, by reason of her beauty and of her other qualities, likened unto the Aurora; but for another cause also is she likened to it, since the Aurora usually brings with it some alleviation of their sufferings to persons who are in sickness: "Another property of the Aurora is that it lightens the pains of the sick; for the heavy dulness of night is counteracted by the cheering loveliness of the Aurora." St. Bonaventure.

O, what a beneficent Aurora is Mary unto us! what salutary influence does she exert on us in our sickness and sorrows! how she mitigates the evils that afflict us! Oh! you souls who stand in need of consolations, when have you ever looked up in vain to this Aurora? All Mary's anxieties have for end to assist the miserable, and hence she wishes nothing else than to dispense her mercies! "Thou hast regard to the poor on all sides; thou appearest to have only one object in view, to show mercy." For how many has she wiped away the tears from their eyes! For how many has she interceded in their necessities! How many has she prevented from falling! For how many has she assuaged their pains! How many has she delivered from dangers! How many has she consoled in their tribulations, even if she obtained for them nothing else! For how many has she secured placid resignation in the most grievous visitations, and the calm of a heavenly spirit!

For these reasons the holy fathers exhort us to place unlimited confidence in her; and the holy Church does not cease to greet her with the sweet title "Our Hope," and to cause all to greet her, "Hail, our Hope!" Not always indeed will she assist us after the manner in which we ourselves desire to be assisted—and why so? For our greater utility. The mother is not good who satisfies all the desires of her children; that mother is at once judicious and affectionate who allows them to cry when, to give them what they crave, would prove very prejudicial to their real interests. Thus acts Mary towards us. She satisfies us when our well being receives no injury from her so doing; and she allows us to lament when what we ask her for would, if granted, conduce to our ruin.

Ever and always then, and in thy temporal as well as in thy spiritual wants, recur to this thrice blessed mother; in thy temptations and in thy tribulations turn to her, and if thou imaginest that she defers consoling thee, and that she causes thee to wait, do not lose confidence, and by no means give way to the imagination that she does not desire to help thee: "for she despises no sinner." St. Bonaventure. Should she not obtain for thee the very graces which thou desirest, she will obtain for thee others more precious; as for example, a resignation so perfect that it will enrich thee with merits, and a tranquillity of such kind that it will blunt the edge of thy tribulations.

Let neither length of time, nor even a momentary dismissal, cause thee to grow weary of invoking her, of praying to her, of weeping before her; rather redouble thy prayer and thy zeal; tell her that thou doubtest not, that thou confidest in her, that thou art assured of her assistance and protection, and she will eventually prove to thee that "no one who hoped in her was confounded."

O my sweet hope! O most gracious Virgin! If no one ever hoped in thee in vain, shall I be the first who finds himself deceived? If all who hope in thee obtain mercies and favors, shall I then alone remain devoid of them? Ah, no, lady! I will not doubt of thy love; I hope, and will forever hope in thee. Thou seest the manifold needs of my soul; thou seest the crosses and tribulations which sorely harass my poor heart. Thou feelest sympathy with me in my situation.

Oh! then come to console me soon; hasten to me with thy mercies; let me immediately enjoy the fruits of the confidence which I placed in thee; and then shall I both in this life and in the next, praise that unlimited bounty which makes thee the sweet hope, and the dear refuge of all who are in affliction. Amen.

THIRTY-EIGHTH MEDITATION.

MARY OUR MEDIATRIX.

FIRST POINT.

MARY PRAYS FOR US.

HIGHLY exalted and singularly powerful with God as is Mary, she employs her greatness to further our welfare, and she sees to our interests with unintermitting assiduity. This is the affectionate service which she charges herself in heaven to render us who are on earth. In Jesus we have a mighty advocate with the Father; and in Mary we have an extremely influential patroness with the Son: "As the Son intercedes for us with the Father, so the mother intercedes for us with the Son." St. Thomas.

Up to the time of Mary's birth, we had no one to represent us with the eternal Word: "Before Mary was born, we lacked a representative with the Son" (Richard St. Victor); but since Mary came into the world, we acquired in her so loving and so powerful an intercessor that she sufficed to produce a complete change in our whole situation in this regard. In fact where is the person in sin, affliction, or misery, on whose behalf she does not approach the throne of her beloved Son? What is the favor which, if it be promotive of our salvation, she does not endeavor to obtain for us by her entreaties? When is the moment at which her love for us is not in action? "Who is he on whom the sun does not shine?" asks St. Bernard; "who is he on whom Mary's mercy does not beam with effulgence?" Yea, of such a kind and so great is the anxiety she feels for our welfare that she busies herself with all persons, and constantly prays for all with more than motherly affection.

Mary in person assured St. Bridget that "no one, so long as he lives, is cursed in such manner as to cease to be an object of my mercy." Esther presented herself but once before Assuerus to obtain favor for her people; Mary presents herself every moment before the divine throne, where she pleads our cause and sustains it with the authority of a mother, with the love of a bride, and with the confidence of a daughter,—and where she prays for the divine forbearance towards sinners, and for graces for them; for consolation for the afflicted, for support for the oppressed, for sustenance for the needy, for strength for the just, for mercies for all. She reminds Jesus of the cares, apprehensions, troubles, anxieties, and sufferings, she endured on his account; she calls to his mind the scourging, nailing, carrying of the cross, and shedding of his blood, all of which he went through for our sakes; and how could the most compassionate heart of Jesus remain unmoved in the midst of so many and touching recollections? How can he avoid lending a favorable ear to the prayers and desires of a mediatrix so amiable, so worthy to be heard, so holy, and, for these reasons so very acceptable to him? "On this account is she an influential mediatrix: influential, because sovereignly pure;

influential, because extremely agreeable; influential, because uncommonly gracious . . . O blessed moment when God deigned to bestow on the world so powerful and so gracious a mediatrix! O delightful the day when such and so great an intercessor was made a present of to the world!" St. Thomas.

Mary troubles herself in heaven about thy welfare; and thou—dost thou trouble thyself about it on earth as much as the case requires? Mary prays for thee, and thou—dost thou pray for thyself? With what zeal and frequency dost thou pray? Art thou perchance one of those who find time for everything else, but no time for prayer? What a wretch art thou if thou belong to that number! Prayer is the key which unlocks the treasures of heaven: "It is the key of heaven," says St. Augustine; "but if thou refuse or neglect to use this key, then the treasures of heaven remain locked." St. Alphonsus Liguori often repeated to the faithful those memorable words: "Who prays is saved; who prays not, is damned."

Examine thyself a little regarding thy prayers, and see whether it be not thy duty to say them more fervently, or to say more of them than thou sayst at present; and entreat thy gracious advocate for the grace to pray well, for this is the most precious of all graces.

SECOND POINT..

MARY SUSPENDS GOD'S PUNISHMENTS.

If God now no longer chastises the world with scourges so dreadful as those wherewith he chastised it in the centuries preceding the advent of Jesus Christ, this favor we have in great part to ascribe to Mary. The world grows no better as it advances in age; yea, much greater than the sins of others are the sins committed by Christians, on account of the ingratitude they involve to God who was born, who lived, who died, and now lies hidden in the Blessed Sacrament, all for the sake of Christians: and yet the punishments now inflicted are by no means so frequent, nor so fearful, as those inflicted in antechristian times. Yes, the holy fathers even say that Mary casts herself into the breach between God and us, that Mary prays, that Mary entreats.

When the Israelites were passing through the desert, God sent them a cool and wide-spreading cloud that overhung them and thus sheltered them from the excessive heat of the sun; and St. Bonaventure tells us that our loving intercessor renders us a like service, in that she shields us from the rigor of divine justice: "Like unto a cloud she protects us from the intensity of the divine anger." A similar expression occurs in the Psalms: "He spread a cloud for their covering."

O how often did this venerable cloud preserve the world! how often did it preserve whole provinces and kingdoms from destruction! There is probably in the Catholic world no city or country, which attests not, by means of public monuments, that Mary has delivered it from some fearful scourge: from hunger or plague, from sword or fire, from inundation, or some other great misfortune wherewith God punishes the injustice of men. Yes! there is no Christian who, in one way or in another, does not experience the loving operations of her protection: and perhaps so palpable are the proofs which thou thyself hast of the truth of this assertion, that thou canst term thyself a very monument to the honor of Mary's mercy. How often did she avert from thy house and head those misfortunes which thy sins merited should come upon thee? How often did she speak to her divine Son in thy favor and preserve thee from his wrath, even when thou neither entreated her to do so, nor invoked her, nor thought of her in any way? "She led me forward," canst thou say, "and yet I knew it not! This loving Lady was all anxiety for my welfare; she saved me from the anger of God, without my perceiving that she did so: she led me forward, and yet I knew it not."

On a certain occasion when an unfortunate dissolute man heard this consoling truth repeatedly inculcated, he contemptuously exclaimed: "Yes, indeed! what good did our Lady ever do to me? from what dangers did she ever deliver me?" He instantly heard this address made to him: "O ungrateful wretch! what good did our Lady do to thee?" And then he saw, plainly as in a picture, all the dangers in which he would have miserably perished had not the most holy Virgin hastened to his protection! On beholding this spectacle, he could contain himself no longer; he burst forth into a flood of tears, he conceived other thoughts, entered into other dispositions, and began to acknowledge and praise the unbounded goodness ot this heavenly patroness.

Wait not for extraordinary lessons such as he received; thank Mary's heart for the benefits which she has conferred on thee to thy own knowledge; and also thank that same heart for the benefits she has conferred on thee, even when thou didst not know that she it was who conferred them. Ah! who can number the latter? Be grateful, then, to her, and be careful not to associate with those unfortunates who desire to remain in their wickedness, who commit sin out of confidence in her mercy, and who so act precisely because she is good. And perhaps it were well for thee to bear in mind that a trait in the character of those wretches is that, while they act criminally, they promise themselves that, whatever happens, she will work miracles for their protection—and such promise they make themselves in spite of the impiety of their lives! Mary will not be treated so meanly: woe to him who would fain avail himself of her protection, for the purpose of continuing to commit sin!

Be afraid of exciting God to anger by fresh ingratitude; and be assiduous in rendering thy most holy mediatrix the thanks thou owest her; and this thou shalt do by leading a life of purity and zeal.

THIRD POINT.

MARY OBTAINS FOR US HEAVENLY GRACES.

Mary, now that she is in heaven soul and body, by no means limits her services to us, to the preserving us from punishment; but, on the contrary, she obtains for us graces and favors of every kind for both soul and body: for the soul, because such favors she has more at heart; for the body, and these manifest to us her goodness, by proving to us that she condescends to succor us in all our necessities. Who can affirm he has received from her no benefits whether of soul or body, or no favors for both? I am satisfied, says St. Bernard, that he should not utter a word in her praise who having often invoked her, experienced not her love: "Who has at any time invoked thee in a spirit of faith, and has ever perceived that thou hast turned thy back on him in his necessities, let him thenceforth omit to praise thee."

The whole world is full of Mary's benefactions; every one finds in her an inexhaustible source of graces and favors. A great servant of God said: "Had I been obliged to hang a silver heart on my bosom for every grace I received from Mary, I should be covered with such hearts from head to foot, and indeed should have more of them than are to be found in the chapels of her sanctuaries." Now were a Christian in a state to see and to know all the benefits which Mary confers on him in the various situations of life, would he not be obliged to make an admission such as that just related? St. Germain used often to say that, if he could interrogate the saints of heaven they would answer him thus: "through Mary's intercession we were saved; the innocent would say to me, through Mary's assistance we were enabled to keep spotless our robes of innocence, and to persevere in good; the penitents would confess they had obtained pardon for their sins through Mary and through her attained to salvation; and all with one voice would extol the power and the mercy of their heavenly mediatrix."

What are now thy views? Thinkest thou she has already bestowed on thee blessings and graces? O how many, how many of every kind, and at all hours! Examine thy life from the tender years of childhood till the present moment, and see and count if thou art able, in how many sicknesses she relieved thee; in how many doubts she gave thee light and counsel; in how many trials she sustained thee; in how many necessities she took care of thee; in how many troubles she consoled thee! And in all this list what wilt thou see? The smallest portion of her favors: those she bestowed on thee are incalculably more abundant than to admit of thy descrying the hand that conferred them. To her art thou indebted for so many heavenly lights, so many interior impulses, for so many wonderful dispensations of Providence entered into, through her, for thy welfare. These and a thousand other such things thou seest not now; but shouldst thou remain faithful to her, the moment will come when thou shalt see all, experience all, and wilt not tire of celebrating the praises of thy most loving mediatrix, and of thanking her with thy whole heart.

Meantime continue, by frequent prayer, by services of every kind, by zeal for her honor, to win for thyselt more and more her approbation, and confide abidingly in her, for the benefits she has already conferred on thee are a pledge of yet others which she will confer on thee hereafter. Make every effort to be a docile and faithful child of her adoption:—docile, by quickly following her inspiration; faithful, by executing the promises thou hast made her. O with what great security wilt thou then be able to say to her, "Well, our mediatrix!"

O my most merciful intercessor! cease not to plead

my cause with God; cease not to stand by me in the midst of so many dangers, and through them all be propitious to me, and pour down thy blessings upon me; cast those loving eyes on me which bring with them graces and favors whithersoever they turn. "Turn thy eyes of mercy towards us." Cause me one day by thy intercession to behold and to enjoy the fruit of thy womb: "And after this, our exile ended, show unto us the blessed fruit of thy womb Jesus." O this—this—is the grace which above all other graces thou must obtain for me, and which I hope to obtain through thy assistance! Yea, obtain for me all other graces of which I stand in so great need in this painful exile; yet assure me of those graces, before all others, those I mean which will conduct me to that happy abode in which it will be my delight to praise and love thee, O clement, O pious, O sweet virgin Mary, for all eternity! Amen.

THIRTY-NINTH MEDITATION.

MARY OUR MOTHER.

FIRST POINT.

MARY—CONSTITUTED OUR MOTHER.

At that moment when Mary gave her consent to the incarnation of the word, she became Mother of all mankind. At that time too she knew by the clear understanding she had of the prophecies, and still more by the heavenly lights she received from her divine Bridegroom, that the Son who was to be born of her would come for the salvation of the human family—but for a salvation to be effected at the price of unspeakable sufferings and of all his blood. This knowledge kindled in her heart an ardent desire for our salvation; and she consented that a body should be found for the person of the Word out of her most pure blood, and at the same time she consented that the blood of this Word made flesh should be the price set upon our salvation.

She became the mother of Jesus, because of her blood she conceived him: she was the mother of Jesus by nature; our mother, by making us her adopted children. From that moment forward when she uttered the pregnant, "Be it done," she began to bear us all in her heart, as she commenced to bear the Word of God in her body: "Is then Mary Mother of Christ only? Certainly not; for she is not only mother of Christ in particular, but likewise mother of all the faithful in general, a fact which fills us with joy exceeding great." St. Bonaventure.

St. Augustine assigns another ground for this motherhood, viz.: since Mary by her love for us contributed to the end that we were born in the Church, she became mother of us all, therefore we are the members of Jesus our head: "She is truly mother of the members, that is, of us, because by her love she co-operated to the end that the faithful, who are the members of that head, were born in the Church." Accordingly the holy apostle Paul styled Jesus "the first born among many brethren:" yea, our Redeemer himself disdained not to confirm the justness of this title by addressing the apostles as his brethren: "Go hence to my brethren."

"O Lady!" exultingly cries out St. Anselm; "if Jesus is our brother then are all we thy children, and thou art our mother: 'If thy Son became our brother, then art not thou, through him, become our mother?'" O truly, yes! the mother of God is my mother likewise. O what a motive for noble and holy joy! what great consolation pious souls derive from this thought! Yes, can one ever picture to himself a greater, a holier, a more lovable mother than this Mother of God? Consider, however, that this bond should serve not only to console us exceedingly, but should also be to us a powerful incentive to lead a life so pure that it will not tarnish the honor accruing to us from so exalted a relationship.

If thou gloriest in having so holy a Mother, thou

must accordingly conduct thyself in such manner that she need not blush at having thee for a son. What will it serve thee to say to Mary, "thou art my mother," if thou be not recognizable as her son?—and thou shalt not be so recognizable if thou followest thy passions and makest thyself rather a child of the wicked enemy. Mayst thou not belong to the number of those who are content with invoking her and with sometimes casting themselves at the foot of her altars, but thereafter take no concern at causing her all possible affliction, and imagine that they have full claim on her loving caresses for the mere reason that she is Mother.

Now be not deluded: "Not every one who says to her, Lady! Lady! shall participate in her special favors; but those who, by leading a genuine Christian life, take the pains to merit for themselves the beautiful name of her children."

SECOND POINT.

MARY—PROCLAIMED OUR MOTHER.

Who proclaimed the most holy Virgin to be the mother of all men, and what was the character of the circumstances in which he so proclaimed her? Our divine Redeemer did so, and did so when he was expiring on Calvary. In those supreme and sorrowful moments our most merciful God designed to give us a new pledge of his love; and this he did by bequeathing us his Mother that she might be our mother also: "Woman," said he to her, with his glance turned to his beloved disciple, "behold thy son;" and thereupon he said to the disciple: "Behold thy mother," as if he were to say: O woman!

that heartfelt and burning love which consumes thee turn henceforward to John, and in him to all the faithful, because I now substitute them in my stead, and desire that thou look upon them for the future as thy children: "Behold thy son."

Two things are worthy of remark in regard to these words; first, that Jesus called Mary not "Mother," but "Woman;" and this he did in order to signify that on that occasion he addressed her not in his capacity of Son, but in his capacity of Redeemer,—not as man, but as God. Secondly; that he wished to comprise in the person of the beloved disciple all the faithful; and for this reason he committed the Virgin to John, not as to his beloved disciple, but as to one of the disciples: "He said to the disciple." Hence he bequeathed her to him not as something personal, not as a legacy which should be exclusively his, but as an inheritance which should be the property of all who were to be his (our Redeemer's) followers. With this understanding she received John as a disciple; that is, she received him from that moment forward, in as much as he might be looked upon as representing all followers of her divine Son; and on his (John's) part, too, he ever looked upon her and treated her as the sweetest mother: "And the disciple took her to himself."

Behold now Mary constituted our mother in virtue of a public ordinance issued in regard to her from the throne of the cross; and indeed constituted our mother in the most solemn and dreadful moment that can ever be possible here below. Shall Mary be ever able to forget the last recommendations and memorial words uttered by her Jesus agonizing on the cross? Ah, no! Mary forgets them not, nor will she ever forget them! Oh, had we but constantly before our eyes so precious a present, and did we know how to praise it as it deserves! She sees herself clothed with the dignity of Mother, and recognizes in us the right of recurring to her as children; and from the moment when she came down from Calvary, she loved us all in the same manner as if she had brought every one of us into the world.

Divine lips of my expiring Redeemer! I render you the tribute of my thanks. What sweeter memento, what present more proportioned to the wants of our heart, couldst thou have left behind thee for us than thy own Mother? Hast thou studied on this affectionate device of thy Lord? He saw that in the troubles of this life we had need of some one to sympathize with us, to encourage us, to inspire us with confidence and love, and to be, as it were, an universal refuge common to us all; and in his last mortal agony, when he was immersed in a sea of sufferings, he was anxious to provide for us such an one; and such an one he found in his most holy mother.

Most loving heart of my Jesus, grant that I may one day know thee; and teach me to hope for as much as possible from a God who, even when he was pierced through on the cross and in the very jaws of death, was concerned only for my welfare.

THIRD POINT.

MARY EXERCISES MOTHERHOOD TOWARDS US.

As Mary was publicly proclaimed our Mother, so also

she was filled with that tender commiseration and that heartfelt love which are peculiarly distinguishing characteristics of a mother. Our Lord enlarged her heart and inflamed it in such a manner that she was enabled to take charge of, and to love, children as numerous as the faithful; and thus is she Mother, not only in title and rank, but also by solicitude, inclination, and benevolence.

What does our lady for us? That which a mother does for her children; she commiserates, reproves, exhorts us; she renders us all sorts of services, she is mindful of us, she prays for us and loves us with ceaseless love. O whoever could give a glance through that heart! What a spectacle would offer itself to his vision! "Can a woman forget her infant, so as not to have pity on the son of her womb? and if she should forget, yet will not I forget thee." Isa. xlix. 15 v. Is, however, a woman capable of forgetting the fruit of her womb and of not sympathizing therewith? And yet thou shouldst know that, were even this the case with a certain earthly mother, it can never occur in the case of our heavenly mother whom God gave us, precisely that she might discharge the maternal offices towards us: "and if she should forget, yet will not I forget thee." Isa. xlix. 15 v.

So long as she lived on earth, she approved herself a most tender mother to all the faithful; and now she continues in heaven to discharge more than ever the duties of her merciful office, and with all the assiduity of the warmest affection. O how many evidences of her maternal solicitude has she not daily transmitted to us, and does she not yet daily afford us! Public proofs of the solicitude with which Mary performs the duties of mother, are, the manifest apparitions which at every time and in every century occurred in such numbers that, in all Christendom, there is scarcely a country which has not been sanctified by her presence; the salutary exhortations which she gives even in our own times, by means of her images,—at one time, by the visible motion of her eyes,—at another, by assuming a sorrowful mien, as if with a view to announce beforehand to the peoples the calamities which awaited them;—the more or less striking miracles which she constantly performs for the relief of sufferers, performs now in this sanctuary, again in that: the unexpected conversion of so many sinners; interior lights and reproaches, the incentives to virtue, consolations, favors, all proceeding from her:—in one word, the balm which she infuses into the wounds, so numerous, of both soul and body. Such are among the public evidences of her maternal love for us.

Art thou aware how many proofs thou thyself hast received of her motherly solicitude? Towards thee Mary discharges the duties of a mother; and thou—dost thou perform towards her those of a child? Dost thou honor her? Dost thou obey her? Dost thou love her? These are the duties which every good child should render unto its mother; perform them generously and constantly, and thereby give her great joy: "Let thy father and thy mother be joyful; and let her rejoice that bore thee." Prov. xxiii. 25 v. Honor her then by rendering her all the services thou canst; love her, but with a love that declares itself by works; above all, be docile and complaisant: "and forsake not the law of thy mother." Prov. i. 8 v.

O Mary! O my most merciful Mother! cast not off from thee a child who takes refuge in thee, and who casts himself at thy feet, there to find pardon and mercy. Ah, Lady! I acknowledge it; a thousand times have I merited thy disfavors, I am not worthy to bear the sweet name of a son of thine! But let not this induce thee to cease to be a mother to me: "Discharge the duties of thy office, perfect thy work." St. Thomas of Villanova.

What mother in the world is there who would cast away from her a son, however ungrateful or unworthy he might be, providing that in a spirit of true sorrow he flung himself into her arms? And thou—couldst thou have the unmotherly courage to reject a son of thine? Ah no! I should be guilty of injustice to thee, were I to call in doubt thy mercy. God has set thee up for a mother to me; Jesus has proclaimed me as thy son; thou art all mercy; I therefore hope to obtain from thee all good. I hope thou wilt receive me as thy child, and wilt cover me in this life with thy protecting mantle, and wilt have regard not to my demerits but to the goodness of thine own heart; I hope that thou wilt so guide me that in the next life I may be able to participate in the treasures which are there in store for those who, here below, are thy docile and affectionate children.

All this I hope I shall obtain through thee, my most sweet and loving Mother!

FORTIETH MEDITATION.

MARY THE GUARDIAN LADY OF THE JUST.

FIRST POINT.

MARY EXTENDS HER LOVING PROTECTION TO THE JUST.

A PRUDENT agriculturist likes all his possessions, and is assiduous in putting them all to rights; he has, however, preference for those which yield him most fruit, and which crown his hope with the most abundant harvest. Upon these he looks more frequently, among these he lingers with greater pleasure, and the trouble he takes with them, will be to him easier and more agreeable.

What are the just? They are chosen vineyards, ("I planted thee a chosen vineyard," Jer. ii. 21 v.)—vineyards which repay the solicitude of their planter by the abundance of their produce. They are obedient children who conform their lives to the desires of the Heavenly Father; who cause him, not affliction, but joy, and return him love for love. Who can then doubt—that Mary bears especial affection towards those,—that they are most dear to her, and—that she extends them a generous share of her protection? She glories in being the keeper of the Lord's vineyards: "They have me the keeper in the vineyards." Cant. i. 5 v.

But what vineyards will she watch over with special predilection, if not over the chosen ones? She rejoices at being the mother of all, "the mother of all the living;" but must she not rejoice more at being the mother of all the just, than at being the mother of wayward children? She does good to all her children; how much more will she manifest her goodness to those of them who are docile and obecient? For these she entertains special affection; of these she takes loving care; these she fills with graces; and these she guards and protects in a very especial manner. The just, while they are on this earth, are not exempt from the dangers, the temptations, and the snares of the evil spirit; to these, the just are exposed as well as sinners, and perhaps more than sinners, on account of the intensity of the envy with which the jealous spirit of hell sees them possess any good. And yet, in spite of all this, what have the just to fear? Mary hides them under the mantle of her protection, and affectionately defends them against the assaults of their enemies.

Unto the just, Mary is that Tower of David against which all the efforts of the evil spirits are powerless. She is unto the just a high tower whence the enemy is descried from afar, a tower of strength which repels every assault; an armed tower, because on it "hang a thousand shields." How many have already been protected in this tower!—St. Justina was a virgin of unsullied purity; the evil spirit directed all his ingenious devices against her in order to cause her to fall; but Justina found herself immured within the walls of this tower. She observed how the evil spirit put forth his strength in such manner, that even the devils themselves acknowledge that she was protected by a mightier arm than their own.—St. Vincent of Paul, reduced to slavery by the Turks, remained for a long time in the houses and employments of unbelievers, was tempted with evil allurements of every kind, and had vicious examples constantly before his eyes; St. Justinian saw himself in the midst of the most irresistible occasions to sin; St. Louis lived amid the dangers of worldly pomp;—but all these holy personages were shut up and defended in this tower, and all the assaults of their enemies were frustrated.

Salvation is thine, if thou belong to so charming a multitude! The evil spirit will indeed lay his snares for thee, will lie in wait for thee, will make an attack upon thee, and when necessary, will strain every nerve in order to possess himself of thee; yet his arrows will not reach thee, and thou shalt be able in joy to address thy Guardian Lady thus: "Thou hast preserved my life from death, and my feet from falling."

The danger consists in going forth out of this tower; that is, in giving up the spiritual life and true devotion. The Devil will entice thee on to tread the paths of sin, that thou mayst walk "in the ways of the ungodly." What then hast thou to do in order to assure thyself that thou goest not forth out of this tower? Hold fast to devotion—to Mary, and keep with great care the grace of the Lord, which is the most precious treasure—the treasure which attracts for thee the eye and the affection of the most holy Virgin.

SECOND POINT.

MARY ENCOURAGES THE JUST TO BECOME PERFECT.

If the just would not fall away from righteousness, they must, while they are on earth, always advance in virtue. If they content themselves with refraining from grievous sins, or if they imagine that the degree of virtue which they possess suffices for them, they are sure to decline in virtue; for to stand still in the way of the Lord, is the same as to go backwards! "Not to advance is to retrograde."

For this reason the apostle exhorts the soul to make great progress and so to assure herself of salvation: "So run that you may obtain the prize." 1 Cor. ix. 24 v. To this contest Mary incites thee, that is, she incites every soul to strive to attain to invincible patience, to unselfish love, and to the constant practice of every virtue. Mary acts as a good mother who exhorts her son to become daily more and more assiduous to advance in learning, and thereby to merit more and more that his teachers be satisfied with him and that his father love him. To gain her end, Mary employs sometimes mere inspirations, whilst she exhorts the soul to stifle that sally of anger, to mortify that curiosity, manfully to overcome gluttony, and to practise this or that work of penance or of charity. At other times, she pours into the soul, unexpectedly, a drop of those consolations which inebriate with delight, and imperceptibly facilitate for it the practice of virtue; sometimes again she withdraws from it every tender affection, and causes it to be seized with disgust for all earthly things, and to feel a certain dryness in every heavenly influence. This she ordinarily does in the case of the negligent, with the view to make them advert to their negligence, and to reproach them with it; and the zealous, too, she sometimes treats in this manner, in order to confirm them in virtue.

At times she accomplishes her end by dispensing special and wonderful graces,—by, for instance, speaking distinctly from her images and declaring her will; thus did she encourage some of her servants to be more circumspect in fixing their hearts on God; thus did she animate the venerable Margaret Alacoque to bear patiently the persecution which caused her to suffer; thus did she give St. Aloysius of Gonzaga and St. Stanislaus Kostka direction to enter the society of Jesus; and thus did she communicate to St. Rose of Lima and St. Magdalene of Pazzi, the manner and way to make progress in the path of perfection.

But who could venture to point out all the means which she employs and all the trouble which she gives herself? It is very difficult to believe that she has not given thyself strong impulses to virtue; how often hast thou, when prostrate before her images, heard her praises proclaimed in that very place; how often hast thou, when reading some book of devotion, observed how her motherly voice aroused thee from thy sluggishness, and urged thee to practise this or that virtue; in brief, urged thee to advance in the way of the Lord?

Examine how thou hast conformed to her well laid plans and if thou thinkest that thou hast conformed but ill, then promise her immediately that thou wilt henceforward hearken to her inspirations more promptly and more generously. Doubt not that she will assist thee to career without stumbling, even to the very summit of the mountain of God.

THIRD POINT.

MARY HELPS THE JUST TO PERSEVERE.

Perseverance in good is absolutely necessary to every one who will be saved; and to continue well for a long time, is not enough; it is moreover requisite to persevere to the end: "Who perseveres to the end, shall be saved." Oh, how many began well and ended badly! What, then, does Mary do? Mary uses her influence with God to obtain for the just that most precious gift; and she induces the just to pray for it with importunity, for although perseverance is a purely free gift, that is, although it cannot be strictly merited as a reward for precedent good works, yet he infallibly obtains it who solicits it after the proper manner. This fact is inferable from our Lord's assurance: "And whatever you shall ask the Father in my name, that will I do." John xiv. 13 v..

What is the end which Mary proposes in the prayer which she makes in heaven for us? What else can her love desire than that she might see us happy with her for ever in heaven? Shortly before the commencement of his Passion our Lord looked up to heaven, and with all the earnestness of his soul, prayed to the heavenly Father for the grace of perseverance for his disciples: "Holy Father, keep them." "Holy Father, take into thy keeping this little company, so that not one who belongs to it may perish."

After the example of Jesus, Mary prays in heaven to the Eternal Father: "Keep them that they may not fall; keep them in thy grace and love to the end, that all may obtain the crown prepared for those who persevere."

Consider, however, that Mary requires the just to co-operate with her, and that on this account she entices them to pray to her constantly; and as nothing constrains one to pray so much as does fear, so she endeavors to maintain in vigor the holy fear of God in their hearts; for this fear is the most reliable weapon of defence amid the dangers of this life: "Happy the man who is ever solicitous." And why happy? Because he confides not in himself, because he is on his guard, because he recommends himself with more zeal and thus attains to salvation.

Oh, how many has she, by inspiring them with holy fear, caused to persevere in good with firmness and resolution: how many souls has she by this means preserved in their innocence even in the midst of the greatest dangers and of the most alluring occasions! Read the lives of the saints, and thou canst not fail to meet with a countless multitude of such souls. The misfortune is, that many repel her maternal solicitude, consider the holy fear of God as a thing adapted to beginners only, repose their confidence in themselves, and in consequence of thus acting, miserably suffer shipwreck.

Glance at thy own life, and ask thyself, didst thou

practise virtue constantly? Perhaps thou also wast zealous for a long time, but then thou didst grow cold and didst suffer thyself to be overcome. Admit now thou wast not well established in the holy fear of God; therefore pray to the Lord with earnestness, and often say with the Psalmist: "Penetrate my flesh with thy fear." Awaken in thee this fear by motives of faith; turn to the Virgin who rejoices to give instructions in this matter: "Come, children, hear me: I will teach thee the fear of the Lord." And the fear of God will preserve thee from dangers, will incite thee to prayer; and God will impart to thee his graces, and thou wilt persevere to the end.

O most august Queen of heaven and of earth! I do not indeed belong to the fortunate number of the just, much rather am I a sinner and indeed a great sinner; but I am fully confident that through thy intercession I have obtained pardon of my sins; and I hope that, notwithstanding all my ingratitude, I enjoy the grace of my God and thy protection. Ah Lady! do not grow weary of knocking at the door of my heart: employ, if necessary, tribulations and threats; I will remain faithful to God, and will persevere in doing good until I die. But for this perseverance, I stand in need of thy love for me; therefore assist me, and abandon me not till thou beholdest me at thy feet, happy in heaven. I confide in thee; and I promise myself that I shall obtain all good from thee! Amen.

FORTY-FIRST MEDITATION.

MARY THE REFUGE OF SINNERS.

FIRST POINT.

MARY AROUSES SINNERS TO CONVERSION.

IN order to reclaim sinners, Mary gives herself as much pains as a tender mother goes to in order to again obtain possession of her fugitive and lost son. Mary herself calls them, goes in quest of them, invites them, and encourages them to return to their God. What is there to which she does not condescend in order to win them over? So affectionately does she look after them and treat them, that she seems even to forget the honor due to Jesus; she appears to have nothing so much at heart as the conversion of sinners; and hence there is no means which she does not employ with a view to effect their conversion. She selects the most efficacious means, the most favorable moments; at one time, by giving them a good thought, she invites them to abandon sin; and at other times, she disposes them to renounce the evil of their ways by giving them interior and unexpected light. She gives them to understand the disorder of their lives, and causes them to feel the weight of their chains. Should all this be insufficient, she incites them by earnest reproaches, by sharp stings of conscience, by most violent uneasiness which tortures them day and night, and inclines them to seek in God that peace which they can never find in giving loose reins to their passions.

How many have already acknowledged with tears in their eyes that to this Mother were they indebted for that thought, or that inspiration, or that sting of conscience, which led them to God? She urges them on by the gracious mien of her images, by a look calculated to excite devotion, by tribulations, by the exhortations of a faithful friend; also, by delivering them from some danger and accompanying the delivery with a certain manifestation as to the hand from which the delivery proceeded. To some she assumes a threatening attitude in their dreams; to others she appears all on a sudden, and by a single glance causes them to melt in tears. At times she speaks to some from her images; occasionally she nods to others from her statues; now and again she causes persons to be removed from dangerous places by an invisible hand; and again on other occasions she terrifies persons by setting before their eyes some fearful example of the divine vengeance: yea, she even recommends some to the father confessors, as to Philip Neri, St. Francis Hieronymus, St. Cajetan, and many others.

Merely read the history of the Church and the lives of the saints, and thou wilt find them both full of the attractions whereby she obtained for herself the title of "hunter of souls," and "charm of sinners." "She opened her hand to the poor, and she stretched out her arms to the needy." O Mary! O dear refuge of sinners! how would the case be with us, were thy love for us not at the same time so strong, so gracious, and so assiduous! How would the case be with me hadst thou, on account of the ingratitude of which I have been so frequently guilty, and on account of my many refusals of thy mercies, suffered thyself to grow weary with me? It were already great kindness on her part, did she condescend to visit with her favors each and every one of those well beloved children who never wandered away from the Father's house. When she shows so much condescension to sinners, even to the most abandoned, to those who are most deeply plunged into vice, to those who are most hardened in sin,—O! then indeed is hers an affection which cannot be sufficiently admired.

Thank this merciful Lady for the motherly assiduity which animated her in thy regard:—who knows how many inspirations, how many impulses, she gave to thy mind and to thy heart? Who knows in how many ways she sought to lead thee to God? What hast thou done in the past? What dost thou now? Wait not for miracles; be intent merely upon not suffering to be thrown away upon thee the evidence which she has given thee of her affection; and if thou ascribe to her thy conversion, then remember to give her a pledge of thy gratitude; and this thou shalt give her by always remaining faithful to her, and by endeavoring to copy after her zeal in gaining souls to God.

SECOND POINT.

MARY RECEIVES SINNERS WITH AFFECTION.

Consider to thy great consolation, that there is in the world no sinner so miserable and so abandoned as not to be affectionately received by Mary, if he only have recourse to her. Jesus never rejected any one who came to him; yea, he even declared that he had come to save sinners: "He is come to save that which was lost."

As Jesus, so also Mary received sinners mercifully; and she assured them that she was their Mother: "I am the Mother of sinners who are willing to grow better." When the prodigal son returned penitent to his father, his father received him with most tender affection: but what would the mother have done on such an occasion? How many evidences of affection would she have showered upon him, how many tears of joy would she have shed, how many caresses would she have lavished on him? How she would have run forth to meet him, how she would have embraced him, how she would have hung on his neck, with what affection she would have pressed him to her bosom, and have covered him all over with kisses and with tears!

Now bear well in mind that sinners, if they choose, can find in Mary the Mother whom holy writ does not mention in connection with the reception of the prodigal son. Mary is not ashamed, nay, it even appears that she rejoices, to be looked upon as the Mother of sinners; she knows that those are the children who are the most worthy of her mercy, and hence the most needful of her affection; she remembers that her dying Jesus recommended them to her maternal heart; she sees them crimsoned with his most precious blood: "They are children," says she, "whom the Lord has given unto me." She forgets the ingratitude and repulses which she met at their hands, and she receives them with a tenderness peculiar to the most tender of all mothers, and becomes their protectress. "Shouldst thou belong to this description of sinners," says the pious Bernardine of Busto, "fear not that she will cast thee off, abominate thee, or turn away from thee her blessed glance. No! thou needst but an earnest will to raise thee from thy sins, and she will instantly stretch out her hand to thee, and her heart will exult at having won thee over more to herself. Even hadst thou committed all sins, let them not be unto thee any foundation for thy discouragement, but turn with confidence to this most glorious Lady whom thou wilt find with her hands full of mercy and generosity."

What more dost thou desire? Hast thou committed even all sins, be not discouraged on that account; and mark well, this is the language which the saints employ one and all:—St. Ephraim calls her "the stay of sinners;" St. Lawrence Justinian, "the hope of transgressors;" St Thomas of Villanova, "the shortest and the easiest path to God." By these epithets, the saints would signify that she is always prepared to receive even the most perverse of sinners.

One day, St. Gertrude saw the most holy Virgin as she held her mantle open and spread out, and the saint saw also the great number of wild beasts that took refuge beneath it; she saw how Mary herself not only did not chase them away, but with great compassion received and caressed them: and from this the saint understood the character of the reception which can be promised themselves at her hands by sinners, who are symbolized by those monsters, and are extremely to be compassionated.

O what good ground has the Church to invoke her as "refuge of sinners!" How much are saints in the right in promising themselves all good when they cast themselves with confiding hearts at the feet of this Queen of mercy! Hasten to throw thyself at her feet; say to her that thou art determined to arise from thy sins, that thou desirest to be saved, that thou hopest from her all assistance, and that thou committest thyself wholly into her hands.

If, on account of having so often broken thy word with her, thou lackest the courage to do this, then go and say to her that thou canst not summon courage to ask for her help, that thou art extremely weak, that thou knowest not how thou canst promise her any thing new; but that thou takest heart, in fine, from the knowledge that she is the refuge of sinners, and that of all those who hoped in her not a single one was confounded. Entreat her with importunity for her help, and hope to obtain from her all good.

THIRD POINT.

MARY HELPS SINNERS TO SANCTIFY THEMSELVES.

Scarce does the sinner think of extricating himself from the labyrinth of his sins, scarce does he make a step of return to God, when Mary immediately hastens to him, and by her graces and favors facilitates and ensures his delivery. She becomes balm and medicine for his wounds: "Thou art become the means of salvation to the miserable."

She knows that their souls, filled with wounds, stand in need of strength and courage, and strength and courage she imparts to them; she knows that by reason of their shortcomings which are so numerous, they are not in condition to remain standing, and she becomes unto them a support, a leader, and a guide. "Truly thou bindest up the wounded, thou bringest the sick to health, and art become to the wretched not only a mother, but also medicine." St. Bonaventure.

Yet this is not the full extent of her love, and she does not content herself with leading them again to the good path and obtaining for them pardon of their sins; but unless sinners themselves struggle against it, she tries to change them into vessels of election, and to sanctify them. There is no grade of sanctity, no privilege however high that has been granted to the innocent, which Mary is not disposed to obtain for her dear captives also. How many favors did she grant, and how many visits did she deign to make, to a Margaret of Cortona, who had been previously a great sinner? And what did she make of Mary of Egypt, who in consequence of her excesses was so very corrupt? A mirror of holiness. What did she make of William of Aquitania, him who was so notorious for his cruelties? A great saint; and she did the same with many others again whom we already know, and with yet countless others whom we shall not know till we are in heaven.

The exhalations which arise from certain slimy marshes are filthy, very disgusting, and contagious;

but, interpenetrated with the sun's rays, ascend from the earth, grow rarefied, and, transformed into a beautiful cloud, even form a certain agreeable aureola or crown around the sun. Something like this takes place with sinners through Mary's intercession; they even become beautiful stars which irradiate her head in heaven. "Come from Lebanon, thou wilt be crowned," says her divine Son to the Virgin; "Come from Lebanon, thou wilt be crowned; come from the dwelling-place of lions, of beasts, and of leopards." Come, O Mother! and thou wilt be crowned; but with what? with lions, with bears, with leopards, with wild beasts.

Albert the Great observes that sinners, by reason of their vicious propensities, are very aptly likened to those monsters, because both have the same intensely evil qualities and inclinations; but sinners, purified from their stains through Mary's intercession, enriched and adorned with the most shining virtues, are even transmuted into so many heavenly stars which are destined one day to constitute the crown of their royal benefactress. They who before were wild beasts, were through Mary changed into stars. Yes, they who were wild beasts before they committed themselves into Mary's hands, were turned into stars after they confided in her and followed her instructions.

Behold what the most hardened sinners can hope for from the most holy Virgin—to become shining stars of her crown hereafter in heaven! O unto how many was so charming a destiny reserved! "Number the stars if thou canst." O how those favored sinners bless the moment when they surrendered themselves to Mary!

O how they thank and will for ever thank her goodness for all eternity!

What then prevents thee from making thy resolution? What dost thou fear, of what art thou shy? A spark of generosity can set thee among those stars, and a mean indecision can cast thee into the abyss of damnation. Listen then to Mary's affectionate invitation: "Come, children, hear me; I will teach you the fear of the Lord."

Ah, most holy Lady! behold me at thy feet; no delay, no indecision, shall be countenanced by me for the future; thine I will be and into thy arms I cast myself. Do with me what is most pleasing to thee, provided thou bring me to good, and lead me securely to salvation. No more sins, no more vanities, nothing more of the world! henceforward let God and my soul be the object of my thoughts and affections; thou wilt be my refuge; in all my temptations and in all my dangers I will have recourse to thee. Be a mother unto me, and act with me in every regard as mother; for, although I am not worthy that thou shouldst do so, yet I desire to be a bright star in thy crown forever in heaven. Amen.

FORTY-SECOND MEDITATION.

MARY THE CONSOLER OF THE AFFLICTED.

FIRST POINT.

MARY BROUGHT TRUE CONSOLATION TO THE WORLD.

MARY was the venerable morning dawn which brought to the world that divine sun which caused us to be born again unto a new life. Before the morning dawn broke and this sun appeared, the world was a vast chaos of errors and darkness. Picture to thyself one of the most remote and unknown countries in the world, on which the sun had not shone for centuries; what would become of such a country? The waters would be turned into ice, the trees would become barren, the meadows and the animals would soon die out; men themselves would, after so long a period of privation, appear with countenances which would make them more like to spectres than to men. Should a beautiful Aurora arise suddenly out of that darkness, and should it bring on that ill-favored firmament a sun so beneficent as in a short time to impart new life to the earth and its inhabitants,—what would in such case be the character of the benefit which the Aurora had brought with it? What sort of life, what sort of consolation, would it have infused into all?

Now know that, before the advent of our Redeemer, the world was in a still more deplorable condition, and the holy Virgin conferred on it a benefit and a more priceless consolation than those which the most beneficent Aurora would have conferred on the dreariest and the most desolate of countries. Mary was the Aurora which brought that sun with it, that sun, I mean which caused the night to disappear in which we all were enveloped: "I caused inexhaustible light to arise in the firmament." His majesty condescended to come down into her womb, became all compassion for mankind, and assumed from her that most holy flesh and blood which he shed on the cross for the salvation of the world: "Out of my womb," said she, "I brought forth the God-Man."

Consider further, as she did not conceive her divine Son without knowing it, but, on the contrary, was aware of and desired her conception of him; so, in like manner, she desired for us all the salvation which could possibly come to us from him. Now ponder upon all the inestimable benefits which redemption brought us, the inestimable treasures of mercy, of blessing and of grace, and then say to thyself: all these are come to us through the medium of that venerable Aurora "of whom was born Jesus." "He desired," can we repeat with St. Bernard, "that we should have all things through Mary."

Dost thou now think it right she should be invoked under the beautiful title of "Deliverer of the afflicted?" If Judith was styled the "joy of Israel," for having preserved the city of Bethulia from being devastated by a terrible army; if Esther was styled the consolation and glory of the Jewish people because she had brought about the repeal of the death sentence unjustly pronounced against them; what then shall be said of this exalted lady, who gave us the author of life, and brought salvation to the entire universe?

O our most loving consoler! how exceeding great is our indebtedness to thee! O how incessantly should we praise thee, thank thee, honor thee! And yet, see how the ungrateful world acts towards her! How many are there who thank her for having bestowed on them such unspeakable benefits? How many are there who render her love for love? Many indeed love and honor her; but many, on the other hand, esteem her not, many even contemn and blaspheme her. Ah, how monstrous their blindness!

Deplore such ingratitude, repair it by thy fidelity, and cause devotion to her not to be so circumscribed as it is at present. Rather make every effort to cause others to honor and love her; and above all, do not permit that any one dependent on thee, or over whom thou hast any influence, should profane the venerable name of so compassionate a consoler.

SECOND POINT.

MARY SWEETENS EVERY AFFLICTION.

Numberless are the evils which afflict us: numberless those which affect the mind, as well as those which affect the body. And yet, among so many sources of pain and anguish, there is not a single one which is beyond the reach of Mary's influence; there is not an evil which the Virgin has not a thousand times remedied.

Painful diseases, fearful dangers, raging persecutions, loss of friends and of wealth, privations of every description, rankest calumnies, imprisonment, wicked temptations, despondency, diabolical obsessions, apprehensions, afflictions, mental anguish, cases of imperious necessity, timidity, remorse of conscience; for all, yea, to say every thing in one word, for all these afflictions, Mary has salutary balm which either banishes the ill altogether, or diminishes it exceedingly, according as the one or the other course is conducive to our salvation.

The consecrated gifts which depend from her images, the history of the Church and the lives of the saints,—all these give the most irrefragable testimony that there is no sickness, however rare and malignant it be, which Mary cannot cure, no distress which she cannot alleviate, no bitterness she cannot sweeten. Here thou findest dreadful and extremely oppressive temptations of sensuality either completely banished, or resulting in brilliant victories; as was the case in a Benedict, a Bernard, a Nilus, an Alphonsus Rodriguez, and in a thousand others, who obtained from her either perfect deliverance or so much strength that, as says the apostle, they found "issue with the temptation." There thou findest sadness, dejection, great mental anguish completely remedied as happened, among so many others, to a Hyacinthe, an Ignatius, a Theresa, who, in their most trying ordeals, were either consoled or wonderfully enabled to bear up against their afflictions.

Elsewhere again thou findest aids afforded by her providence; witnesses of this fact are Cajetan of Theina, Francis Regis, Clara of Assisium and a thousand others, whom she succored by giving them money or the means wherewith to sustain life. In other cases thou findest comfort imparted to persons who were calumniated, oppressed, ill-treated, and immured in darksome prisons; thus did she, for instance, console the venerable Spinelli in the midst of the most cruel insults that had been offered him, and she signified to him that this consolation was afforded him in consideration of the zeal wherewith he strove to propagate her honor. Thus did she console, by personally appearing to her and by speaking affectionate words to her, the blessed Germana when she was being mercilessly beaten by her step-mother; thus did she deliver Jerome Miani from prison, and restore him to complete liberty.

Thou findest, besides, instances of those who deplore their lack of talents and of knowledge, being abundantly furnished by her with both knowledge and talents. Through her agency, an Albert the Great, a Suarez, an Alvarez de Pazzi, became the wonder and admiration of the world. They are numberless,—and history is full of examples of them,—who were tormented by the bad treatment of their relations, or stung by remorse of conscience; and yet in every case they found consolation in Mary.

In one word, what affliction is there in which thou findest not always flowing the vein of consolation and of refreshment opened by this loving mother? Conclude from all this, that however grievous and bitter thy tribulations may be, thou canst always find consolation and remedy at the feet of thy loving mother—Mary.

Be well convinced that thy trouble, whatever its character, is neither the first she lightened of the kind, nor will it be the last. Those thoughts then crowd upon thee;—that there is no consolation for thee, that the ills which afflict thee are without remedy, that it is in vain for thee to busy thyself with prayer;—those and the like thoughts are snares of the evil spirit, devices to discourage and to mislead thee, and all to the end that thou mayst omit prayer and neglect to flee to this merciful consoler.

Do what lies in thy power, continue with patient confidence to knock at the door of her heart, and she will cause thee to grasp as if with the hand the truth that with great right is she styled "the consoler of the afflicted."

THIRD POINT.

THERE IS NO ONE IN AFFLICTION WHOM MARY DOES NOT CONSOLE.

It is not difficult to convince others that the most holy Virgin tempers all that is bitter; but for him who is actually in a state of affliction, it is difficult to believe that he would be consoled by recurring to her. The weight of one's own sins, the stratagems of the wicked enemy, preclude from the afflicted heart the heavenly balm of hope, and at the same time cause superhuman consolation to appear an utter impossibility: and yet what else is all this than an extremely subtle device of the wicked enemy?

Certain it is that many there are who, in their afflictions, do not merit to be consoled by the most holy Virgin; but why do they not merit to be consoled by her? Is she, in bestowing her favors, governed by the merits and demerits of him who prayerfully addresses himself to her? Woe to us were the case so! She is the Queen of mercy: and who are the subjects of her kingdom, asks St. Bernard, if not the miserable? "Thou art the Queen of mercy; and who else than the miserable are the subjects of mercy?" Thus we see that it is necessary, only to belong to the number of the wretched, in order to be entitled to confidence in her goodness.

Art thou a sinner? Art thou unworthy of her graces, because thou hast a thousand times abused her goodness? Art thou loaded so heavily with unrighteousness that thou hast not the courage to cast even a glance at her images? If so, then truly art thou of the number of the wretched; if so, then hast thou all claim to turn to her, and to place in her thy confidence.

Dost thou imagine that thy case is still worse? that all is over with thee? Know then that the saints salute her with the title, "Hope of those in despair," so sure are they that she rejects no one, that she suffers herself to be moved to compassion, and receives every one who recurs to her with confidence and perseverance. Yea, some remark that if even Judas, after his atrocious crime had, instead of yielding to despair, sought out Mary and cast himself at her feet, she would have greatly commiserated him on account of the evil consequences of the deed he had perpetrated; she would have received him with maternal affection, have consoled him, and worked out for him pardon of the most crying sin of which he had been guilty.

Who is now the one that is to be precluded from the right to confide in Mary? No one! no one! But knowst thou well what it means to confide in Mary? It means to obtain graces, to find mercies, to meet with consolation, protection, help of every kind. Sincere and lively confidence exercises unspeakable influence over every good heart; how much more influence, then, does it exercise over the most tender, the most sympathetic, the most noble heart that God ever gave to a mere creature! Of all those who placed their hope in this heart, not one was deceived, and not one remained uncomforted. No, not one: "No one who has hoped in thee was confounded." The afflicted of every description, most inveterate sinners, persons who were bestialized in a manner by crime, persons so debased by squalid wretchedness that the world would not have deigned to look at them,—such persons confidently recurred to her, and were comforted by her; Mary sent not one of such empty away: "No one who hath hoped in her was confounded."

A poor sinner, expelled the city by reason of her filthy and scandalous doings, and abandoned by all, had in her wretchedness and dreadful isolation come to the brink of the grave; and in this situation she turned to Mary and said to her: "Thou art the refuge of those that are forsaken; just now I am forsaken by all; thou art my only hope, thou alone canst help me; oh, have pity on me!" The most holy Virgin did not suffer the tears of this unfortunate to roll down in vain; and in the mercy peculiar to her own heart, she worked out for her pardon of her sins and refreshment after death. No! "Not one who has hoped in her was confounded."

What then art thou that thou dare not hope to receive consolation from her, if thou castest thyself with childlike confidence at her feet? Turn to Mary, conquer thy opposition, pray to her and address her: "Holy Mary, assist the miserable, help the desponding, comfort those who mourn." O Mary! O most merciful Lady! who accountest it thy glory to befriend the wretched, to console the afflicted, behold at thy feet one in misery and affliction who groans under the burthen of his tribulations. Cast a look at the many wounds of my soul, at the many wounds of my heart; thou knowest the remedy for my ills; thou hast now the power to deliver me from them; ah! infuse into my heart a drop of that salutary balm which will cause me to forget all the bitterness of my condition. Hasten to help this poor sinner who confides in thee, and grant that he may be able to celebrate on earth, and afterwards in heaven, the praises of his merciful consoler. Amen.

FORTY-THIRD MEDITATION.

MARY THE HELP OF CHRISTIAN PEOPLES.

FIRST POINT.

MARY PRESERVES THE CHRISTIAN PEOPLE FROM ERRONEOUS DOCTRINES.

THE evil spirit loses neither time nor opportunity to sow tares in the evangelical field, and to stifle in it the corn of excellent quality; and by this is meant the propagation of the spirit of error among Christians, in order to corrupt the precious deposit of their faith. Ah! by how many artful inventions, and with what great activity, he endeavors to misguide them and to lead them into error. Woe to the watchmen who are not vigilant!

What, however, does Mary do amid such dangers? Mary, the guardian Lady, the Mediatrix, the Mother of the Christian people, "is solicitous in all things and on every occasion for the miserable. She inspires faith, strengthens hope, banishes distrust, and transforms pusillanimity into courage." St. Bernard. She opposes weapons to weapons; she animates faith, confirms hope, encourages the vacillating, infuses the spirit of strength and zeal: she is in every way solicitous for the protection of her people. And not content with this, she exhorts, with the earnestness characteristic of a mother, pious souls to multiply their prayers. She exhorts the most zealous of her servants to redouble their efforts; she exhorts the learned to take up the pen for the defence of truth; she exhorts the pastors to raise their voice to give warning of the snares that are laid for their flocks.

Often, too, does she herself disclose the snares of the enemy, and teach the manner and way in which he can be combated and overcome. Herself brought from heaven a formula of faith to St. Gregory, Bishop of Neocæsarea, in order to guard his flock against the then prevailing errors; she encouraged St. John of Damascus to write against the Iconoclasts, that is the image-breakers; and by a miracle she restored to him his right hand, which they had cut off out of hatred to religion. She instructed St. Dominic as to how he should extirpate the heresy of the Albigenses; she taught St. Ignatius the manner and way to oppose with success the turbulent machinations of Luther and Calvin; and she did the same in the case of many other holy personages;—facts attested in every page of history.

So clearly did the Church recognize the hand of Mary in the extirpation of heresies, that she (the Church) could not refrain from congratulating her on having alone eradicated all heresies and brought them to naught: "Rejoice! O Virgin Mary, thóu alone hast banished from the world all heresies."

In her Immaculate Conception Mary crushed the head of the infernal serpent, and so often as he raises it to the detriment of her chosen people, she continues to crush it in like manner.

Happy those Christian countries which correspond

with the maternal designs of the most holy Virgin! The poisonous breath of the serpent will not be able to infect them. The tares will indeed crop out, but will be stifled again. Mary will help those who die faithful to her, to maintain in its integrity and vigor that faith which is the root of all that is good. O may the Christian people always render themselves worthy of so admirable a protection! O may they always in every danger flee to her!

But ah! in many quarters devotion to Mary grows cold and is on the decline. People are no longer solicitous to inspire the young with this devotion. This devotion is no longer practised with so great affection among those who are grown up. People are ashamed to appear as clients of this exalted lady; they remove her statues from the streets and from the houses where gratitude for favors received had erected them, as a most handsome adornment and as a most powerful protection. Is it, then, any wonder that the evil spirit possesses so great power, and that the people are infected with poisonous teachings?

If God has set thee up as a watchman over the evangelical field, if thou art a pastor of souls and art solicitous to preserve in them the deposit of faith, then remember always that in thy greatest necessities the channel through which flow the most powerful means of assistance is Mary—that Virgin whom the Church invokes and entreats under the beautiful title of "Help of Christians."

SECOND POINT.

MARY ASSISTS THE CHRISTIAN PEOPLE WHEN THEY ARE PERSECUTED.

The assistance which the most holy Virgin grants to Christian people in order to preserve them from error, she also grants with a view to sustain them in that constant struggle which all the enemies of God, who are sworn to effect their damnation, evoke against God and the Church.

How many fearful and bloody persecutions! and yet in them all the helping hand of Mary plainly appears. The Roman Pontiffs who are the lawful interpreters and the most incontestible witnesses in the case, declare that the finger of Mary appears in a wonderful manner throughout all those persecutions: "The Christian people often experienced, in a wonderful manner, the most manifest assistance from her to overcome the enemies of religion." Consult the pages of history, and thou shalt find a thousand proofs of this fact. She calmed the fearful storms which set all Christendom in commotion in the time of Paul II.; she healed the wounds which half a century of schism had inflicted on the Church in the days of Boniface VIII.; she rendered great assistance to the Church when it was oppressed during the pontificate of Gregory IX.; she combated the fury of the Turks in the time of Urban II.; she saved almost the whole of Christendom from falling under the dominion of the Mussulman who, during the pontificate of St. Pius V., had already devastated the greater portion of the Christian world. And who is ignorant of what assistance she rendered the Christian family in the times of Pius VII.—times which come nearer our own day? Who has not heard of the assistance which, in more recent times, she rendered in order to enable Pius IX. to return to his pontifical chair?

During those and many other persecutions, so visible was the assistance rendered by the Virgin that peoples and their pastors considered it a strict duty of gratitude to perpetuate, by means of public monuments, the memory of the assistance which they obtained from her on such occasions.

Imagine not, however, that she has furnished only those aids which were cognizable to our senses. No! the greatest portion of the waters which the earth receives into its bosom, is not that portion which falls from the clouds in a manner visible to all; on the contrary, the greatest portion is that which descends on it imperceptibly and in ways which we never discover. In like manner, the assistance which Mary gives and which we see not, is more abundant than those others which fall under our senses. Could we see all things, we should observe that there was not a single victory which Christian weapons obtained over the enemies of the Church, that there was not a single storm of persecution, in which she did not furnish powerful or appropriate assistance.

If thou livest in one of those sad periods when God allows the Church to be persecuted on account of the sins of her children, or from other inscrutable designs of his Providence; if thy lot is cast in such an epoch, lose not courage. Here on earth the Church must combat; she will be assailed, but her victory is secure, for "the gates of hell shall not prevail against her." Adhere firmly to the principles and the teachings of faith. The more thy necessities increase, the more shouldst thou confide and pray. Prayer has lost nothing of its power, nor has Mary's arm grown shorter.

Entreat her to hasten to assist thee; "Let not thy help be far away from me." Encourage all to pray; and as regards thyself, fear nothing; Mary will annihilate the enemies of God and of the Church, and will turn struggles into victories and persecutions into triumphs.

THIRD POINT.

MARY'S ASSISTANCE IN TIMES OF PUBLIC DISTRESS.

There is no public visitation, whether of hunger, famine, earthquake, or of any other misfortune, in which the Christian people, as if from natural instinct, did not hasten to cast themselves at Mary's feet and stretch out their hands to her in an imploring attitude. The Christian people act after the manner of a child who, beaten by the father, runs to the mother and takes refuge under her protecting mantle. And why does the child act so? Because it always finds protection in the mother. Just this is the very case with the Christian people. They know from continuous experience that, in their misfortunes, Mary's protecting mantle is their securest refuge, and that no one has recourse to her in vain.

"In all storms, in all trials and adversities, when

there is plague, hunger, war, tribulation of any kind, we all flee to thee," says St. Thomas of Villanova, addressing her; "thou art our protection, our refuge." Yes, dost thou not see with what great assiduity Christian kingdoms and countries endeavored to secure her protection? Dost thou not see how particular countries and kingdoms chose her for their special patroness, how they rivalled each other in testifying to her their gratitude and their love? Is there in all Christendom a people that would not have desired to place themselves under the protection of Mary? If there be, then go ask why are there so many sanctuaries, so many temples, so many chapels built in her honor; examine into the origin of so many public monuments consecrated to her with so much ceremonial splendor; examine into the cause of so many vigils faithfully kept in her honor, of so many solemnities celebrated on her account, of so much homage paid to her in all places; and thy examination will induce the conclusion that all these evidences of devotion to her originated with Mary's having preserved or delivered those peoples from some grievous calamity.

That city was devastated by plague, this by hunger, and yet another by war: earthquake threatened to bury one quarter, water came on the point of swallowing up a certain province, fire to reduce to ashes whole districts;—the Christian people in their desolation turned to Mary, consecrated themselves to her by vow, and she mercifully covered them with the mantle of her protection, and shielded them from the wrath of God. Joshua, the valiant leader of the people of Israel, set up twelve large stones in the river Jordan, in order thereby to keep green in the minds of the Hebrew people the memory of the benefits they had received; and when they evinced astonishment at what he had done, he said to them: "When your children shall ask their fathers to-morrow, what mean these stones? answer thus: 'those stones are erected in commemoration of the great miracles which God has wrought in our favor.'"

What are the many monuments erected to Mary, and the many festivals celebrated in her honor? They are perpetuators of the memory of the wonderful deeds which Mary performed on behalf of the Christian people; they are incontrovertible memorials of the calamities from which she preserved those people, they are evidences of gratitude and love. Men do not so easily honor Mary for her dignity and elevation, and out of pure unselfish love; then their honoring her so much, is a sign that in so honoring her they find much advantage.

Let us learn from this, how much we can promise ourselves from Mary when tribulations press hard upon us; let us also learn that the most effectual means to get rid of them when they are upon us, or to ward them off when they threaten us, is to have recourse to Mary, and to recur to her in a spirit of humility, zeal and sincere penance. God does not change; aroused to anger by so many iniquities, he is willing again to be propitiated. Well is it for us if his most holy Mother will plead our case! And yet what is done by the Christians of our day, to procure on their behalf so loving a course on the part of

Mary? Where are the public and special prayers, the good works and the promises?

Ah, what indifference, what callousness! But as to thee, do what thou canst; place thyself, thy interests, thy family, thy country, under her mantle: "We fly to thy protection, O holy Mother of God! O Lady! despise not our petitions, at this time especially when we are in so great distress; despise not our prayers in our necessities;" save us from all the chastisements which we merit, and keep us constantly under the mantle of thy protection, Virgin most glorious and ever worthy of all praise! "But deliver us from all evils, O thou ever glorious and blessed Virgin!" Amen.

FORTY-FOURTH MEDITATION.

MARY'S LOVE FOR HER CLIENTS WHILE IN THIS LIFE.

FIRST POINT.

MARY'S SOLICITUDE FOR THE WELL-BEING OF HER CLIENTS.

A WISE and prudent Queen indeed loves all her subjects, but she entertains special affection for and feels special interest in those who make up her court, and who, by their greater fidelity to her, and the greater services they render her, really deserve her special protection. Precisely so, stands the case with Mary; she loves all; yet she receives in a particular manner those who truly profess to honor her in a particular manner. For these she evidences her solicitude, and even if she does not exempt them from the troubles of this life—troubles to which she was more subjected than any one of her venerators—yet, in order to enable them to go through those troubles, she gives them all the assistance that is compatible with their well-being.

Jesus came to heal the diseases of the soul, but he did not disdain to heal the diseases of the body also; he sanctified Martha and Magdalene, but he comforted them too by raising Lazarus to life. Those who loved him most ardently he desired to distinguish, by working on their behalf one of the most splendid miracles recorded in his Gospel. Such a distinction the Virgin also grants to her loving children by conferring on them most distinguishing graces in the tribulations and necessities of the present life: "For thou," such is the loving address of Ephraim of Syria to her, "thou art the helper of the afflicted, the patroness of the oppressed, salvation to those who are frail, a port in the storm, assistance and refuge to all who are in necessity."

It is nevertheless certain that she has still more at heart the spiritual welfare of her clients, their advancement in virtue, their fidelity and perseverance in the ways of the Lord. These are the objects she has in view,—and what stone does our blessed and merciful Lady leave unturned with a view to their accomplishment? She stands by her affectionate clients; she defends them, protects them, guides them and conducts them, as it were, herself into a secure harbor. This solicitude was represented to the virgin, Mary Magdalene of Pazzi, under a most beautiful symbol. She beheld some ships sailing on an immense sea which was agitated by fearful winds and storms; one of the ships tossed in every direction by the surging waves, and another rolled right and left on its side; this one struck on a sand-bank, that one indeed pursued its due course, yet struggling with great effort against the mountainous waves: in short, all the vessels were in great danger, and very hard set. One alone appeared to be privileged; one alone ploughed the waters securely and triumphantly, without receiving detriment from either winds or waves. At the helm of that ship stood a majestic Lady, who with one of her hands commanded the sea, and with the other directed the ship calmly and amid the benedictions of the passengers.

O that fortunate ship! O those thrice favored souls who took passage therein! Knowest thou what this ship symbolized? It symbolized the legion of Mary's clients who, amid the storms of the raging sea of this life, were protected by her, and were, by the lights and graces received from her, conducted to the haven of a happy eternity. The holy father Bonaventure clearly expresses the same thought, when he assures us that just this was the loving destiny of Mary our star: "This is truly the destiny of our star, that she leads those who sail on the sea of this world, in the ship of innocence or of penance, to the shore of the heavenly fatherland."

Hast thou good ground for believing that thou shalt obtain a place in this blessed ship? Or hast thou merited that the most holy Virgin take a particular interest in thee? Bear in mind that she takes such interest in those souls who truly profess to be particularly devoted to her service: use all thy industry to render thyself worthy of her special interest in thee. If thou wilt take easy and secure means to effect this object, then become a member of one of the societies established in Mary's honor; perform the exercises faithfully and affectionately; and should anything seem difficult to thee, remember that without taking some pains, and without going to some trouble, no one will be saved.

So convinced was St. Charles Borromeo of the

advantages accruing to souls from being connected with such pious associations, that in his diocesan conventions he strongly recommended father confessors to persuade their penitents by every possible means, to enroll themselves as members of such associations. In membership thou wilt have light, means of salvation, good examples, directions of every kind; and advantages of this sort cannot fail of facilitating for thee the path of salvation, or of winning for thee the special protection of Mary. This was the very answer which St. Liguori gave to Lord Kitterdam, who inquired of the saint what he (Kitterdam) should do in order to assure himself of the salvation of his soul.

Then become a member of some society, it will be unto thee a blessed ship which will bring thee into port; and if thou art perchance already in such a ship, then renew thy spirit, redouble thy zeal, and make thyself always more and more worthy to be numbered among the children of the most holy Virgin.

SECOND POINT.

MARY'S GREAT GOODNESS TO HER CLIENTS.

Mary condescends to be so good to her clients that no one can help admiring her condescension. What is the extent of her condescension? She appears to forget her greatness in order to serve him who serves her. Thus the very learned Idiotus expresses himself: "She loves those who love her, yea, she is a servant to those who are servants to her." There is not a single good office of affection which a mother renders her children, which Mary does not render those who love her.

St. Dominic was very much afflicted at the stiff-neckedness of the Albigenses, and in his afflictions he invoked Mary's assistance with warm tears. The result of all this was that she appeared to him, and thus affectionately addressed him: "My dear son Dominic, behold here present her whom thou invoked, and who is now come to thy assistance." She appeared to St. Stanislaus Kostka, of the Society of Jesus, when the saint was seriously ill, and she placed the child Jesus in his arms. When St. Catherine of Sienna was troubled at not knowing how to acquit herself of the duties imposed on her by obedience, she had recourse to Mary, and Mary hastened to sympathize with her, to instruct her and to console her. When St. Columba was shut up and forsaken in a room, the blessed Virgin brought him his daily nourishment. She thanked St. Idlefonsus for having defended her virginity against the Hebridian sect; she thanked St. Benno for his efforts to have her birth solemnly celebrated; Father Martin Guttierez she thanked for his zeal in propagating, and in successfully propagating among the public at large, the doctrine that her merits surpassed the merits of all the saints taken together. She turned away from Thomas of Kempis with a countenance indicating displeasure, with the view to remind him of having forgotten his religious exercises; and she often furnished the blessed Hermann with money, when he was yet a boy. With a snow-white handkerchief she wiped the sweat from the forehead of St. Alphonsus Rodriguez when, exhausted by a long and fatiguing journey, he was no longer well able to stand on his feet. She informed a captain who had rendered an humble service to a poor blind person for the sake of her name, that, as part of the reward for what he had done, he would be elected emperor; and this captain was Leo, the second of the name. A poor Turk who used to light the lamps faithfully and affectionately before her image, she compensated by commanding him to become a Christian, and she gave him the name of Joseph.

Who could now point out the thousandth part of the affectionate allurements which Mary employs in regard to her clients? They are so great and of such a kind that the sensual spirit of the world cannot bring itself even to believe them; and yet for those souls who are a little experienced in the loving ways of Mary, and who have some knowledge of how affectionate and sympathetic is the heart of this exalted Lady—for such souls she has always sweet consolation at hand.

O how encouraging is the maternal confidence with which she treats her dear clients! and who will not strive to attain the happiness of knowing her more and more, of serving her, of loving her? Who will not take every pains in order to conquer constantly new degrees of love of her? Admire her goodness; but do not covet extraordinary favors unless it were her affectionate presence with thee in thy last moments—a favor which several saints solicited for themselves, and also, to their unspeakable consolation, obtained.

Exert thyself to obtain the same favor, by the great humility and the great purity of thy life—two virtues which she enthusiastically esteems; and then, when thou hast done this, let it suffice for thee to know that she protects thee from heaven above. Bear in mind that if thy life be humble and pure, thou wilt meet with many an occasion to experience the unspeakable goodness of Mary.

THIRD POINT.

MARY GIVES HER CLIENTS A PLEDGE OF SALVATION.

Sterling devotion to Mary takes root only among the honored people, that is among the elect who shall praise God for all eternity: and "I took root among the honored people." My elect, says our Lord to her, are destined to be that favored soil on which devotion and love to thee, O Mother, shall take root and flourish! "Take root among my elect:" and the Virgin seems to answer that she will abide only with those, and "my habitation is in the assembly of the saints."

Happy those souls who are thoroughly established in this devotion! They have good grounds for hoping that they belong to the number of the chosen few; and this is the view entertained by the saints also—by the saints of early as well as by those of recent times. The blessed Simon Rosas said to a member of his congregation who was tortured with great mental anguish: "Fear not, my son, only persevere in thy devotion to Mary, and heaven is thine." St. Alphonsus Liguori used often to repeat: "If I honor Mary, I am secure of heaven." St. Philip Neri, St. Charles, the blessed Leonardo of Port Maurice, and many other personages of sainted memory, declare that devotion to Mary is a clear sign of predestination to glory; and this same doctrine can be said to be the universal belief of the ancient fathers.

St. Anselm says whoever is privileged with frequently thinking on Mary, and thinking of her with tender affection, has, in this life, a strong sign that he will attain to eternal felicity: "Let him to whom it is given to think often on her with affectionate emotion, take this favor for an infallible sign that he shall be saved."

This, however, does not imply that merely thinking of her suffices for salvation; but the meaning of the saint's expression is, that it is impossible to occupy one's thoughts frequently with Mary without, at the same time, entertaining great affection for her; and the affection which we feel for her facilitates for us the imitation of her virtues, and it is in this imitation consists the principal fruit of the homage we pay to our blessed Lady.

Still more plainly does St. Bonaventure teach the doctrine, that affection for Mary is a sure sign of predestination. This learned client of hers maintains that devotion to her is, as it were, a mark set upon the forehead of those whose names are registered in the book of life: "Whoever bears on his forehead the sign of her name, shall be written down in the book of life; even as the angel marked the foreheads of all those who were to escape extermination." Ezech. ix.

The same teaching is delivered in very plain terms by Saint Bernard, who calls devotion to the Mother of God, "the most certain sign possible that salvation shall be attained by its possessor." St. Liguori's "Glories of Mary." Other saints confirm this doctrine, and maintain that there is no more beautiful sign of gaining eternal salvation than is devotion to Mary.

O what powerful incentives to thy heart are the

facts just stated! If thou art one of Mary's clients, then art thou secure of gaining heaven. Observe nevertheless that, by reason of its very results, this devotion must be deeply rooted: "I took root." A plant is considered deeply rooted when it buds, blossoms, and brings forth fruit. Is thy devotion to Mary rooted deeply enough to stand this test? Examine a little the character of thy devotion, and, from the flowers and fruits which grow upon it, conclude whether it be or be not a pledge of heaven for thee. Entreat Mary, however, to grant thee the charming grace of this deeply rooted devotion to her; say to her that thou desirest it, and indeed that thou desirest it, cost it what it may. O Mary! make me one of thy clients, I ardently wish to become one; I long for this pledge of my salvation; I desire to love thee on earth, in order that I may always love thee in heaven. Tell me what dost thou desire me to do? I am willing to do all things to the end that I may belong to thee; but deign thou to assist me; let devotion to thee take root in my heart, and indeed take root so deep that neither the evil spirits, nor the world, nor the flesh, can ever again be able to shake, much less to eradicate, it. Amen.

FORTY-FIFTH MEDITATION.

THE ASSISTANCE WHICH MARY GIVES HER CLIENTS IN THEIR LAST MOMENTS.

FIRST POINT.

MARY PROTECTS HER CLIENTS AGAINST THE ASSAULTS OF THE EVIL SPIRITS.

Mary does not act as those worldly friends act, who forsake us in the hour of our greatest need ; on the contrary, she proportions the greatness of the help she gives to the greatness of the necessity, and redoubles her solicitude according as the distress of her clients increases. She does as a mother whose anxiety at her child's bedside augments with the danger of the child's condition ; and which is the most dangerous moment ? Certainly the moment of death. Then it is that the evil spirit redoubles his assaults, because he knows that but little time remains for him : "the devil is come down unto you, having great wrath, knowing that he hath but a short time." Apoc. xii. 12 v. The sins committed, fear of the judgment to be undergone, the sickness which weighs heavy on the departing, render it easy for the enemy to make his assault.

But notwithstanding all this, what has a soul to fear who is devoted to Mary ? Nothing. At that hour Mary becomes their shield and assures them of victory : "The desires of those who are departing she not merely complies with, but even anticipates," says St. Jerome. Our blessed Lady herself attested this fact to St. John of God, who complained that he did not see his royal patroness come to his assistance. She then appeared to him, affectionately reproached him with his lack of confidence in her, and said: "John, it is not my custom to abandon my clients at their last moments. I am by no means accustomed to forsake my clients in their embarrassment at this supreme hour."

And what does she do? She does not suffer them to be tempted, and this favor she grants to very many who never enjoyed so great tranquillity and peace of mind as at the hour of their death; or if she allows them to be tempted, the temptation will serve to beautify their crown all the more. In this manner the evil spirits furiously assailed the venerable Father Emanuel Padian of Jesus—a Father who was very devout to the Virgin—but what happened? She descended visibly into his room, and her apparition was as a flash of lightning which put the evil spirits to flight and constrained them to cry out: "Ah we affect nothing; for she who is without stain has him under her protection." They made an attack on Father Caspar Haywood—another very devoted servant of Mary—but scarce had he invoked her, when he could exclaim, "I thank thee O Mary for having come to my assistance!" They fearfully assailed St. Andrew of Otrellins; but the temptation was for him a most glorious triumph. During the struggle he raised his eyes to a statue of Mary, and thereupon he expired most placidly in her arms.

Whoever is defended by so mighty a Lady, can at no time be vanquished, and has nothing whatever to fear: "Mary is for us," exclaims St. Antoninus; "who is against us?" O God! what a consolation will it be for us at the end of our life, when the question will turn upon our eternal salvation, to behold the Queen of heaven at our side in order to succor us, and to comfort us, by assuring us of her protection! Rejoice then, devout souls! Mary does not forsake at the hour of his death him who served her and loved her in the hour of his vigor. O she will not permit the evil enemies to assail the devout soul; or if she permit them, she will cause the contest to conduce only to the increase of thy merits and of thy glory!

Let then thy enemies and their assaults be ever so dreadful, the bare name of our defender is a name of terror which disperses and puts them to flight. If we abide steadfastly in the service and love of Mary, says Richard of St. Lawrence, she will grant us courage, protection, and victory, at the hour of our death. Let us often say to her: "Defend us from the enemy and receive us at the hour of our death." Let us frequently recommend to her our last hours, and let us repeat with great piety the words of the angelical salutation, "Pray for us poor sinners, now and at the hour of our death." Amen.

SECOND POINT.

MARY SOFTENS THE AGONY OF THE DEPARTING.

Mary does not disdain to diminish with maternal affection the sufferings and the pains which death brings in its train. She does not content herself with leading the souls of her clients to salvation. She desires also to make the momentous step less painful and less terrible to them: "Then," said she to St. Bridget, "then will I, who am their most loving Lady and Mother, come to meet them when they are departing, in order that I may give them consolation and relief."

Dost thou understand? She goes to them not as their Lady, not even as their affectionate Lady: but she goes to them as their Mother, and brings them not only consolation but likewise relief; relief from the pains, relief from the anguish, relief from the sufferings, whatever their character. She sends them when they are in need of it, spiritual or corporal assistance; she infuses heavenly peace into the heart; she assures them interiorly that she will protect and assist them; she exhorts them to bear patiently the pains and trials of their condition, that thereby they might escape the fires of purgatory, or at least abridge the term of their confinement in prison: she announces to them the time of their departure; she grants them relief by consoling them in every manner.

No proof of what is here advanced, can be required by any one who was ever present at the death of one of Mary's clients who were favored in this regard, and whose breath was a breath of affection for her. Adolphus, Count of Alsace, who afterwards became a Franciscan monk, was tormented with great fear in the closing hours of his life. Then appeared to him the Virgin accompanied with several saints, who, in accents of gentle encouragement, said to him: "My dearest

Adolph, why then dost thou dread death so exceedingly?" St. Liguori's "Glories of Mary." St. Mary of Ogny saw the most holy Virgin at the death bed of a poor widow, and saw how, like a compassionate nurse-tender, she sought to mitigate the sufferings which the widow was enduring. So consoled at the time of his death was her extraordinarily great servant Father Suarez, that he said he had not the remotest idea that it could possibly be to him so agreeable a thing to die: "I could not have imagined that death was something so charming." In recompense of his devotion to Mary, the Duke of Zeria was so filled with joy that he called his first-born to his bedside and said to him: "My son, devotion to Mary is the most glorious inheritance I bequeathe to thee in these my last moments. I have no sweeter consolation than the reflection that I was a true servant of this heavenly Lady."

If we gave free scope to our pen in adducing those charming proofs, our task would never be finished. Oh, what ought not a soul devoted to her, promise itself? Very often she causes the person departing to lose the memory of the mortal agony in the consolations which she imparts; happy the one who understands and knows how to secure so great a boon! Perhaps the performance of those services which promote her honor come difficult to thee at present; perhaps it is burthensome to thee to increase thy prayer on the days specially set apart in her honor; perhaps it is burthensome to thee to visit her altars, to perform the nine days' devotion which was instituted as a preparation for her festivals; perhaps burthensome to thee to celebrate the month of Mary:—but if all these things put thee to some inconvenience at present, a moment will arrive when the services thou shalt have rendered to Mary will be thy most precious and most sweet consolation: "For in the latter end thou shalt find rest in her, and she shall be turned to thy joy." Eccl. vi. 29 v.

What thou dost now for Mary thou wilt certainly find again; Mary is mindful of it and she will begin, in the hours of thy greatest need, to make thee taste those joys which await thee for all eternity.

THIRD POINT.

MARY BRINGS THE SOULS OF HER CLIENTS TO HEAVEN.

As star differs from star in magnitude and glory, so likewise the clients of the great Virgin differ from one another in point of merit. There are certain of her clients eminently full of merits, and who far surpass the others in this regard—a spotless innocence of life, an indefatigable zeal in imitating her virtues, an intensely strong and tender affection for her, wonderfully endear thee to her. How then does Mary treat those well beloved souls? As they themselves while they live, try to become like unto her, so she obtains for them the grace to become like unto her in their death. She died out of pure love, and causes those servants to die out of pure love also; she died in the midst of the most precious consolations from heaven, and in like manner she causes her clients to spend their last moments amid heavenly consolations. St. Vincent Ferrier wrote that the Virgin deigns to receive the spirit of her departing clients: "the Virgin receives the souls of the dying."

This maternal solicitude she evinced to thousands, by filling them, through her most affectionate presence, with unspeakable joy, and then by bringing their souls to heaven. Contemplate for a while the death of a saint Bernard of Clairvaux, of a John Francis Regis, of a Philip Neri, and of so many others who have not as yet had the honor of being raised on our altars. O how their cells were resplendent with heavenly light! O what visits! O what joys! Stanislaus Kostka, a youth whose morals were as pure as an angel's, burned with the desire to be in Heaven with his dear Mother on the festival of the Ascension. The Virgin acceded to the earnest desires of her well beloved, and assured him that she would grant him this grace. On the vigil of the Ascension he was, contrary to all expectation, reduced to the last extremity; and then the most exalted Queen of Heaven, surrounded with a multitude of virgins, comes down into the humble little cell of Stanislaus, draws near to his bed with an eye fixed on his countenance, and a gracious smile on her own, and invites him to follow her. O what heavenly moments! O what unspeakable joy did Stanislaus find in this invitation! He contemplated his exalted patroness, a glow came over his countenance; and having placidly expired in her arms, he takes his leave of this world, in order that he may for all eternity behold the glories and victories of his most holy Mother and Lady! "Mary receives the souls of the dying."

Graces of this kind are truly extraordinary; yet do not think they are so rare as that they occur only every century:—But a few years ago, and a similar grace was accorded to a very innocent country maiden who was very little known to the world, but thoroughly known to the Queen of Virgins. Mary has at all times her favorites, and she distributes at all times her graces; thou imaginest that thou shouldst not hope for so much, but who forbids thee to long for that affectionate assistance which she renders in an invisible manner?

Would it not be great happiness to have her invisible at thy side, to assure thee of victory over thy enemies, to assuage thy pains? Who loves much ought to hope for much: only love her with thy whole soul, and then fear not thou also to entreat her in the words of her great servant Alphonsus: "O Lady, pardon me my boldness; assist, thyself, at my death, in order to rejoice me with thy presence; and because thou hast shown this grace to so many, I, also, wish to obtain it. If my boldness is great, greater still is thy graciousness which seeks out the miserable. In thy graciousness I trust. . . . O Mother! I await thee, let me not go away uncomforted: let what I ask be granted, let what I ask be granted! Amen."

FORTY-SIXTH MEDITATION.

THE ASSISTANCE WHICH MARY AFFORDS HER CLIENTS AFTER THEIR DEATH.

FIRST POINT.

MARY ASSISTS THE DEPARTED.

So great is the sympathy which the most holy Virgin feels for her servants, that she does not think it enough to protect them during their lives and to help them when they are dying, but she also comes to their assistance when they are enduring thes corching flames of purgatory. This fact she herself revealed to St. Bridget and confirmed to Father Carvaglio, another of her very devoted servants, when he recommended himself to her in consequence of the great fear of the purgatorial torments: "I am," said she to him, "the compassionate mediatrix of my clients, not only in this life, but also, and still more, in the life which is to come."

Yes! how can her maternal heart forbear helping them at a time when they most need her affection, and are not in a condition to help themselves? No! In order to assist them, she leaves no path untrodden and forgets no means whatever. She inspires the faithful to offer their prayers to God, to give alms, to fast, to practise penitential works of satisfaction also; and before all else, to cause the holy sacrifice of the mass to be offered up—and all these things to be done with a view to succor the souls in purgatory.

To the performance of these works of mercy, Mary disposes and animates us, sometimes by interior exhortations, and sometimes by exterior and wonderful communications; and she obtains for the departed themselves the grace of being able to solicit assistance, a grace accorded to Innocent III., who appeared to St. Luitgar and asked him for help. Yea, Mary recommended, and even had a hand in, the institution of pious works for the relief of those poor souls; such works, for example, as are the associations which were established for the assistance of the poor souls, the society known by the name of the "Association of Poor Souls," a society already established in very many cities, the night bell which invites the faithful to say the *De profundis*; the generous practice, inspired by affection towards the souls in purgatory, of performing many works of satisfaction, and of placing in the hands of Mary and of committing their merits to her distribution.

Whoever could thoroughly know the origin of those so numerous exercises of piety, would not fail of descrying in them all the operation of that tender-hearted and beneficent Lady, who could not at all endure that the eastern Christians who were reduced to slavery by the Turks should pine away in their chains, and receive no assistance whatever. How many helps do not the souls devoted to her receive during the month of Mary alone? In every place where this admirable devotion obtains,—and now more than ever before, it can be said to be practised throughout the whole Catholic world,—

prayers are offered up for those souls in particular who honored Mary; and O what refreshment for so many souls! Admire the good fortune of her clients who are in purgatory, and do thou imitate in like manner her zeal in procuring for them relief and assistance.

If thy duty be to preach, if thou be a father confessor, or if thou hold some other position of prominence, if thou preside over spiritual conferences, associations, and exercises of devotion, or if thou instruct and form youth,—if any of those duties devolve on thee, then use every effort to inspire those who are subject to thee with love for the souls in purgatory, and especially for those souls who most honored Mary. Be their merciful ambassador and see faithfully to their interests. Thy zeal on behalf of those souls will prove most acceptable to the Blessed Virgin; she will consider as done for herself that which thou dost for those her cherished souls; and doubt not that, in the hours of thy distress, she will know how to give thee an abundant reward.

SECOND POINT.

MARY MITIGATES THE SUFFERINGS ENDURED IN PURGATORY.

Not only does Mary excite the faithful living in this world to help her departed clients, but herself assists them with all her efficacious power; "for she has jurisdiction over the domain of purgatory," says St. Bernardine. There is in that prison no suffering which cannot be assuaged by her prayers; not an hour passes in which she does not pour cooling rain on the flames.

"I am," said she one day to St. Bridget, "the mother, of all the souls who are in purgatory; for all the punishments which they have to undergo for their sins are rendered more mild every hour by my prayers." (St. Liguori's "Glories of Mary.") Yea, she even added that her mere name gives them most desirable refreshment, as the words of a friend afford consolation to a poor forsaken patient. "If they but hear my name, they rejoice as a poor bedridden person when a comforting word greets his ear."

All this is confirmed by St. Bernardine of Sienna, already quoted by St. Bonaventure, by St. Vincent Ferrer, and by many others, who never tire of sounding the praises of her love. But does the Virgin evince this charity for every one? Most certainly; for she confesses that she is the mother of all; still, however, the charity which she evinces for her clients is far more generous. Led on by the impulse of thy own good heart, thou wouldst, were thou but able to do so, give assistance to all who are in need, but yet thou wouldst, with still greater love and generosity, assist those who show themselves more attached to thee, and render thee more services and more honor than others render thee: and couldst thou desire that Mary who is grateful for the smallest services offered her, should not distinguish her favorites by manifesting to them greater affection?

O in what manner, and how greatly, does she distinguish them! "Although she offers help and refreshment to all," says Novarino, "it is chiefly to her own that she offers them." St. Bernardine acknowledges that Mary entertains this marked predilection for her clients, and describes her as if she were visiting purgatory, where, in the midst of the flames, she recognizes the souls who were devoted to her, and tempers their burning sensations: "I come to keep my clients in the hour of their necessities and of their tortures."

O how important it is to serve and love Mary in this life! Pattern after the compassion also which the most holy Virgin feels for the souls in purgatory; do not content thyself with exhorting others to assist those holy souls, but do what thou canst on thy own side to help them; and if thou desirest to be numbered among her distinguished clients, then put all thy good works in her hands in order that she may dispose of them to thy best advantage. Offer to God a perfect sacrifice, and let this sacrifice consist of thy spiritual goods. The offering of this sacrifice is an act of heroic love which many pious persons perform; and if thou imitatest them in making this sacrifice, then have no fear whatever that thou shalt be lost.

On this very subject our divine Redeemer addressed to St. Gertrude these words: "I will generously increase thy glory as a reward of the charity with which thou hast given up all claim to the merits of thy satisfactory works." Whoever becomes poor from love, will be enriched with the riches of God.

THIRD POINT.

MARY HASTENS THE DELIVERANCE OF THE POOR SOULS IN PURGATORY.

Mary by her mediation abridges the sufferings of her clients who have passed to another life. Just as a royal princess obtains from her father, sometimes one, sometimes two, sometimes three, years' remission of the punishment which a prisoner has to undergo,—so this exalted queen of heaven, as the dispensatrix of the divine treasures, emancipates her dear clients before the time from the prison of torture, and brings them triumphantly to heaven.

Novarino teaches this doctrine very plainly when he says that his belief is that, by Mary's merits, the time of their sufferings will be shortened in the place of purification: "I am disposed to believe that through Mary's merits the sufferings of the souls in purgatory are not only assuaged but even abridged." (St. Liguori's "Glories of Mary.") Others before and after him maintained this same doctrine; and the Church herself took the lead of them all in this matter. She tells us that it is a pious belief, that the most holy Virgin delivers souls from purgatory before the expiration of the term of their imprisonment, and consequently that she conducts them to their heavenly fatherland before the allotted time: "The pious belief obtains, that the most blessed Virgin brings the souls in purgatory, as soon as possible, to their heavenly home."

Writers of great authority put forward the belief that, on the day of her glorious assumption into heaven, Mary obtained from her divine Son the privilége of bringing with her to heaven all the souls who were detained in that prison of intense sufferings; a privilege which was so abundantly conferred on her that Gerson exclaims, "that the fire of purgatory was emptied of its occupants on that day: the fire of purgatory remained without a soul in it." The most distinguished writers add that the same honor is accorded to the Virgin on her principal festivals, so that on those days she abridges the sufferings of some, mitigates the sufferings of others, and again emancipates others entirely, and conducts them with her to the eternal joys of heaven, as a dear prey seized upon by her love and power: "But I would incline to the belief that on every great festival of the Virgin several souls are delivered from sufferings."

So firmly does St. Liguori believe that the privilege here mentioned is granted to Mary, that he exhorts her clients to entreat for themselves this favor and to hope that they shall obtain it; he goes even farther, and encourages them to hope for complete preservation from those sufferings. He says if we serve her with especial love, why should we not look forward with hope to the grace of entering into heaven immediately after our death, without having aught whatever to do with purgatory?

Hast thou a confidence so beautiful? Do not lose courage, strive to become a true and zealous servant of Mary; strive to procure her affection more for thee, and then repose in her all confidence, for her liberality can grant far more than anything for which thou canst hope. O most powerful queen of heaven and earth! I believe that thy power is very great to deliver souls from the place of purification, especially the souls of thy clients; I believe thy heart is so tender that thou canst not brook the defeat of allowing those to suffer long in purgatory. I promise myself that I shall obtain from thee the favor of not suffering long in that prison; and to this end thou must not only assist me at the hour of my death, but also thou must deliver me from the flames of purgatory and land me safely in heaven!

Those who love thee expect this much at thy hands, and shall not be deceived; this much I also hope for—I who, although a sinner, love thee with all my heart, and love thee beyond all things, God alone excepted.

FORTY-SEVENTH MEDITATION.

THE MANNER AND WAY IN WHICH THE CHURCH HONORS MARY.

FIRST POINT.

THE CHURCH HONORS MARY IN A PARTICULAR MANNER.

HOLY CHURCH pays to the blessed Virgin an honor shown to none else—an honor higher than that which is rendered to the saints, and less than that which is rendered to God. Holy Church gives to her less honor than to God, for the reason that the most blessed Virgin is only a mere creature; she shows more honor to her than to the saints, for the excellent reason, too, that the very close union obtaining between God and Mary, raises her as much above the saints as heaven is above the earth, and as it were, transfers her to a sphere quite other and far higher than theirs.

Where indeed is there to be found a union more intimate than that obtaining between the mother and the child? And yet this is the very union which obtains between God and the Virgin—a union which does not exist between him and any of the other saints, but between him and Mary alone. By a series of astounding miracles, God prepared Mary for himself: he announced her to the world as the repairer of all which the world had lost: and when the appointed time had come, she clothed the eternal Word with her immaculate flesh, brought forth the Son of God,—true God and true man,—nursed him with her most pure milk, and reared him with every possible circumspection.

But where are the visual organs powerful enough to bring within their sphere Mary's great exaltation? and where is the intelligence mighty enough to measure the greatness of her dignity! The saints are indeed great before God, yet in a last analysis they are but servants. Mary is his mother, and if her humility lead her to look upon herself only as a handmaid, this very humility becomes to her a ladder by which she ascends to the throne of the Queen of all the saints.

In what manner then should Mary be honored? Next after God, she must be considered worthy of receiving the greatest honor. Now behold how much higher is the honor which is in fact shown her, than that which is rendered to the saints; and observe, likewise, how nearly the honor which the holy Church pays her, approaches to the honor which she (holy Church) pays to God. As the honor rendered to Jesus is universal, so also is the honor rendered to Mary: there is no people to whom was announced the name of Jesus, to whom the name of Mary was not in the same breath proclaimed: there is not a single temple built in honor of Jesus, in which is not to be met with also some special monument erected in honor of Mary. The Church addresses her a prayer received from on high, as is the "Hail Mary;" she invokes her and gives her titles which, strictly speaking, are applicable to God alone; titles such as "our life," "our hope." She applies to Mary the words of praise which holy writ speaks of the Eternal Wisdom: "From the beginning and before the world was I created." Eccl. xxiv. 142 v. She entreats her for graces in the same manner as she entreats God, just as if grace came from Mary as from its source: "Loose the bonds of the guilty, bring light to the blind, turn away evils from us." In the most sublime ceremonies and in the holy sacrifice of mass, in the recitation of the divine office, in public and special prayers, the Church associates the Mother with the Son most intimately; having invoked Jesus, she invokes Mary next, she prays to her for assistance, and appears unable to approach the throne of God otherwise than in the company of Mary.

The Church is the teacher of all the faithful; and her direction is the secure line of conduct to be followed by every good Christian. Learn from her that thou owest the most profound reverence to the most Holy Virgin. Conclude from all this, how sincerely and how immensely should Mary be honored. Honor, then, her who is thy holy patroness, invoke her, entreat her; win for thyself her protection, rendering her all sorts of good services: and do not forget that Mary should be all the more distinguished than the angels and saints, the more she is raised above them. The difference between their condition and Mary's, is that between the condition of the king's mother and that of his subjects.

SECOND POINT.

THE CHURCH HONORS MARY IN EVERY SORT OF MANNER.

The Church gives clearly to understand what and how great is her zeal for Mary's honor. What are the marks of reverence, what are the protestations of affection, which she does not offer her? With public solemnities she commemorates the mysteries of her life; she causes the learned to defend them in the schools; she causes preachers to expound them in the pulpits; she causes them to be sculptured in marble; and not content with all this, she distributes her images on all sides, in order that, as they are a most powerful protection to Christian families, so also they might be a most beautiful adornment to Christian houses. The Church presents her to the homage of the faithful in the different stages of her existence: as a child in swaddling clothes, as a maiden in the temple, as a bride at the altar, as a traveller on the mountains of Judea, as the Mother of Jesus in the cave of Bethlehem, as immersed in grief at the foot of the cross, as glorious and triumphant in heaven. The Church composed complete offices of the blessed Virgin; she praises her with holy canticles and celebrates her noble deeds in appropriate hymns. She consecrates to her majestic temples; she dedicates to her churches, sanctuaries, and chapels, in every part of the Catholic world; she establishes under her name, spiritual and military orders, societies and conferences; she proclaims her as the patroness of kingdoms, cities, and empires, and as a compassionate helper of all Christian people. In tribulations and dangers, she lifts up her hands to her imploringly, and seems to have no dearer refuge than Mary's bosom.

Under how many supremely glorious titles does she invoke her? With what great zeal does she not defend her privileges? How much solicitude, how much painstaking, how much diligence, are evinced in her course, when one of Mary's privileges is assailed by false teachers! See what the Church did for her in the third Œcumenical Council, in which she defined and defended the divine maternity against Nestorius. Behold the zeal which she evinced in recent years, for the definition so ardently desired of the doctrine of the Immaculate Conception! What activity on the part of all Catholic bishops! With what energy the pastors of the most distant people overcame the obstacles and faced the dangers that lay in their way! What great zeal, what joy, in the bosoms of all the people of Christendom! The Church embraces every opportunity, employs every means, takes every pains, to further the interests and the honor of the holy Virgin; and after all this, she (the Church) acknowledges that she is incapable of praising her in a becoming manner; and filled with this conviction, she bursts forth into the exclamation: "I know not with what praises I should extol thee."

Dost thou honor her as much as ever thou canst according to thy condition and thy capabilities? What are the pious exercises by means of which thou recognizest her greatness, and winnest for thyself her protection? Whatever be the character of thy devotions, never forget one devotion which is competent to all the faithful, extremely agreeable to the Virgin, and highly profitable to thyself:—the devotional exercise here meant is the thrice holy Rosary:—honor her, then, with this offering of praise: "Bring unto her a sacrifice." Let no day go by without doing her the homage of saying the beads in her honor; say them with recollection and love, say them in conjunction with thy family; and if this beautiful custom obtain not already in it, use thy best endeavors to introduce it at the earliest moment possible. Say them for thyself in the secrecy of thy chamber; say them before her image in the churches; say them during thy voyages and journeys; and let the Rosary be the most telling sign that thou art in very truth a loving servant of Mary.

THIRD POINT.

THE CHURCH ENCOURAGES US TO HONOR MARY.

The Church does not content herself with encouraging the faithful by her example to honor Mary, but she also does what she can by the exercise of her authority to that end: she exhorts, entreats, entices the faithful, she even renders it obligatory on them by her command, as is the case in regard to the celebration of the vigils of her festivals and of her festivals themselves.

What is it that the Church leaves undone, in order to promote Mary's interests? Three times in the day, morning, midday, and evening, she invites the faithful by the ringing of bells to greet her,—and this she does out of pure anxiety that no part of the day should pass without the faithful having recourse to Mary. The Church devotes Saturday in every week to her honor, and desires that the faithful should evince every anxiety to merit her protection. In the course of the year, there is scarcely a single month on which she does not endeavor to prepare her children to celebrate one of her festivals with faith and love; she always furthers whatever can increase devotion to Mary. How many pious exercises for that very purpose has she approved! What a superabundance of indulgences has she granted! What else can be the object of the Church in dispensing so many spiritual treasures, than by them to entice the faithful to do homage to the Virgin? Yet more; she is desirous that her ministers should inspire the faithful of both sexes with devotion to Mary and should root it deeply in them; and for this purpose she erected over the whole Catholic world Mary's chapels, established her associations, attached to those associations favors, enriched them with graces and privileges, and facilitated the obtaining of them by throwing them open to all the different states of Christian society,—to men and women, young and old, noble and vulgar, poor and rich, —that all might be enabled to know her more and more, and to increase in confidence in her, and in love of her.

The same is to be said of so many other exercises, very pious indeed, which the Church favors and recommends. The design which she has in furthering those exercises, clearly appears from the papal bulls, and is never aught else than merely to propagate every honor to her that is practicable, and to inspire her children with zeal in rendering her all the homage in their power; and this course the Church pursues in the conviction that, by so acting, she confers an inestimable benefit on her children.

And what dost thou do in regard of this important matter? Dost thou encourage others to honor Mary? Art thou on the alert to seize the opportunities of honoring her that present themselves, and to avail thyself of them to further the interests of her honor? A loving heart easily finds means to praise the person beloved: but shouldst thou find nothing but difficulties in praising her, shouldst thou lack time, shouldst thou forget her, shouldst thou not know what to do or to say,—this is a bad sign, it is a sign thou dost not love her, a sign that thy heart is cold towards her. Divest thyself then of thy sluggishness, arouse thy zeal once more, pray to Mary for pardon as regards the past, and for newness of spirit as regards the future. O my most loving Mother! forgive me my lukewarmness; already a thousand times have I promised thee that I would exhort others to honor thee, and that I would burn with zeal to the end that thou mightst be glorified.

And yet, however, not only have I not, alas! kept my promise, but even I myself also have omitted to cast myself often at thy feet, omitted to offer thee daily the small tribute of my services, and to distinguish thy festivals by making due preparation for their celebration. Pardon me, O Mary! I acknowlege my infidelity and ingratitude. I repent of having so ill corresponded with thy mercies; I entreat thee a thousand times for pardon of my negligence; and, confiding in the goodness of thy heart, I this very day renew the promise to embrace with more assiduity the opportunities of propagating thy honor, and also the promise to be more faithful in serving and in loving thee. But do thou, O Lady! assist me; thou beholdest my weakness; thou beholdest my inconstancy. Ah! strengthen my resolutions, re-animate my spirit that I may commence to be grateful to thee, and that I may bring forth those precious and prized fruits which are so dear to thy heart: "My flowers are precious and prized fruits."

FORTY-EIGHTH MEDITATION

THE LOVE WHICH THE SAINTS CONCEIVE FOR MARY.

FIRST POINT.

THE LOVE WHICH THE SAINTS BEAR TO MARY IS AN ACTIVE LOVE.

HOWEVER numerous are the saints, there is not amongst them a single one who, during the time of his or her natural life on earth, did not pay sovereign honors to Mary. All of them,—of every age, sex, and condition; of every place and period of time, —all raised their eyes and hearts to this star of heaven; all looked upon her as their most cherished hope next after God.

Love for Mary appears to be a distinguishing characteristic of sanctity. But love is a fire that cannot remain concealed; and hence in the case of the saints, this fire always reveals itself by performing various and manifold services and exercises of devotion. Frequent recourse to her in time of necessity, preparation for her festivals, by watching, fasting, giving alms, and doing works of penance; a previous devotion of three or nine days; even long pilgrimages to her sanctuaries, and pilgrimages bound up with many privations; watching for whole nights before her images; carrying around and distributing her likenesses;—these are exercises which can be called more or less common to all and each one of the saints.

A great number of them showed much diligence in introducing new forms of serving her, new means of serving her, new ways of serving her; and this they did in order that their love of her might be ever in action. Who could number those forms, means, and ways? Cardinal Thomassin tied about his wrists two ribbons and wrote on them: "I belong to Mary, let no one touch me:" and in times of trouble and temptation, he raised up those ribbons as a sign that he was one of Mary's subjects, and thus did he pray to her for assistance. On an appointed day every year, St. Gertrude solemnly chose her for protectress and Mother, and consecrated herself to her special service. St. Ignatius of Loyola always bore on his breast her image, pressed it to his bosom when he sought for help in his necessities; and by rendering Mary this homage, he could assure himself of being delivered from many dangers. St. Angela of Foligno began no work, how little important soever, without first praying to Mary for her blessing; and on one occasion when she was praying to her for it, she heard from her this answer: "Receive thou my blessing, and my Son's blessing also." On every Saturday in the year, and on all the vigils of her festivals, St. Charles Borromeo fasted rigorously on bread and water; St. Hyacintha Marescotta desired to have Mary's name written on all the objects designed for her (the saint's) use; and when she was not able to visit her in the churches, she sent thither a multitude of maidens in order that these, in her stead, might be able to visit her and pray to her. St. Ambrose Sansodonio gave more abundant alms to the poor every Saturday, with the view to confer honorable distinction on this day consecrated to the Virgin. St. Magdalene, of Pazzi, often rendered her the service of procuring by sacrifice and prayers refreshment for those souls in purgatory who had been devout to her.

Read the lives of the saints, and thou canst not fail to be struck with the activity of the love which they bore her:—there is no mortification practicable to which they did not subject themselves, no possible evidence of magnanimity and fortitude which they did not afford in their works of devotion to Mary.

What, then, are the pains thou takest which reveal the love that thou feelest for her? What mortifications dost thou practise, what proofs dost thou furnish her, that thou really lovest her? If thou canst not lay a finger on thy mortifications, thy inability is a sign that thou art not constant in the practice of any; and if thou lovest not Mary, then what kind of a fire burns in thy heart? whither dost thou direct thy affections?

Oh, miserable that thou art! Why dost thou defer any longer to enkindle in thee so precious a fire? Use every effort to make it burn brightly. The services which the saints rendered Mary were the fruit of their love for her; those which thou renderest her will be unto thee the means of acquiring love for her: therefore, make immediately a firm and practicable resolution to serve her, and say with the venerable Berchmanns: "I will not rest till I obtain a most tender love for Mary, my most sweet mother; I will not desist, till I acquire a tender love for Mary."

SECOND POINT.

THE LOVE OF THE SAINTS FOR MARY IS AN OVERFLOWING LOVE.

The saints were not content with loving Mary themselves; but they labored with unspeakable zeal to make her known, were it possible, to all creatures, and to incite them to love her: yea, they would have ardently desired that the whole universe glowed with so excellent a love.

Commence with the apostles who imparted to the faithful their reverence and affection for her; pass thence to the fathers and the doctors of the Latin as well of the Greek Church, and remark what they in their homilies and discourses said of her. What brilliant sentences of praise did they indite upon her virtues and privileges! What plenitude of eloquence was theirs when they came to speak of her goodness! What affectionate encouragements, what tender and warm exhortations, to love her! To name in this place only some of the saints, were to be guilty of an injustice to them all, so common to all is the zeal to enkindle in every heart love for the holy Virgin.

Then figure to thyself what so many apostolic men did for her,—as a St. Bernard who was to her a most zealous panegyrist and client; a St. Dominic who propagated so extensively the pious exercise of the holy Rosary; a St. Francis Xavier who placed all his missions under her protection; a St. Francis Regis who, in so many ways, propagated and promoted her honor; a St. Alphonsus Liguori, who seized upon every opportunity to speak of her in public as well as in private.

Represent to thyself what great pains so many others gave themselves to build in her honor new temples, new pulpits, new altars; to celebrate her fesitvals with greater pomp; to circulate more and more the books which treat of her glories; to inform the hearts of youth with love of her. What did not St. Philip Neri alone do in this very connection? Think of the countless volumes which had for avowed object to defend her privileges, to celebrate the praises of her virtues and of her mercy,—in short, to propagate her honor. How many books of every form, in all languages! How much sweat did the friends of God in every age pour forth in order that they might have the consolation of enkindling in their fellow-men that flame which glowed so intensely in themselves!

Yes! and even with all this they would have declared themselves not satisfied; their desire would have been to offer their lives for the honor of their Lady; yea, they obliged themselves by vows to do so, as did, for the defence of her Immaculate Conception, so many religous orders, and so many men distinguished for learning and sanctity. So ardent was the desire of St. Hyacintha Marescotta, although a woman, to lay down her life for the honor of the Virgin, that she (the saint) often repeated that she would shed her blood to the very last drop, in order to enkindle and to maintain in the faithful love for the most holy Virgin.

Such are the thoughts, such the actions of the saints; and how dost thou aim at promoting Mary's honor? what hast thou done, and what dost thou now, in order to win for her new clients? If God has given thee a talent, then thy bounden duty is to embrace every opportunity to use it for Mary's honor: if he has given thee beauty, then shouldst thou know how to use it in a manner promotive of Mary's honor: if he has granted thee riches, then omit not to contribute to the adornment of Mary's churches, and to the circulation of those books which are calculated to excite confidence in her, and to enkindle love for her in the hearts of all.

It thou reducest to practice this advice, fear nothing; for the little thou shalt have done, she will know how to prize according to the sincerity and the ardor of thy desires.

THIRD POINT.

MARY IS THE MODEL OF THE LOVE WE SHOULD CONCEIVE FOR HER.

The love which the saints bore to Mary, can be styled a model love in a twofold regard; first, because they point out to us the manner and the way in which it behooves us to love her; and because, secondly, they assure us, by the beauty of their love, that this way is right and that this manner is holy.

The way they point out to thee, thou canst follow by filially and constantly recurring to her by performing those works of mortification which they themselves performed; by rendering her those services of so many different kinds which they knew so well how to render her; and as to thy honoring her after the manner in which the saints honored her, then must thou love her without measure, that is, as much as thou art able, for thus did the saints love her: "Look, and do according to the model."

See what the saints did; see how in all their needs they fled to her with great confidence, how they prayed to her with fidelity and constancy, how they employed every diligence to know her, and how they spent themselves in order that she might be honored. Seek to imitate them, and thou shalt reach the same goal which they have reached. They assure thee, moreover, that thou canst not go astray by imitating them; for in heavenly matters the saints and the friends of God are the best instructed. What they did for the most holy Virgin was sanctioned by their virtue and wisdom; and, before all, by the Church which recognized and, as it were, set her seal upon, their sanctity.

Now consider that they honored and glorified her more than they did all other pure creatures taken together, and in doing so they felt no apprehension that they were doing too much; as well because the honors shown to Mary redound all to God in a last analysis, who is the primary object of our worship—"All the honor rendered to the Mother," says St. Jerome, "redounds to the Son"—as also because God himself was the first who gave himself to us as a model in honoring her. He himself loved and honored her more than he loved and honored all other creatures.

What a consolation is it now for thee to know that thou goest to render service to so great a lady, and that the love thou bearest to her has in it nought that is reprehensible! Mayst thou know how to derive profit from the examples of the saints, and learn to take those examples as a pattern and an encouragement unto thee! A traveller who sees a very vast number going before him on the same road, and is aware that it is the right road, feels his courage and strength redouble, and becomes filled with joy. Mark now this is the very fruit which thou shouldst derive from this meditation—a generous impulse in the love and service of Mary: and if thou wilt easily secure this impulse, then recommend thyself to those saints who were distinguished clients of Mary; and first of all to her well beloved spouse, and to St. John the Evangelist, to whose care the most holy Virgin was entrusted by the expiring Jesus.

O Mary! it is a great grace for me to be able to love thee, and to know that thou despisest not the love of a poor sinner! But of what use is this knowledge to me, unless I attain to sincere love of thee? Ah, Lady! since thou hast already shown me so many mercies, refuse me not this one now; I will love thee, and truly I will love thee more than I will love all creatures else. Grant me the grace to do so! enkindle in my heart a true love for thee. And how could I refrain from loving thee—thee, who art so amiable and so much beloved? I will ever purify my heart more and more; I will be more faithful in honoring thee; I will pray with more zeal; in fine, I will do everything that is pleasing to thee. But deign, O my august sovereign, and my sweetest Mother, to remember, on thy part, that I yearn after the grace of loving thee with all the powers and with the utmost strength of my poor sinful soul in this world, in order that I may love thee for ever in heaven. Amen.

FORTY-NINTH MEDITATION.

THE HONOR WHICH CHRISTIAN PEOPLE RENDER UNTO MARY.

FIRST POINT.

THE HONOR RENDERED TO MARY—AN HONOR OF VERY ANCIENT ORIGIN.

THE teachers whom the Christian nations follow in honoring Mary, are the apostles themselves.

Dionysius styled the Areopagite, a very ancient author, proves that many of them, among whom was Peter the apostle, had come from various and distant countries, for no other object than to feast their eyes once more on the greatest work that God had done to show forth his glory. This work was Mary: Mary the masterpiece of the works of his hands. The holy apostle, just mentioned, most urgently recommended all to honor her; and this recommendation they embodied in the consecration of temples to her: thus did St. James in Saragossa, St. John in Asia, as also St. Peter in Rome. Many others likewise whose names are lost, erected temples in her honor whilst she yet lived. Among numberless means employed for promoting and propagating this honor, were the venerable missals, which were transmitted to the first churches as containing the rules and regulations of the divine worship; and, from these missals can be gathered at the faithful were taught, as also what they believed and practised. Who then can correctly determine the high station accorded to the Virgin, in those monuments of earliest Christian antiquity?

Who can express her dignity, her holiness, her immaculate purity, the sublime laudations which were prescribed to be rendered unto her,—and prescribed in every one of those primitive documents? Who can express the confidence she excited in the hearts of the faithful, and the exhortations that were addressed to them, in order to induce them to venerate and to invoke her? Furthermore, the holy fathers and the most ancient authors, commencing with those of them who might have seen her, speak of her in terms so redolent of humble and affectionate veneration, that it is very easy to perceive therefrom the honor paid her in those earliest Christian times, and also the confidence which the faithful reposed in her.

The propagation of the honor due to Jesus went hand in hand with the propagation of the honor due to his august Mother: by the same spirit of faith which animated the first, was the second also animated. The fruit appeared united with the tree; the pearl was not divorced from its shell. In the most ancient images Jesus is represented with Mary; the faithful are seen prostrate before Son and Mother,—before him as their God, before her as their mediatrix.

Thus the honor paid the most holy Virgin was congenital with the very Church herself, and came through the course of so many centuries uninterruptedly and constantly down to us, with this modification however, that accordingly as it was propagated and increased, so also it grew in strength and affection; even as a river which, issuing from the mountain in which it takes its rise, becomes constantly of greater force, and widens its bed, until in the end it bears more resemblance to a sea than to a river.

Oh, how greatly does God glorify this humble Virgin who glorified him exceedingly here on earth! Look at the source whence springs the honor thou renderest to Mary; and see whether that honor could possibly have been sanctioned by an authority more legitimate, whether that honor could possibly have had a more continuous duration, or could possibly have employed a more welcome reception.

Oh how well founded, according to this, were the exhortations wherewith thy good parents, and thy good grand parents sought to induce thee when thou wast yet young, to be devout to Mary! How edifying is the example which thy family gave thee when, prostrate before her image, they prayed to her and taught thee also to pray to her! O what sweet confidence did thy heart then feel! With what zeal and affection didst thou render her thy services!

Has this confidence, this zeal, wherewith thou wast animated towards Mary in thy first years, increased with thy advancing years? Dost thou, at the present time, feel that thou hast those dispositions, and that those dispositions in thee are of a lively and operative character?

SECOND POINT.

THE HONOR PAID TO MARY—AN UNIVERSAL HONOR.

The unanimity of the peoples of the universe in honoring Mary, did not recently commence to obtain, for it dates back centuries and centuries. Run over, in thought, the Catholic world, from one end of it to the other:—see how many nations are scattered in all parts of the earth,—nations different in temperament, in customs, in language! All those venerate, honor, and love Mary; thou canst not find, I will not say a province or a city, but even a village worth speaking of, in which are not to be seen splendid marks of the honor paid to the Mother of God: on the summit of the steepest hills, in the most wretched valleys, in the most remote forests, there is, provided but a handful of Christians be there, certain to be also there a little church or chapel consecrated to Mary. This chapel or church is the dearest treasure unto the poor country people; thither do they hasten in their necessities and dangers, thither do they bring their gifts; and on greater festivals, this offering of their gifts becomes to them a subject of pure joy and an occasion of holy emulation.

Whose tongue can tell what the piety of the faithful to Mary has done in cities, and generally in richer neighborhoods? Already those sanctuaries which are most famous for the concourse of pilgrims, for the solemnity of the sacrifices, for the multitude of miracles performed there,—those sanctuaries number one thousand six hundred! And the faithful stop not even at this;

they represent her under a thousand forms; they set up her statues everywhere,—in the houses, on the streets, in the heart of forests, in the deserts, on the fields, even on the sails of ships and on the banners of armies. They try to outdo each other in testifying generous gratitude to their most unselfish and bountiful benefactress. This is what the faithful do in order that they may have Mary constantly before their eyes. They give her as many honorable titles as there are wants, however trifling those wants, of human life—hence they style her: "Holy Mary of help—of peace—of mercy—of health—of graces—of consolation—of hope—of refuge—of light:"—and they give her a thousand other appellations besides.

Also thou must not imagine that those multifarious honors which she receives were rendered her by the poor classes only, or by the untaught populace. No, no! there is in all Christendom no station so elevated as that its occupant glories not in prostrating himself before her images, and seeks not to secure for himself her protection, by rendering her most sincere homage; personages conspicuous on account of their dignities, such as princes, kings and emperors; men distinguished for knowledge, such as learned masters and doctors of all sciences, personages distinguished for piety, as the saints of all times and of all places. Persons of every condition, of every sex, of every age—beginning with children who commence to lisp, and continuing to those who have attained to decrepit old age—all raise their eyes to this loving mother; all invoke Mary; even sinners the most wretched, even evildoers the most inveterate, call upon her in their dangers, and render her now and again some worship.

O charming star of heaven! Who is there in this sorrowful land of exile, who does not offer thee, with sweet affection and tender confidence, at least some tribute of veneration and love? The veneration which is shown to Mary has no other limits than those of the Catholic world. Consider that, at the same hour in which thou offerest to the most holy Virgin thy prayers and other evidences of thy esteem for her, perhaps a countless multitude of pious souls, dispersed in all the countries of the world, send up to her throne their prayers, their sighs, and their desires, and send them up in a spirit of faith and with sincere devotion.

Mary knew how to affectionately distinguish thee among so many peoples, among so many souls, and thus did she distinguish thee,—by privileging thee beyond so many others, by bestowing on thee the most exceptional mercies and favors. And thou—dost thou know how to signalize thyself among her clients, by manifesting through thy works thy gratitude to her, thy fidelity in glorifying her, thy zealous love for her? Ah! who knows how many far surpass thee in gratitude and fidelity to her, even though they have less means, less knowledge, and less instruction than thou hast? Resolve, and resolve in all earnestness, to be more generous and constant in honoring her who has approved herself so generous towards thee.

THIRD POINT.

THE HONOR PAID TO MARY—AN HONOR SUPREMELY EXALTED.

He who first honored the most holy Virgin on this earth was not a man, but one of the purest spirits who stand before the face of God,—one of those heavenly spirits who ceaselessly chant eternal canticles before the divine throne. The archangel Gabriel was the first who honored her on this earth; he came down from the highest heaven in order to honor this modest and retiring Virgin; he visited her in the lowly dwelling where she lived concealed from the eyes of the world; he opened his interview by addressing her words of most profound reverence, words which now constitute the fond prayer of Christian peoples: "Hail, full of grace, the Lord is with thee, blessed art thou among women."

Consider further that the archangel Gabriel came not in his own name; no! he came as ambassador of the Most High; he came in the name of the most holy and adorable Trinity: "There was an angel sent from God." In the name of the three Divine Persons, and of all the heavenly citizens, he reverentially saluted this humble Virgin; thus God himself and his holy angels are the first to give us the example of honoring Mary, —an example which renders it incumbent on us also to honor her. Can the veneration paid to Mary possibly have a higher origin, a more exalted leader?

Consider, moreover, the end for which the archangel was sent to Mary: this end was to commune with her about the execution of that mercy which constituted the only hope of Adam and Eve, the yearning of the patriarchs and the prophets, the expectation of all nations;—the end for which he was sent, was to confer with her regarding the incarnation of the Son of God, and the redemption of all mankind.

O how much more palpable becomes the sublime character of the veneration we pay to Mary, when that veneration is viewed in the light of the object proposed to be accomplished through the archangel's mission. God asks for her consent through the ministry of the angel; and immediately when she consents to accept the incomparable honor of the divine maternity, then instantly is accomplished the great mystery of the Incarnation of the Wòrd: "Behold the handmaid of the Lord, be it done unto me according to thy word"—"and the Word was made flesh, and dwelt amongst us."

Is it indeed possible to conceive a greater honor? The Father has the incommunicable privilege of begetting his Son eternally, and nevertheless confers on Mary the privilege of begetting that same Son in time: the Son of God becomes in very truth, her son; and she becomes, in very truth, his Mother. The Holy Ghost descends upon her for the purpose of performing this miracle; he fills her with lavish superabundance of all his graces, and becomes Mary's bridegroom.

Behold, how God honors Mary! How then do we honor her? What praises do we render her? What canticles do we sing in veneration of her? What solemnities do we celebrate in her honor? Conclude from all this how greatly are those selfish and haughty souls deceived, who would consider themselves lowered if they performed the exercises of devotion to Mary—exercises which those souls despise and look upon as fit only for common minds and for weak females. O spirits truly vulgar, despicably vulgar indeed, and utterly blinded by the fume of pride!—spirits who are not capable of soaring above the earth, and of grasping the sublimity of that veneration which is being testified to the most exalted and the most holy of all mere creatures!

Entreat her to cast on those desolate souls a look of pity. O most august Queen of heaven and of earth! whom the angels and the saints glory in serving, deign to cause all creatures to know thee, and to glorify in thee that God who has exalted thee so exceedingly! Triumph, by thy mercy, over those souls who are widely separated from him in consequence of their vicious lives; let those souls be thy conquests, those the glorious triumphs of thy goodness; enlighten so many poor blind souls; give so many poor hearts that now grovel in filth and corruption, a yearning after a more sublime end. O that all would love thee! Over me, however, exercise thy amiable dominion, and permit not that I should be indifferent and callous in the midst of so many others who honor thee; yea, cause me, from this moment till the last breath of my life, to be one of those clients who are animated with fidelity to thee, and with most glowing love. Amen.

FIFTIETH MEDITATION.

MEANS OF OBTAINING DEVOTION TO MARY.

FIRST POINT.

REMOVE THE IMPEDIMENTS TO DEVOTION TO MARY.

LIVING in sin is the first and the greatest impediment to devotion to Mary.

How thinkest thou that, in one and the same heart, there can tabernacle a sincere readiness to do that which is pleasing to the most holy Virgin, and at the same time the will to do that which of all things she most hates and abhors? She, the whitest of lilies, purer than the light—and sin the most horrible and loathsome monster there can ever be in this world! She, all love to her adorable Jesus—and sin, the cause of his dolorous passion and ignominious death! How wilt thou that she acknowledge for her servant and client, him who bears this monster in his soul, him who does not banish it from him, him who hates it not? No! The will to commit sin and devotion to Mary can never dwell together in the same person; they are as antagonistic to one another as are light and darkness. To imagine otherwise would be to form quite a strange, nay, a shameful, idea of the Virgin; and hence, when devotion to Mary takes possession of a soul, this devotion must, say the saints, put sin to flight, even as a medical remedy banishes disease:

Should thy soul, unfortunately for thyself, be ever defiled with sin, then banish it without delay, for sin is the greatest obstacle to thy becoming one of Mary's true clients. Render her this service,—the service not to defer a moment to get rid of the sin that is in thee; and hold for certain that she will assist thee in a wonderful manner, because she declares herself to be the mother of those sinners who desire to emerge from the abyss of sin: "I am the Mother of sinners who wish to mend their ways." Yea, so great is her condescension that she never sent away from her any one however impious, who prayed to her to assist him in his efforts to abandon the path of sin: "She never despised any sinner, how wicked soever he might have been, provided he prayed to her."

Our natural sluggishness is a second obstacle, and a great obstacle it is indeed, to true devotion to Mary. This sluggishness produces in us a certain loathing and disgust in the performance of all our spiritual exercises; and as it causes them to appear so burthensome to us, we perform them in so perfunctory a manner, that we had almost as well pretermit them altogether. This sluggishness is to the mind what fever is to the body. What art thou good for, when thou art attacked with fever?—for nothing; and the same is the case with him over whom sluggishness wields the sceptre. By halves he wills, by halves he wills not: "the sluggard wills and wills not." In every thing he does, he feels disgust and reluctance; to day he passes over one exercise, to-morrow another; and, ere long, he omits them altogether.

Is this, perchance, the course of things as they took

place in thy regard? If thou wilt obtain true devotion to the Virgin, thou must eradicate this evil plant of sluggishness; thou must heroically overcome thyself; thou must struggle against the inclinations which mislead thee, must struggle against thy proclivity to prefer thy own selfwill to Mary's honor; thou must evidence to her that thou honorest her, not only at the moment when thy soul is heated with a little zeal, but likewise in every circumstance, however discommoding, and that thou honorest her even when, in order to honor her, it is necessary for thee to vanquish thyself. When, on a certain occasion, the blessed John Villani remembered, late at night, that on the day just gone by, he had not rendered to Mary his accustomed tribute of devotional services, he instantly arose from his bed, and returned not till he had performed all the omitted exercises.

Mayst thou, on a similar occasion, know how to do in like manner! In this way will there be opened up to thee the unencumbered and smooth path to solid devotion to the Queen of heaven; thou shalt go along that path with ease; the mortifications, which at first come difficult to thee, will appear not only easy but agreeable, and thou wilt soon experience how sweet and how enjoyable a thing it is, to love and serve Mary.

SECOND POINT.

PERFORM THE EXERCISES PROMOTIVE OF DEVOTION TO MARY.

Meditation is, according to St. Thomas, the first milk of true devotion. The reason there were so many holy souls inflamed with love for Mary is that, by means of meditation, they discovered in her so many beauties, privileges, and treasures, that they were constrained to love her: "a fire burned in my meditation."

Believe firmly that there is not a single exercise so promotive of love and devotion to her, as is the exercise of meditating on her dignities, her virtues, and her glories. Father Suarez, as holy as he was learned, spent on all her festivals not less than two hours in this exercise of devotion. So much is not required of thee; but it is desired that thou often devote to it some of thy leisure time; and if thou dost this, thou shalt always know her better and better, and the flame of her holy love will increase more and more in thy heart. Meditate on her dignities, which are a shoreless sea; and should these prove too high a subject for thee, then meditate upon her mercies, upon the benefits which she sheds upon us in so great abundance, upon the graces and favors she has conferred on thyself.

Oh, what an easy and rich matter for meditation do all these suggestions offer thee! How then canst thou find it difficult to reflect on them—on how often she delivered thee from dangers—on how often she consoled thee in thy tribulations—briefly, on how often she approved herself a watchful and an affectionate Mother to thee! St. Bernard, speaking on this subject, says: "The idea of mercy is more agreeable to us; we recal mercy oftener to our memory; we invoke mercy more frequently."

If meditation be in no wise to thy taste, then replace it with the reading of those books which treat of it. This is the counsel which St. Theresa gives thee—learn of others what thou canst not learn by thyself. Oh, how many devout thoughts will then rise up in thy mind! how many affections of gratitude and love will then be excited in thy heart! what an impulse wilt thou feel within thee to try to honor her!

Frequent invocation of her is another exercise which is likewise highly profitable in this connection: in doubts, in perplexities, in dangers, think on Mary, invoke Mary! let her not depart from thy lips, let her not depart from thy heart;—this is the advice of the exquisitely devout saint who, when he one day greeted her in her image with the usual "Hail Mary," heard her answer him straightway, "Hail Bernard."

And in order to aid thy memory as to the practice here recommended, study to have her before thy eyes, by adorning thy rooms, thy books, thyself, with her images. Whoever loves a person wishes to have that person's likeness before his eyes:—if thou lovest her, O how agreeable will it be to thee often to gaze upon this most charming countenance which, after God, is the joy of the blessed in heaven!

Happy Christian houses! if from them were banished the abominable representations of shameful pleasures; and if instead, were to be seen there no more beautiful ornaments than the picture of the purest of all virgins! How much less sin would then be committed, how much greater would then be the incentive to the practice of virtue!

Besides the things that have already been mentioned, it will be most agreeable to her, and most profitable to thyself, that thou approach Holy Communion on every one of her festivals without any exception whatever: there is no better way of honoring Mary than to honor her in Jesus and with Jesus. So well did St. Charles Borromeo convince those committed to his spiritual charge, of the utility of receiving Holy Communion as a means of honoring Mary, that at Milan it was received as universally on Mary's festivals as on Easter Sunday itself, so great was the number of those who, with a view to honor her, approached the holy sacraments on those days. Thus the faithful made, in regard to the reception of the sacraments, no distinction between Easter Sunday and the festivals of Mary.

By persevering industry a barren soil is rendered fruitful; and in like manner thy heart, although cold, will, awakened by those and the like exercises, be inflamed with love for the most holy Virgin; and she will recompense thee for all thou shalt do for her, by striking in thee those firm roots which she strikes only in the elect: "And I struck roots in the honored people."

THIRD POINT.

PERFORM THY EXERCISES OF DEVOTION TO MARY—PUBLICLY.

Nothing takes away so much from the practice of virtue as does human respect. St. Ignatius of Loyola used to say: "Who has great fear of the world will never do any good." And why? Because such a one directs himself according to the judgment of the world, and confines himself to doing that which the world allows him to do.

If then thou desirest to become one of Mary's clients and to limit thyself to doing only that which is not displeasing to the world, rest convinced that thou shalt never become one of her clients. The world will reprove thee when, on her festivals, thou approachest the thrice holy sacraments; it will reprove thee when thou permittest thyself to be publicly seen before her altars—when thou takest part in the processions which are held in her honor—when thou enrollest thyself in her associations—when thou showest zeal for her glorification. Now if thou allowest thyself to be put to shame by the small talk of the world, thou shalt never have the courage to perform those pious exercises which thou also wouldst like to resolve upon performing, and never wilt thou attain to genuine and solid devotion: "Who fears man will most assuredly fall."

What remains, then, for thee to do? Never blush to honor her at any time, in any place, by rendering her public services: "I will fulfil my vow before the eyes of all his people." Oh what joy wilt thou, by this course, cause to thy heavenly Lady! What admiration and praise is not earned from a prince by a soldier who, in the combat, casts himself into the midst of the enemies, thereby incurring a thousand dangers! With what benevolence and complacency will not the prince look upon him!

Salvation is thine, if on due occasions thou wilt but approve thyself a valiant and fearless client of Mary! She will look down with complacency upon thee from on high: she will rejoice to have thee for her servant, and she will load thee with favors. A young student of a famous university was accustomed on vacation days to repair from the school to assist at the public devotional exercises of the month of Mary; his companions laughed at him, and made game of him; but when this did not cause him to desist from his usual practice, they passed from mockery to the most vulgar abuse and threats. The pious youth did not suffer himself to be moved by all they said and did; and with eyes lifted up to heaven he broke forth into this exclamation, "Never Lady! is it to be verified in me that I am ashamed to appear as thy client: from this time forward, I shall come from the university, not only on vacation days, but on every day, to render thee the honor to which thou art entitled."

O thou noble and blessed soul! How many graces wilt thou have obtained for this course from the Virgin! Believe now that such a generous-hearted procedure confers on thee more power to become a client of Mary, than would a hundred unimpeded exercises performed privately within the walls of thy own dwelling. It is very certain that thou shalt not lack opportunity to imitate the course of that young student: when the opportunity presents itself, then remember that Mary looks upon thee from the high heavens above; prove to all persons that thou art willing and ready to endure every sort of contempt and abuse for her sake; show to all that thou esteemest the privilege of being in her service too highly, the privilege and that thou dreadest too exceedingly, to bring down upon thee her contempt; and that these two dispositions which are sincerely thine, give thee the noble courage to trample under foot the low mockery of the world: "This do and thou shalt live."

O most holy Virgin! I am determined to obtain devotion to thee, cost what it may; my passions will put a thousand obstacles in my way; but I hope that with thy assistance, I shall conquer every difficulty and completely triumph over every obstacle. I will very carefully fly the dangers, in which were I placed, I might have the misfortune to offend thee! I will practise the mortifications which thou art anxious I should practise; and I will endeavor with all my heart to overcome human respect which was but too often the cause of my fall.

All these things, O Lady! I promise thee: yet please do not forget that I am very weak; thou canst make me very strong. Make me so, O Mary! cause me to despise the judgments and the foolish babbling of the world; grant that I may heroically overcome myself, in order that I may one day participate in the reward promised to the victors. Amen.

FIFTY-FIRST MEDITATION.

QUALITIES OF DEVOTION TO MARY.

FIRST POINT.

CONFIDENCE IN MARY.

GENERALLY speaking, Mary's clients place in her that affectionate confidence which good children have in their mothers. Notwithstanding the high position to which the most blessed Virgin has been raised, notwithstanding how great and how exalted is our blessed Lady herself, yet however she is, in a last analysis, our Mother,—and indeed the most tender, the most compassionate, and the most solicitous, of all mothers. And what are her clients? They are children who distinguish themselves from others, by the fidelity with which they serve her, and by the love which they bear to her.

Now, who is ignorant of the fact that, between the mother and the children, there obtains a mutual and a very close relationship of affection and confidence? They obey her, they esteem her, they honor her; but at the same time they look upon her as something all their own; they betake themselves to her as to a place of safety, and act towards her with that freedom which they certainly would not permit themselves when dealing with their father.

In this manner act with her the clients of the most

holy Virgin. The saints who always held the first place among this multitude, acted towards her with so great confidence, and called upon her with such affectionate expressions, that these expressions sometimes would offend against truth if they were taken in their strict sense, and on this account, must be understood according to their milder signification. St. Philip Neri called her "his delight;" St. Bonaventure, "the soul of his soul;" St. Bernardine, "his beloved;" St. Herman, "she who is espoused to him by love;" St. Augustine, "his Lady."

All the saints without a single exception call her, "their mother." And often did they turn to her as to their mother; they unbosomed themselves of their tribulations to her, and banished all bitterness from their hearts by praying to her, by sending up their sighs to her, by weeping before her; and with so great confidence and so intimate conviction did they promise themselves that they would obtain from her light and mediation, that not even a child could begin to be more confiding in its earthly mother.

What consolation is it not, to have here on earth the mother of God herself as confidante of one's secrets, as patroness, as mother? Of such a character and so great is this consolation that it sweetens all which is bitter, enlarges the heart by inspiring it with most precious hope, and mantains in it tranquillity even in the midst of the storms which would throw it into commotion. St. Paschal Bailon used to console himself in misfortunes, with the thought that our dear Lady herself would plead his cause; and, whenever any adversity befel him, that illustrious servant of God would say: "Our Lady will attend to this matter:" and thus he kept his peace of mind and remained under her protection.

Do not fancy that such confidence is a privilege enjoyed by the saints exclusively; no, it is a privilege of all those souls who are really entitled to call themselves her clients: "If we often greet her with some service and prayer, she cheerfully greets us as often with some benefit and consolation." (St. Bonaventure.)

Art thou one of Mary's clients? Then shalt thou also have the happiness of placing in her such confidence. But dost thou know when it becomes difficult for thee to feel in thy heart that confidence? It will be difficult for thee to feel it when thou shalt experience the stings of conscience in consequence of some fault thou hast committed. Then shalt thou be as that little son who has not the courage to present himself before his mother, for he knows he has forfeited her caresses, and on this account it is that he approaches her timidly, downheartedly and irresolutely.

If such was the cause why thou didst confide so little in Mary, then pray to her for pardon; promise her that thou wilt speedily and earnestly improve: and do not fear that she will cast thee off. Does a mother ever cast off a child who, in contrition, throws himself at her feet? Make the experiment immediately; and thou shalt experience how a childlike and affectionate confidence is so peculiar to those who love her, and so ennobling a characteristic of every one of her true servants.

SECOND POINT.

SOLIDITY OF THE DEVOTION TO MARY.

The devotion to Mary must be solid devotion; that is, it must not be one of those superficial devotions which are taken up with too little consideration, and which consist in the performance of some external exercises; but thou must put thy hand to the work of purging thy soul of its faults, and of enriching it with virtues: "Extirpate and destroy; destroy and tear down; build and plant."

A land yet uncultivated can be transformed into a lovely garden; but the stones and weeds must be previously got rid of, and in their stead, choice seeds must be sown, and choice flowers must be planted.—True devotion must aim at doing something like this in the soul, before it can deserve to be termed solid devotion.

Doubtless this process may be somewhat troublesome to thee, but it will in the end recompense thee for thy pains; for if the venerable Virgin beholds thee struggling and working with the view to please her, she will give thee abundant assistance in all the assaults which thy passions and the evil spirits will make upon thee. In such cases turn to her with thy inmost soul, assure her that thou wilt prefer to die rather than to offend her beloved Son; and the victory—fear not—will be thine.

In like manner thou must, from love of her, flee the dangerous occasions of sin, flee certain places, certain misleading and captious writings; thou must, in short, flee all the occasions which can expose thy weakness to the danger of committing sin. O what a sure sign will thy flight of the occasions of sin be, that thy devotion is solid! The same anxiety to please the Virgin will incite thee to enrich thy soul with virtues; to do so will not come difficult to thee if thou love her, for love presses one on to imitate the beloved, and produces also similitude. Cast thy eyes on Mary's virtues; observe how she acted; and in forthcoming cases, try to form in thyself like virtues.

Art thou prone to anger?—Mary was extremely gentle; then let thy love for her put thee on thy guard not to allow thyself to be guilty of either words or actions proceeding from ill temper. Art thou given to curiosity? Mary was exceedingly uninquisitive and discreet: then, out of love for her, keep a watch on thine eyes. Mary was extremely humble, extremely pure, and full of the love of God and her neighbor. How many occasions shalt thou have for the exercise of humility, of purity, and of charity? If thou art in the church, think of Mary at Nazareth; if thou art at table, think of Mary at the wedding feast of Cana:—in every one of thy actions then thou canst, by remembering Mary, imitate her virtues.

Should thy devotion bring forth such fruits, rejoice, for then indeed hast thou every reason to rejoice; thou hast an exceedingly agreeable pledge that thou shalt thank her and love her for all eternity. Should, however, thy devotion not bring forth such fruits as yet, do not let this consideration cause thee to lose courage; but set to work with energy, and endeavor to make it bring them forth after a time. Oh, how greatly will the Virgin approve of thy efforts! Oh, how she will give them her blessing from heaven!

THIRD POINT.

PERSEVERANCE IN THE DEVOTION TO MARY.

There are many who do not reap the fruits of their devotion to her: "Perseverance crowns the work." Happy he who has that gift; unhappy he who forfeits it!

Many young persons commence with great zeal; but they become cold and forgetful of all exercises as their passions and years grow upon them. Some cleave very closely to the Virgin when they are in trouble, but as soon as the trouble is over they take leave of every thing that concerns her honor; and it occurs even to pious and spiritual souls that by reason of their multiplied occupations, or out of lukewarmness, they neglect to render to Mary the tribute of mortifications and of services which they formerly offered her with so much affection. Is it it then any wonder if, on her part, the Virgin show herself towards them less generous and somewhat reserved in dispensing her graces?

Who is to be saved?—Our Lord says, "He who perseveres to the end." Who will enjoy abundantly the fruits of his devotion to Mary? Who will be more affectionately defended, protected and sustained, by her?—He who perseveres in devotion and love to her. One of the holy fathers remarks that devotion to Mary should not be as a wild stream which sometimes contains a vast quantity of water and overflows its banks, and at other times loses all the water it had, so that its very bed could be seen dried up. Not like such a stream must be devotion to Mary; but it must rather resemble a river which always contains within its banks nearly the same quantity of water, and ever faithfully gives up its due tribute to the sea.

Such must be the character of our devotion to our Blessed Lady! That tribute of prayers, services, mortifications, virtues, of the payment of which we acquit ourselves to her is a tribute which we must render to her perseveringly. Oh, how many more souls would there be in heaven now, had they but persevered in honoring Mary! How many would have led a christian, blessed, and tranquil life, had they but remained faithful to her! But alas! many who at one time loved her tenderly are now indifferent in her regard; many who prayed to her every day, and communicated on her festivals, now pray no more to her, and no longer approach the holy sacraments. And as is the case to-day, so was it yesterday.

O inconstancy! exceedingly to be deplored! Influenced by the thought of this inconstancy, St. Liguori, her world-renowned client, cried out to her: "Blessed Virgin, if I persevere in serving thee, in loving thee, and in recurring to thee, I am sure of my crown!"

Wilt thou be certain of thine? Wilt thou, in life, in death, and after death, enjoy her special protection? Wilt thou sing her praises throughout the whole length of a happy eternity? Abide steadfastly and perseveringly in prayer and devotion to her.—Circumstances will arise in which it will be inconvenient and burthensome to thee to render thy usual services to the heavenly Lady. Then, more than ever, bear in mind that her service demands fidelity; and then more than ever, pray to her for perseverance, for "he who perseveres to the end shall be saved."

O Mary! for the sake of the love thou didst bear thy blessed Son, I pray thee grant me the grace to honor thee always in this life, in order that, in the life which opens just as this closes, I may love thee for all eternity! I feel in my heart a tender confidence in thy goodness; I sincerely desire to lead a life well-pleasing in thy most pure eyes; but O Lady! I fear my inconstancy and my sluggishness. I am not afraid that thou wilt first abandon me; but, ungrateful wretch that I am, it is possible that I may by degrees give up thy service. Oh! confirm me, strengthen me, and cause me, by persevering till my death in devotion to thee, to be so fortunate as to enjoy the fruits of my devotion to thee! Amen.

FIFTY-SECOND MEDITATION.

MOTIVES TO PROPAGATE DEVOTION TO MARY.

FIRST POINT.

PROPAGATE DEVOTION TO MARY OUT OF LOVE FOR THY NEIGHBOR.

God has commanded each and every member of the human family, to contribute as far as affection and prudence dictate to the well-being of each and every other member; and bear in mind that this command extends, as has just been stated, to each and every individual, and not to those persons only who, in virtue of their office, are bound to devote special attention to the interests of others. The general precept then here spoken of is given to all whose circumstances enable them to be of service to their fellowman.

Wilt thou obey this command with ease and success? Exert thyself according to thy condition, to propagate with much zeal devotion to the great Mother of God; then this command will lie lightly on thy shoulders, as great sacrifices are not required for the propagation of honor to the most holy Virgin, since the name of Mary is so charming, that by itself it makes its way to the hearts of the most hardened. And thus care to thy neighbors' welfare will be not only easy for thee, but likewise thou shalt assume it with success; for if thou by thy toils but succeed in adding a single soul to the number of her clients, then canst thou say that thou hast saved a soul.

The saints are unanimous in this matter, and they therefore spare no pains and sweat in the conviction, that increasing the number of Mary's clients is a most efficacious means of leading souls to salvation. St. Alphonsus Liguori felt that he could not refrain from writing on this subject the following words: "If the statement be true,—and I also hold it for true and indubitable,—that all graces are dispensed only through Mary's hands, and that all who are saved, are saved by means of this Mother of God; then, in virtue of the consequence necessarily resulting therefrom, it can be said that the salvation of all depends upon preaching about Mary, and upon confidence in her mediation." (Introduction to "Glories of Mary.") Thus highly do the saints esteem, and thus efficacious do they consider, devotion to Mary!

How much good then shalt thou be able to work in thy neighbor, if thou give thyself the pains to inspire him with this devotion, to propagate and increase it where it already exists, and to introduce it in places where it has not as yet obtained a footing? Who knows what fruit will be one day brought forth by those words, which now as chosen corn-seed thou sowest in the hearts of the young! Who knows how many souls will one day praise the zeal which thou hadst in persuading them to honor Mary, and to enkindle in them a lively confidence towards the Mother of mercies! O what consolation, O what joy, shalt thou feel in heaven, whenever any soul ascribe to thee the beginning of the fulness of graces and blessings it received, and consequently ascribe its eternal salvation to thee!

If thou have unfortunately scandalized thy neighbor, then is incumbent on thee the most strict obligation to repair the injury thou hast done him. How helpful towards this end shalt thou find an anxious and working zeal to spread devotion to Mary! How easily canst thou, by this means, lessen or efface altogether the sins which thou hast committed in the sight of God! In this way thou shalt confer on thy neighbor a very considerable benefit: and this is true, whether it be justice or mere charity that obliges thee to be solicitous for his salvation.

O! didst thou but understand what a boon is zeal for the propagation of Mary's honor, and didst thou but know how to make use of that zeal! Perhaps the day is yet to come whereon thou wilt thank Mary for having moved thy heart to propagate her honor from the motive of love for thy neighbor; for when all is over, thou shalt discover that thou hast wrought more good than thou couldst ever have believed or imagined.

SECOND POINT.

PROPAGATE HONOR TO MARY OUT OF GRATITUDE TO HER.

If thou hast received favors and graces from the Most Holy Virgin, then by all means art thou bound to offer her thy sincere thanks. There are ties which bind the receiver to the giver of a benefit; and he who ignores them, or recognizing, despises them, is worse than the wild beast.

Now cast a glance at Mary's image, so redolent of affection; go through the years of thy life, and examine if thou canst say that she has never interposed for thy best advantage—that she has never done thee any good! Oh, how much good on the contrary has she done thee in every necessity and at every time! The mercies which she has shown thee are, certainly, more numerous than the days which thou hast lived.

Dost thou desire to be grateful to her therefor? Then do not content thyself with recompensing her watchfulness over thee, by leading a moral and pious life. Go something farther; do for her what thou wouldst do in order to attest thy thankfulness to a person of the world who was thy greatest benefactress. What wouldst thou do? Thou wouldst declare thyself not satisfied with thanking her, with honoring and praising her thyself; but when opportunity would offer, thou wouldst sound forth in the hearing of others the praises of her affection, and the advantages accruing to thee therefrom; and thou wouldst aim at securing for her the admiration of others; and if the occasion presented itself of rendering her a great service, this service would not appear great in thy eyes, however great it might be in itself.

Well now! act in this very manner towards thy heavenly benefactress. Be not only devout to her, but be unto her an active and zealous servant; manifest thy gratitude by rendering her the service on which she sets such high value: that is, the service of promoting love and honor to her more and more. Let everything that is calculated to increase in others gratitude and love to her, and is calculated to conduce to her glorification—let every such thing be an object of thy most assiduous study! As often as thou art in a state to do it, speak of her to young and to grown persons; praise her goodness and her mercies; promote her honor, by contributing according to thy condition in life, to the beautiful celebration of her solemnities, to the distribution of her images and of such books as are fit to excite and foment in souls confidence in her. Encourage others also to adopt this course; encourage them by frequently appearing in public before her altars and at her processions, but appearing always full of the spirit of recollection; encourage them likewise by approaching the Holy Table on her festivals, in order worthily to receive her Jesus.

And if thou wilt render her a service supremely agreeable to her, then bring back and lay at her feet some erring sheep. A more welcome thanksgiving than this, rest assured, thou canst not offer to Mary; for nothing can be more pleasing to a mother than to see one taking every pains to lead back to her her fugitive or lost son. Mary herself oftentimes declared this fact, by reproaching even in an audible voice, some of her servants with being too cold and supine to embrace such favorable occasions of promoting her honor; and the same she declared, by thanking other of her clients for being animated in this regard with zeal warmer and more sustained.—To which of these two classes dost thou belong? To the ungrateful, or the grateful? To those whom she reproaches, or to those whom she thanks?

Ponder on the countless benefits which Mary has

conferred upon thee; ponder on the labors which thou undergoest for her sake: and having done these two things, then draw thy conclusion. Resolve, however, to begin immediately to prove to her by thy deeds, that her mercies have not fallen on barren and ungrateful soil.

THIRD POINT.

PROPAGATE HONOR TO MARY FOR THY OWN ADVANTAGE.

How laboriously soever thou shalt work to propagate devotion to Mary, the whole will fall out in the end to thy own immense advantage. To co-operate with God to the salvation of souls, is a work sovereignly meritorious; but how greatly will this merit be enhanced, when besides thus co-operating, thou aimest at the propagation of Mary's honor? Even this twofold end he accomplishes who truly endeavors to propagate devotion to Mary. He co-operates to the salvation of souls, for this devotion is the most powerful means to effect it; he causes the Virgin to be glorified anew, because the number of her clients and devout servants is increased by his efforts. He does likewise two things which are extremely agreeable to God; as well because God is extremely desirous to see that humble creature more and more honored and glorified, whom he himself honored and glorified more than he did all else; as also because nothing gives him greater pleasure than to see sinners return to the right path through the mediating action of his most Holy Mother.

What merit, therefore, will he not acquire who exerts himself to render his divine Majesty so acceptable a service? Certainly, he who so exerts himself, will acquire a merit which assures him of the choicest blessings in this life, and of eternal glory in the next. And how canst thou think that God will not bless him abundantly, when he inflicts terrible—terrible—chastisements on any one who places impediments in the way of her service? He very often exhibits more zeal for his Mother's honor, than for his own; and if he bear patiently the sacrilegious insults offered to himself, it would seem as though he cannot bear so patiently the indignities offered to the practice of devotion to his most holy Mother. It is therefore to be reasonably concluded that he rewards even in this life, those who undertake to defend and to increase this devotion. St. Bonaventure says, that doubtless "much good is in store for her panegyrists." (Introduction to St. Liguori's "Glories of Mary.") But a fact yet more important which is this, that eternal life is clearly promised to them: "They who elucidate me shall have eternal life." (Eccl. xxiv. 31.) He who will labor to make me known and loved, shall have eternal life for his reward. The Church and the holy fathers commonly apply these words to the Virgin; and their signification is, that she will assist with so many graces the souls who are zealous for her honor, that in the end they will be saved: "they will have eternal life."

Now raise thy spirit heavenward, and see how many souls of every age, sex, and condition, obtained in this way a high throne in that blessed kingdom! How many souls are there, who shine like unto the brightest stars and surround our most august Lady ! Dost thou know who those souls are ? They are those who glorified her on earth by their words, works, and good example—those who were more affectionate to her than were others, and who zealously encouraged to love her all those with whom they came in contact.

O precious reward ! O sweet hope ! This reward awaits thee also, if thou wilt but nerve thyself to make so delightful an acquisition, and put forth all thy powers in order that it may not escape from thee.

I also, O Lady ! am desirous of one day becoming a companion of so charming a multitude. I am also desirous of drawing nearer to thee, of loving thee, of venerating thee, of praising thee for all eternity ! Among the choirs of the blessed, I behold some who were one day as I am now, and who at this time surround thy throne ! I behold among them souls who were not associated with thee by love, but who became so associated by thy assistance. This thought gives me fresh courage. I am a poor sinner ; yet I feel within me a sweet hope, a holy fire, which serves me as a guarantee that I shall receive so paramount a grace. Thou, most holy Virgin ! didst overload me with mercies and favors ; thy goodness it is, if I am on the right path of salvation ; thy gift, if I know thee and love thee ; thy boon, if I hope to love thee throughout all eternity in the midst of the angels and saints. Multiply now in me thy mercies ; cause me always to know thee more and more, and to teach others always to know thee more and more ; cause me to honor thee, and to make others honor thee more and more; cause me to love thee in this world, and to cause others to love thee, more and more; for if I do these things in the present life, I hold for certain that I shall know thee, honor thee, and love thee in a far higher degree for all eternity. Amen.

THE END.

APPENDIX.

Extract from the Dogmatic Decree of the Œcumenical Council of the Vatican on Papal Infallibility:—

(From the *Catholic World*).

"Nevertheless, since in this present age, when the saving efficacy of the apostolic office is exceedingly needed, there are not a few who carp at its authority; we judge it altogether necessary to solemnly declare the prerogative which the only begotten Son of God has deigned to unite to the supreme pastoral office.—Wherefore, faithfully adhering to the tradition handed down from the commencement of the Christian faith, for the glory of God our Savior, the exaltation of the Catholic religion, and the salvation of Christian people, with the approbation of the sacred Council, we teach and define it to be a doctrine divinely revealed: that the Roman Pontiff when he speaks *ex cathedra*,—that is, when in his exercise of office of pastor and teacher of all Christian peoples, and in virtue of his supreme apostolic authority, he defines that a doctrine of faith or morals is to be held by the universal Church,—possesses, through the divine assistance promised to him in the blessed Peter, that infallibility with which the divine Redeemer willed his Church to be endowed, in defining a doctrine of faith or morals; and therefore that such definitions of the Roman Pontiffs are irreformable of themselves, and not by force of the consent of the Church thereto. And if any one shall presume (which God forbid), to contradict this our definition, let him be ANATHEMA."

Extract from the Dogmatic Decree on the Immaculate Conception of the most blessed Virgin Mary, pronounced at Rome by our Holy Father, Pius the Ninth, on the 8th of December 1854, in the ninth year of his pontificate:—

"Wherefore, after we poured forth, in all humility and with fasting, our own and the public prayers of the Church, without intermission, to God the Father through his Son, that he would be pleased to direct and to confirm our mind with the strength of the holy Ghost; and after having implored the protecting favor of the whole court of heaven; and having with sighs petitioned the Paraclete Spirit—and thus while under his inspiring influence—we, by the authority of our Lord Jesus Christ, of the blessed Apostles Peter and Paul, and by that invested in us, do, to the honor of the holy and undivided Trinity, for the glory and adornment of the Virgin Mother of God, for the exaltation of the Catholic faith, and the advancement of the Christian religion, DECLARE, AND PRONOUNCE, AND DEFINE, that the doctrine which holds that the Blessed Virgin Mary, in the first instant of her Conception, has been, by a special grace and privilege of Almighty God, and in view of the merits of Jesus Christ, the Savior of the human race, preserved and exempted from every stain of original sin, is revealed by God, and consequently is to be believed firmly and inviolably by all the faithful. Wherefore if any persons should have the presumption, which God forbid, of thinking in their hearts contrary to what has been in this respect defined by us, let them be made aware, and let them further know, that they are by their own decision condemned; that they have suffered shipwreck of the faith, and have fallen away from the unity of the Church, and that moreover, by their own act itself, they subject themselves to the penalties imposed by the law, if they should either by word written or oral, or by any other external sign, attempt to give outward expression to the erroneous views they form in their hearts."

THE PRAYER OF ST. BERNARD TO THE BLESSED VIRGIN.

Remember, O most gracious Virgin Mary, that never was it known, that any one who fled to thy protection, implored thy help, and sought thy intercession was left unaided. Inspired with this confidence, I fly unto thee, O Virgin of virgins, my Mother. To thee I come; before thee I stand, sinful and sorrowful. O Mother of the Word Incarnate, despise not my petitions, but in thy mercy hear and answer me. Amen.

www.ingramcontent.com/pod-product-compliance
Lightning Source LLC
Chambersburg PA
CBHW022028110726
47901CB00006B/1684

* 9 7 8 3 7 4 3 6 5 7 9 9 1 *